The INSECT APPRECIATION Digest

Everything you ought to know about insects (that your parents didn't teach you)

F. Tom Turpi

Purdue University
West Lafayette, Indiana

The Entomological Foundation

Third printing, 1997

For information:
The Entomological Foundation
9301 Annapolis Road, Suite 300
Lanham, MD 20706–3115
http://www.entsoc.org

Library of Congress Catalog No. 92–074776

ISBN 0–938522–44–2

The

Insect Appreciation

Digest

Everything you ought to know about insects!

Chapter 1
The Study of Insects

Chapter 2
The Insect

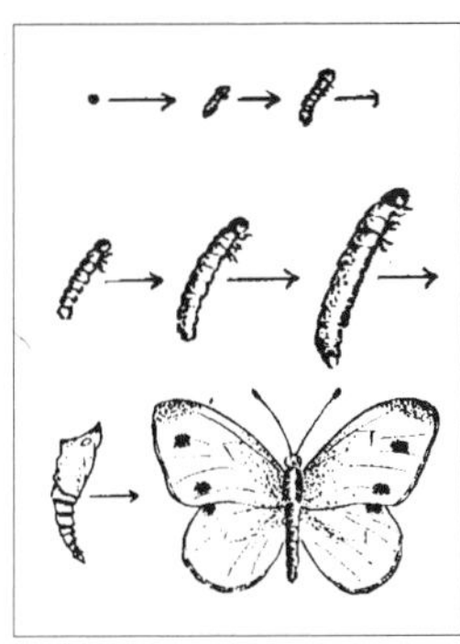

Chapter 3
Insect Biology

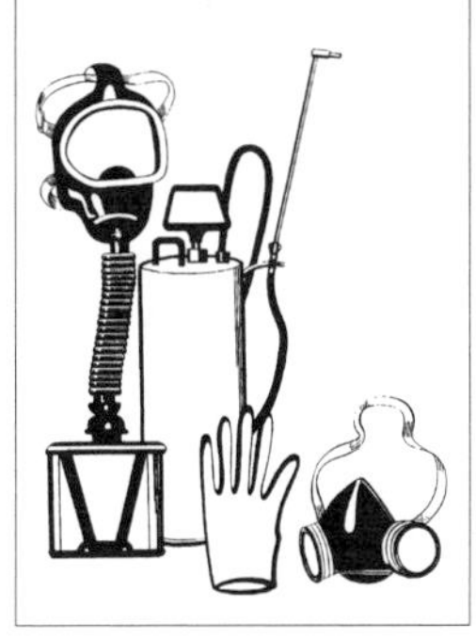

Chapter 4
Interaction With Humans

Chapter 5
Insects and Human Culture

Insect Control

Ol' Bug Scout cleans up pretty good when he gives a speech.

Graphic Designer: Sandra Stephens-Reeves

Chapter 1

The Study of Insects

Entomology and Entomologists

Entomology is the study of insects. The word entomology is based on the Greek *entomon* which was used to describe the creatures we know today as insects. The Latin word *insectum* which is based on *insecare* — meaning to cut in, a reference to the cut-in appearance of these animals — is the basis for the English word **insect**. Another term sometimes used for insects is **hexapod** which is based on the Greek hex (six) + podos (foot) — a description of the six-legged nature of these creatures. The study of insects could just as well be called hexapodology or insectology but entomology is the word that has come to be used to describe this branch of science.

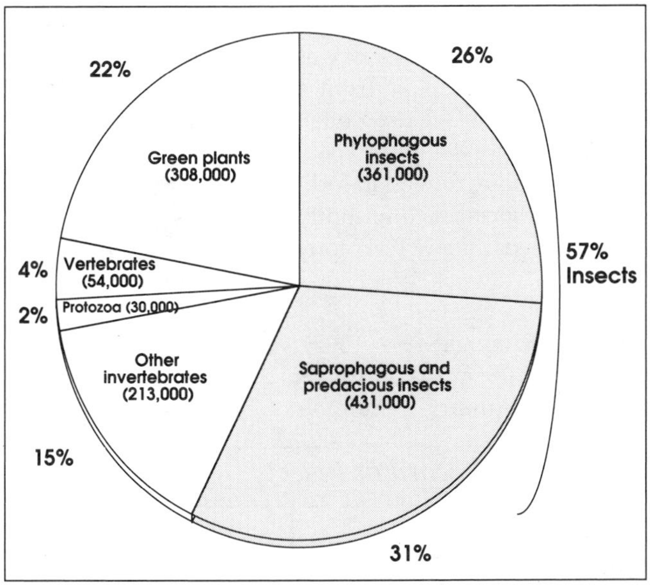

22%
Green plants (308,000)
26%
Phytophagous insects (361,000)
4% Vertebrates (54,000)
2% Protozoa (30,000)
Other invertebrates (213,000)
15%
Saprophagous and predacious insects (431,000)
31%
57% Insects

The *Biological Pie:* Insects, other animals, and plants.

Why is there a science called entomology? The study of insects could be a part of biology. To be sure a biology course would be incomplete without including insects. However, the specific study of insects as the science of entomology can be justified in several ways including the following.

- **Insects are the dominant group of animals** on the surface of the earth and in fresh water. There are over 1 million kinds (species) of insects described and many more (some say as many as 10 million) that have not yet been named. Insects make up about 80% of all known animals. It has been estimated that there are as many as 230 million insects on the surface and in the top 9 inches of soil in an acre of meadowland. They play essential roles in the balance of nature including that of predators, parasites, scavengers, and as food for other animals (and plants).

- **Insects represent a biological system vastly different than ourselves.** Their physiology and structure are completely different than ours. They fly and are cold blooded. They don't think and they survive in conditions that humans would find totally intolerable. The "alien" insects and humans in many ways represent the pinnacles of evolution on the earth.

- **Many insects are valuable to us.** Insects produce goods such as honey and services such as control of undesirable pests. They also are the pollinators of many of the fruits and vegetables that we eat. Insects are research animals used in scientific inquiry in many areas including the study of medicine.

- **Some insects are harmful**. While less than 5% of the insect species are considered harmful, those that are cause considerable loss each year. Insects destroy our crops, animals and our possessions, they transmit human diseases, and just plain annoy us with their presence.

- **Insects are interesting creatures.** Because of their diversity of form and living habits many people (other than students of entomology) are fascinated by them. Insects add to the natural beauty around us.

People Who Study Insects

Entomologists are people who concentrate on the study of insects either as a career or as a hobby. Most people who practice entomology as a hobby are interested in insects because of the beauty and diversity of these creatures. They are primarily collectors and taxonomists (classification, especially of plants and animals according to their natural relationships) of insects. →

Most entomologists who make a living working with insects are employed in colleges or universities, with federal governments, or with companies dealing with pest control or products for pest control (the pesticide industry). Professional entomologists also work for museums and zoos, industries other than pest control, and as consultants working to solve insect-related problems for clients.

An understanding of insects is important to anyone who is an agriculturalist, naturalist, or biology teacher. There are also many scientists who do biological research at either the cellular level or organismal level who use insects as their model organism.

A Short History of Entomology

Early study of insects was associated with need and the earliest records of entomological activity are from East Asia. In 4700 BC silkworms were being grown for their silk that was used for guitar strings and fishing lines. In ancient China honey bees were maintained for their honey and wax. Ants were also employed by the Chinese people as biological control agents for insect pests on citrus.

In the Middle East early entomology was associated with magical powers that the people associated with insects. King Menes in the first dynasty in Egypt made the oriental hornet the symbol of his kingdom. In Biblical times the Philistine city of Ekron had a god named Ba'al Zebub — the god of the flies. The sacred scarabaeus is commonly associated with the ancient Egyptian civilization. This scarab beetle was the personification of their sun god.

During the Middle Ages, a time when science was rejected and symbolism flourished, insects were not forgotten. The fly became the symbol of the devil and sorrows, the ant was the symbol of the provident worker, the bee stood for virginity and wisdom and the moth represented the temptations of the flesh.

The 1700s was a time when scientists were naturalists and they began to systematize and describe things in nature including insects. It was during this time that Carl von Linne, known today as Linnaeus, founded the science of systematics. Linnaeus started the classification of insects and he named thousands of insects. Many of the names given to insects by Linnaeus remain today and such names are indicated by an "L" following the name. Another entomologist who described and named many species of insects was J. C. Fabricius, a student of Linnaeus.

Carolus Linnaeus

Early American entomologists were biologists or practiced entomology as an avocation, a hobby. Some entomologists consider Frederick Valentine Melsheimer (1749-1814) to be the "Father of American Entomology." Melsheimer was an ordained minister and came to America as the chaplain in a regiment of Hessian dragoons. He remained in America as a minister but practiced entomology throughout his life.

Thomas Say

Another early American entomologist was Thomas Say (1778 - 1834). He was from a wealthy Philadelphia family in the drug business. He helped found the Philadelphia Academy of Science and eventually moved to Indiana as a participant in the socialist community at New Harmony. He died at New Harmony and is buried there.

Charles Valentine Riley (1843 - 1895), known as C. V., was one of the most controversial figures in the history of American entomol- ➔

The Geologic Record of Insects			
Geologic Period	**Millions of Years**	**Key Events**	**Insects**
Cambrian	600	Marine Invertebrates	
Silurian	425	Land Plants	
Carboniferous	310	Insects, Amphibians	Roaches, Mayflies
Permian	280	Glaciers	Dragonflies, Cicadas, Lacewings
Triassic	230	Reptiles	Ants, Bees, Bugs
Jurassic	185	Birds, Dinosaurs	Flies
Cretaceous	135	Seed Plants	Butterflies, Termites
Tertiary	60	Mammals	Fleas
Recent		Civilization	Lice

Small is Beautiful to Bugs

In nature bigger isn't always better, especially when it comes to insects. Even though they are small and some can't be seen without a magnifying glass, insects are one of the most successful creatures on earth.

Smallness has its advantages. For instance, insects can hide in cracks and crevices too small for most animals. Many insects escape death simply because they are overlooked due to their size. Gardeners, notorious for their desire to smash insect pests, frequently don't even know insects are around until damage begins to appear.

Another advantage to being small is that the smaller you are the less food you require. Many insects live their lives on food wasted by larger animals. When it comes to food and insects, a little dab will do 'em.

A little wasp, which is a parasite of eggs of other insects, is only about 1/3 mm long. On the other hand, one of the largest insects is the Goliath Beetle. This mammoth among insects weights about 1.5 ounces. A weight that makes it a little heavier than hummingbirds and shrews, the smallest birds and mammals.

Their small bodies also make it possible for insects to do some marvelous things. For instance some grasshoppers have been observed to jump nearly 10 times their height and 20 times their length. If humans could do as well, just think what the world records for the high jump and long jump might be! Some beetles can drag 120 times their body weight. An average human by comparison would be able to drag about 9 tons.

Although it's an advantage for insects to be small, the way they're built means they can't be much larger. For instance, insects have an exoskeleton which would become too heavy for large animals to carry. Also, insects supply oxygen to their cells though a series of tubes that carry air to all body tissues. Larger animals cannot use this approach. They depend on blood in a circulatory system to supply the oxygen needed by tissues.

To insects being small is indeed beautiful. It is a key to the success of these creatures. How successful are they? In the United States it has been estimated that insects average about 400 pounds per acre compared to the weight of humanity of only 14 pounds per acre. They may be small, but what they lack in size, they make up in numbers. ■

ogy. It was through his efforts that entomology became part of the U. S. Department of Agriculture. He was a pioneer in the practice of biological control and is known for his efforts to introduce the Vedalia beetle, a ladybird beetle, into the U. S. for control of the cottony cushion scale on citrus.

One of the first teachers of entomology was John Henry Comstock (1849 - 1931). J. H Comstock spent his entire teaching career at Cornell University.

The Success of Insects

It can be argued that insects and humans are the two most successful creatures on earth. Of course humans represent a single species and "insects" many species but the comparison between the two is frequently made. We are successful primarily because of our ability to think, to reason, and this, combined with our ability to use tools (it's the opposing thumb that makes the task easier) allows us to manage our environment. Insects on the other hand manage to exist in their environment. Indeed they are very successful. The success of insects hinges on several biological considerations including the following.

- ✔ **Skeleton.**
  The insect has an exoskeleton that is very adaptable. It provides protection against the outside world and especially against moisture loss. It was the skeleton that allowed insects to invade the land before most other animals.

- ✔ **Size.**
  Insects are small, at least when compared to many other animals including humans. Some of them are even microscopic. This small size has allowed them to creep into and live in spots inaccessible to other organisms.

- ✔ **Flight.**
  Insects use flight to escape enemies and to inhabit new areas.

- ✔ **Metamorphosis.**
  By changing forms from the immature to the adult stage many insects are able to utilize different food resources.

- ✔ **Reproduction.**
  Insects can produce tremendous numbers in a short time. This is due to two aspects of their reproduction. They lay lots of eggs and have a short generation time.

These biological considerations make insects adaptable organisms. In general it is the adaptability of insects that is the key to their success. They can respond quickly to changes in environmental conditions or even control measures such as pesticides.

Insects and Other Animals

Insects have been been represented on the earth for over 350 million years. Among the earliest of the insects were the cockroaches. Cockroaches were around when the first amphibians roamed the earth. These roaches survived the glaciers that wiped out the dinosaurs. By the time birds where taking flight for the first time insects were flying everywhere. Seed plants in part were able to develop because insects were there to act as pollinators. When mammals showed up insects - the fleas - developed to feed upon the hairy creatures.

"Insects have been around for 350 million years, Humans for only 10,000 years!"

Lice are one of the more recent developments in the insect world. It is said that lice owe their lifestyle to the development of civilization, or the lack thereof. When we live in crowded conditions we provide the kind of habitat in which lice thrive.

Insects certainly were on the earth long before humans and will probably be here long after we're gone. Such was the sentiment of the entomologist W. J. Holland, who concluded his book "The Moth Book" with the following which he entitled "The End."

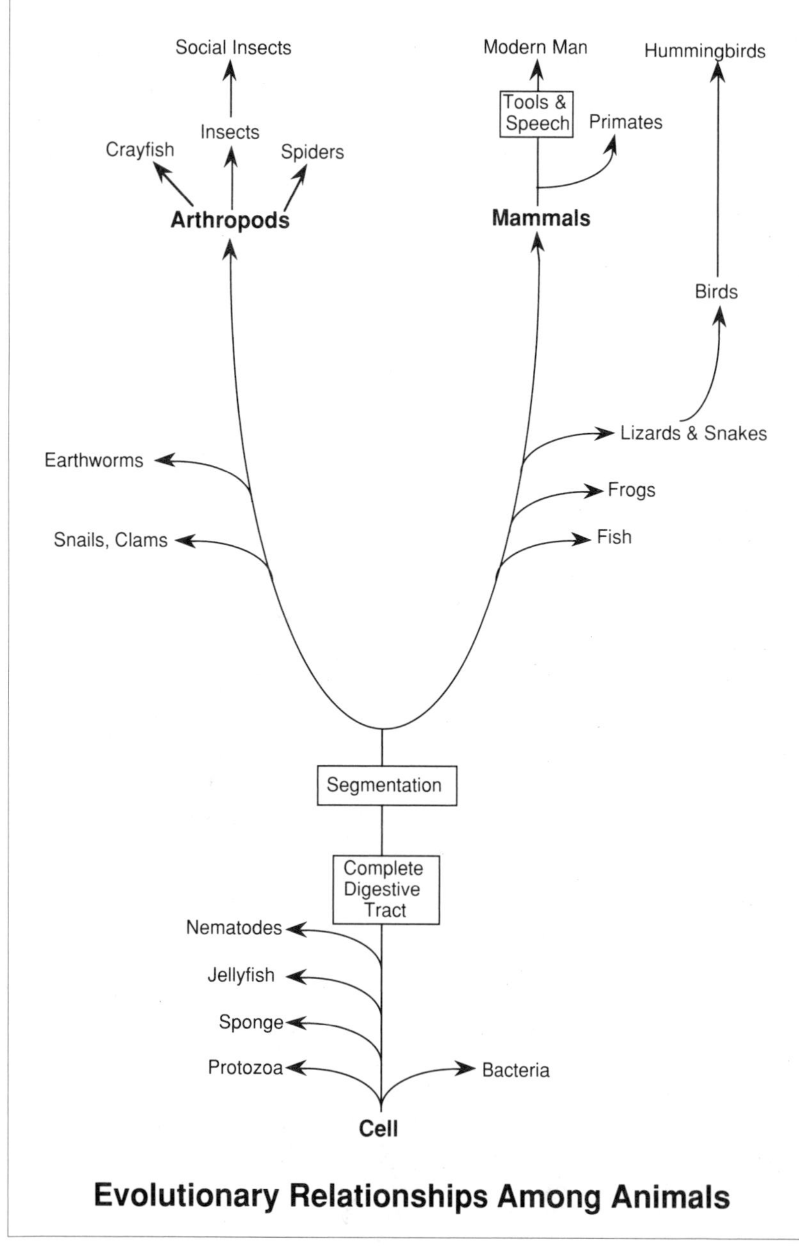

Evolutionary Relationships Among Animals

When the moon shall have faded out from the sky, and sun shall shine at noonday a dull cherry-red, and the seas shall be frozen over, and the ice-cap shall have crept downward to the equator from either pole, and no keels shall cut the waters, nor wheels turn in mills, when all cities shall have long been dead and crumbled into dust, and all life shall be on the very last verge of extinction on this globe; then, on a bit of lichen, growing on the bald rocks beside the eternal snows of Panama, shall be seated a tiny insect, preening its antennae in the glow of the worn-out sun, representing the sole survival of animal life on this our earth,— a melancholy "bug."

Certainly the success of insects as a life form is secure. In fact it has been suggested that the pinnacles of biological evolution to this date are three. The human being with our ability to think (although this is questionable in many instances) coupled with our ability to use tools. The energetics of the hummingbird. And social insects. Even "archy" the cockroach recognized the latter accomplishment when he wrote:

the bees got their
governmental system settled
millions of years ago
but the human race is still
groping

from archy and mehitabel

➔

Common Arthropods

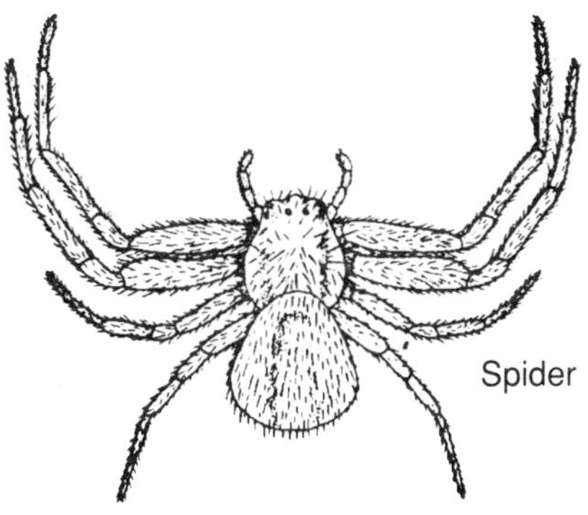

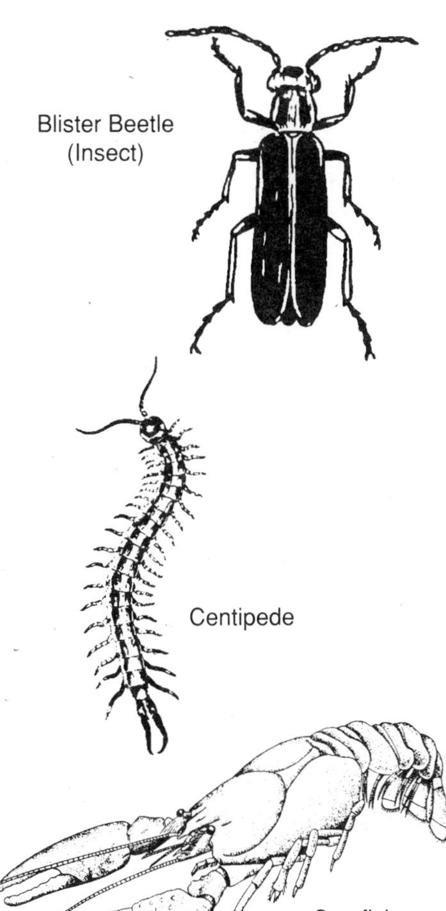

"Crustacea (lobsters, crayfish, shrimp) are dominant arthropods in water, insects on land."

Insects are part of the phylum of animals called Arthropods. Arthropods are named for one of their dominant physical characteristics — that of jointed limbs (from the Greek arthr = joint; podi = foot). Arthropods are also covered with a hard shell or skeleton known as an exoskeleton. In addition to insects, arthropods include such common creatures as spiders, ticks, millipedes, centipedes, lobsters, crayfish and crabs.

The major arthropods can be separated according to these characteristics. Insects have 3 pairs of legs, 3 body divisions, and usually have wings. Spiders and mites have 2 body divisions (they appear to have lost their head), 4 pairs of legs, no antennae, (although sometimes palps on the mouth may resemble them) and no wings. Lobsters and crayfish have several pairs of legs, 2 pairs of antennae and no wings. Centipedes and millipedes have many pairs of legs and no wings. ■

Entomology and Entomologists

1. About what percentage of all named organisms are insects?

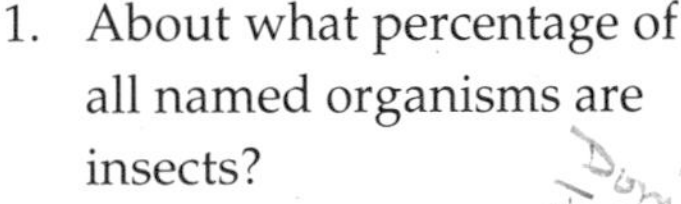

2. What are five good reasons to study entomology separate from biology?
3. What is the etymological (the origin of words) basis for the word entomology? Insects? Hexapod?
4. What are the common names of three insects used extensively by the Chinese people nearly 5000 years before the time of Christ?

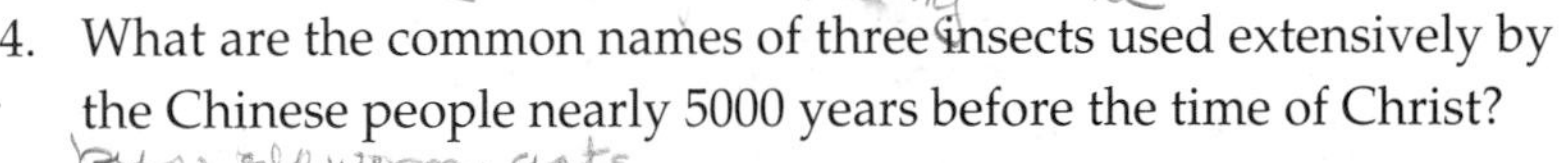

5. Name an early American entomologist who was associated with the socialist experiment at New Harmony, Indiana.
6. What are five biological factors that contribute to the success of insects?
7. Name a key geological event that was associated with the development of these insects. Butterflies. Fleas. Lice.
8. To what animal phylum do insects belong? What are the common names of other animals in this phylum?

Bugs Bad Rap

"Bugs bad rap" could be a music critic's negative review of the latest album of a rap group. Or it could be a Disney release of a new Bugs Bunny cartoon. Bugs bad rap, however, is a commentary on the negative attitude that most people have toward insects.

In her Pulitzer prize winning book, *Pilgrim at Tinker Creek*, Annie Dillard summarizes that attitude with these lines. "Fish gotta swim and bird gotta fly; insects it seems, gotta do one horrible thing after another. I never ask why of a vulture or shark, but I ask why of almost every insect I see. More than insect – the possibility of fertile reproduction – is an assault on all human value, all hope of a reasonable god."

Annie Dillard has hit the nail on the head. Most of us view insects in the light of the bad things they do. To be sure, insects bite and sting, they transmit diseases to plants and animals, they destroy our crops and possessions, and they generally make nuisances of themselves.

The insect world, in the view of humans at least, really lends credence to the old saying that "One bad apple can spoil a barrel of good ones!" In fact less than five percent of all known insects are bad. They are the ones that grab the headlines and spoil our patio barbecues.

As Paul Harvey might say, the other 95 percent of insects are "the rest of the story." Indeed insects provide valuable goods and services to humankind. The most obvious are products like honey and silk. But insects provide animals for research in medicine, genetics, population dynamics and basic biology.

In nature, insects are important to the grand scheme of things. They provide food for many animals. They pollinate the plants that provide many of our fruits and vegetables. They take a leading role in recycling. Insects are johnny-on-the spot for road kills. Otherwise roadsides would be littered with dead animals. Termites turn dead wood into humus. And the billions of tiny insects that inhabit the soil help keep it aerated and "alive."

In the uneasy relationship between humans and insects, the insects provide far more benefits than harm. Consequently, "Bugs" do get a bad rap.

■

Insect Collection

Insect Collecting Equipment

Large insect collections may be made using a small amount of inexpensive equipment. Nets and killing jars are the most essential, although a few other items mentioned later will come in handy and enable the collector to obtain a larger variety of specimens.

The Net

A net serves two purposes. One is to *beat* or *sweep* foliage. This means that the net is swung back and forth so that it scrapes the tops of plants and collects insects that are feeding or resting there. The other use for the net is to collect bees, wasps, butterflies, dragonflies and other flying or wary insects. A suitable net is one that is sturdy enough to sweep plants, yet light and porous enough to be swung through the air. Such a net can either be purchased or made at home.

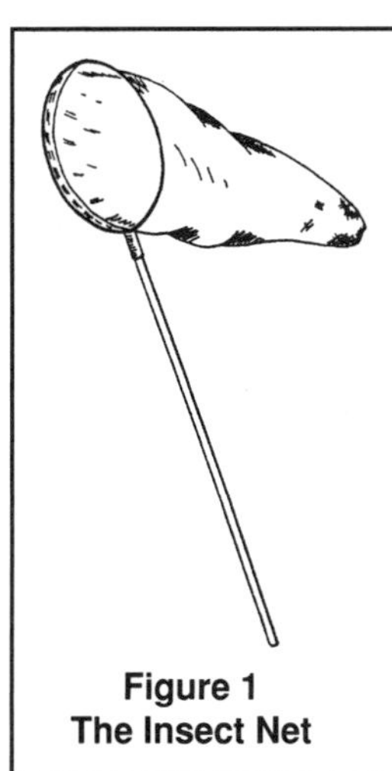

Figure 1
The Insect Net

A net (Figure 1) consists of a handle fitted on a heavy wire loop. A bag is fastened to the loop.

Select a strong, lightweight handle about 3 feet long. A 3/4 inch dowel rod is ideal for this purpose. Cut two grooves along the sides at one end as shown in Figure 2a. These grooves cradle the bent arms of the hoop and should be cut as deep as the thickness of the wire. Make one groove about 3-1/2 inches long, and the other 2-1/2 inches. At the end of each, drill a small hole through the handle.

To make the hoop, bend a 4-foot length of about 1/8 inch durable steel wire, preferably piano wire, into a hoop with short arms at each end as shown in Figure 2b. Take care that the arms and little hooks at their ends are bent just right to fit along the grooves and into the holes in the handle. After fitting the hoop to the handle and properly attaching the bag, you are ready to make the joint fast between the handle and the hoop.

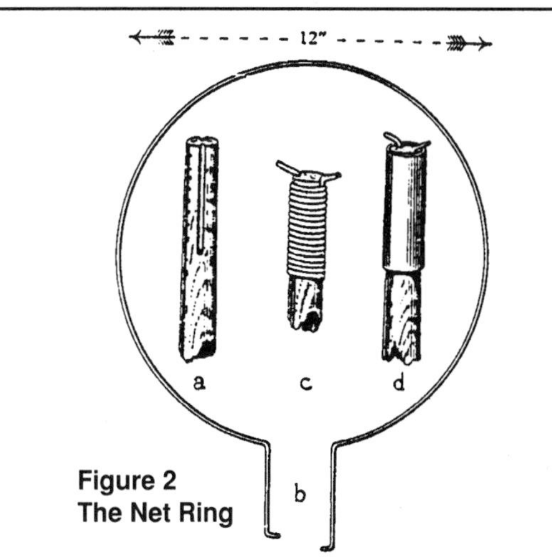

Figure 2
The Net Ring

Two grooves of unequal length are cut on opposite sides of handle at one end (a). These grooves terminate in small holes into which the bent arms of the wire hoop or ring (b) are fitted. The joint may be wrapped with a wire (c) or fitted with a sliding ferrule (d).

Wrap the joint tightly with fine wire (Figure 2c) or better still fit the handle with a sliding metal ferrule (Figure 2d). A short piece of 3/4 inch copper or aluminum tubing will fit snugly over a dowel rod of that diameter.

The bag should be cut out and made cone-shaped as shown in Figure 1 and should be twice a long as the diameter of the hoop. This length lets you loop the bag over the rim and thus prevent the escape of insects. An ideal material for making the bag is nylon mosquito netting available from surplus stores. A good quality marquisette or similar material can also be used, but cotton mosquito netting or cheese cloth is not satisfactory.

To construct the net bag, cut out two pieces of net material the size and shape shown in Figure 3. Place these together, one directly atop the other and sew from point "a" to point "b" to point "c." This seam should be about 1/2-inch in from the cut edges. Fold the outer edge (from the seam to the cut edge) back onto the body of the net and sew around once more, this seam being about 1/8 inch from the cut edges. To make a loop for the wire hoop, use a strip of heavy muslin 5 x 44 inches. Fold it

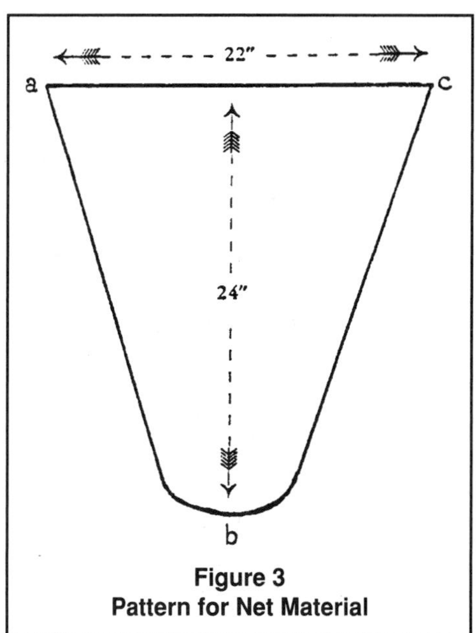

Figure 3
Pattern for Net Material

→

lengthwise to form a hem around the top of the bag. The top edge of the net should be placed between the two sides of the folded muslin. Tuck the cut edges of the muslin in such a way that the edge of the net and the tucked edges of the muslin overlap at least 1/2 inch. Combine these by twice sewing completely around near the middle of the overlap.

The Killing Jars

After insects have been collected, they must be killed quickly without breaking or otherwise damaging them. A killing jar is used for this purpose. Every collector should have at least two such jars - one large enough for butterflies and moths and another for beetles and small insects.

Jars that use ethyl acetate or 1-1-1 trichloroethane as the killing agent can be made at home. The ethyl acetate is safer and excellent for use by young people and beginning collectors. These chemicals can generally be purchased at drug stores. The chemical 1-1-1 trichloroethane is also sold as Engine Cleaning Fluid (use the fireproof one), and may be found in other spot removers. Regardless of the chemical you use, select a jar of heavy glass having a large mouth and a screw cap. Do not use plastic jars.

Ethyl acetate or 1-1-1 trichloroethane jars:

Pour about 1 inch of wet plaster of Paris (more for large jars) into the bottom of the jar. Let it harden, and then dry thoroughly in the oven. After removing from the oven, saturate the dry plaster of Paris with the killing agent; pour off any excess liquid that does not soak in. Put the screw cap lid on the jar. Then put a label on the jar saying "INSECT KILLING JAR" - also list the chemical you have used for the killing agent. The jar is now ready for use; however, keep it tightly capped when not in use. When the jar loses it killing strength, dry it out again and recharge.

Cyanide jars:

Killing jars containing sodium or potassium cyanide may be preferred by advanced collectors: however, their construction and use is no longer recommended. Collectors requiring cyanide killing jars can purchase them from biological supply houses. This suggestion is being made since restrictions governing the sale of cyanide makes it difficult to obtain.

How to Use Killing Jars

Always keep a piece of clean, crumpled paper in each jar to absorb moisture and keep the specimens from becoming rubbed or broken. A successful insect collector makes it a practice to mount and label all specimens within a few hours after they are caught. Insects left in the killing jar for a day or two will become soft and ruined, whereas those taken out but not pinned will become too brittle to handle.

Never put damaged or mutilated specimens in the killing jar. Most insects are so plentiful that there is no excuse for wasting time and energy trying to mount and label anything less than a perfect specimen.

How to Pin Insects

Insect pins may be obtained from any dealer in entomological supplies. Do not use common pins, since they will rust and soon ruin what may be valuable specimens. Pins come in several sizes, but number 2's and 3's will be found the most useful.

Any insect that is large enough to support a pin without breaking or otherwise being distorted may be pinned directly through the body. Insert the pin through a definite part of the body from top to bottom (Figure 4a). The place of insertion depends upon the type of insect. The following rules have been set up for pinning different types of insects so

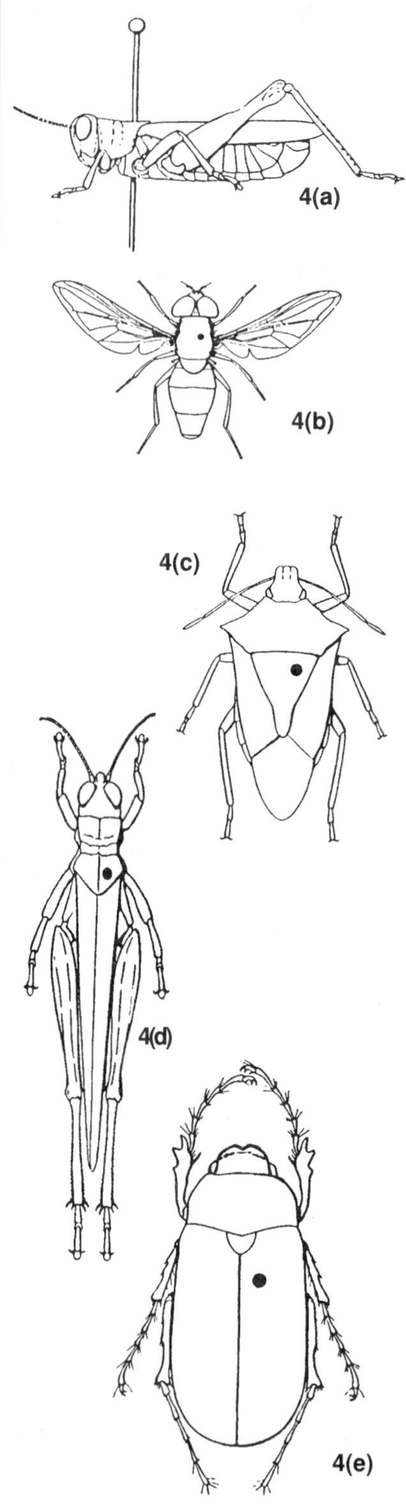

Figure 4
Side view (4a) of a pinned grasshopper. The black dots show the location of the pins in the fly (4b), stink bug (4c), grasshopper (4d), and beetle (4e). The pins are inserted through the insects from top to bottom, leaving 1/4 to 1/3 the length of the pins projecting above the backs.

➔

that the pin may be placed firmly through the heavier parts of the body without destroying important identifying characteristics.

1. Bees, wasps, flies, etc.: Pin through the thorax between bases of fore wings and just to right of middle line (Figure 4b).
2. True bugs: Pin through the scutellum, which is the triangular area between the bases of the wings (Figure 4c).
3. Grasshoppers, crickets, etc.: Pin through the prothorax or "saddle" just to the right of the center line (Figure 4d).
4. Beetles: Pin through the fore part of the right wing cover near the center line (Figure 4e).
5. Butterflies, moths, dragon flies, etc.: Pin through center of thorax between the bases of fore wings (Figure 5a and 5b).

About 1/4 to 1/3 of the pin should project above the specimen.

As each specimen is pinned, straighten the legs, antenna or wings so they will dry in the desired position. Soft-bodied insects, such as crickets or walking sticks, can be held in position by blocking them up with pieces of light cardboard placed on the pin. These temporary supports should not be removed until the specimen has become thoroughly dry.

The Pinning Block

The appearance of a collection is vastly improved if all the specimens are placed at a uniform height on the pins. This is easily done by using a "pinning block" (Figure 6). Such a block may be made either of wood or metal. Metal blocks, of course, must be purchased, but wooden ones can be made at home.

The wooden block is cut out of a soft piece of wood 1-inch square and 4 inches long, or it may be built up by gluing together four pieces of 1/4 inch finishing lath. Small holes are drilled through each of the four steps, which are 1/4, 1/2, 3/4 and 1 inch high, respectively. After an insect is placed on a pin, either the head or the point of the pin is inserted in the desired hole and the specimen adjusted to the proper height. The block is also very useful to adjust labels to a uniform height upon the pins.

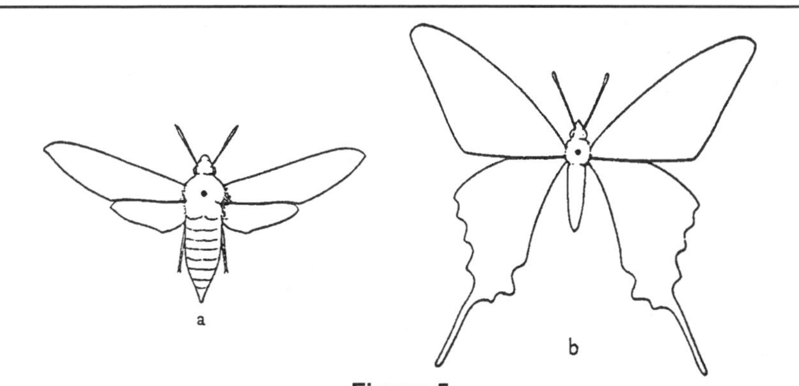

Figure 5
In both moths (a) and butterflies (b), the pin is thrust through the center of the thorax between the bases of the fore wings, just to the right of the mid-line.

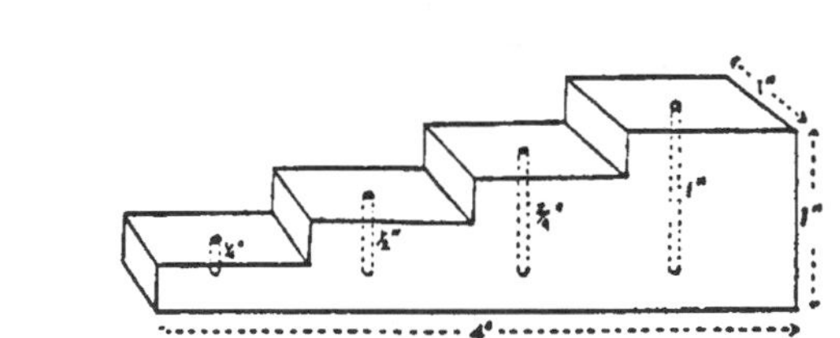

Figure 6
The pinning block. This device is used to adjust both insects and labels to their proper heights on the pins.

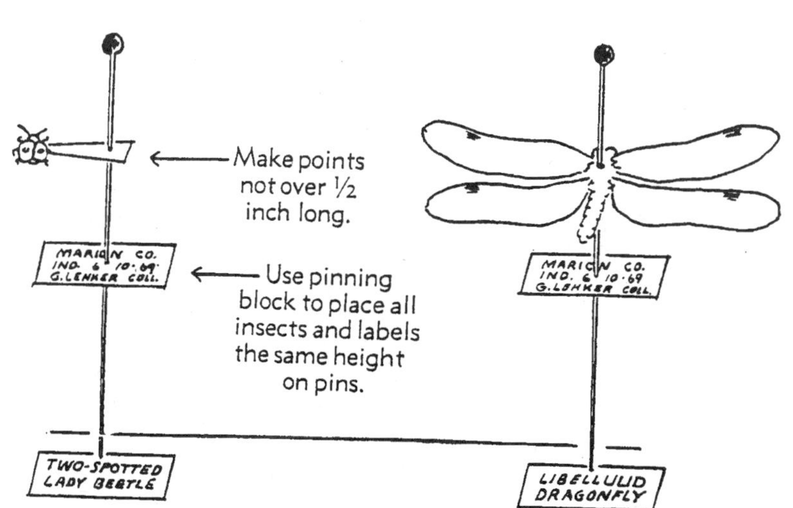

Figure 7
Mounting small insects and labeling. Insects too small to be pinned may be mounted by the card point method (left). All others should be mounted directly upon the pins (right). Note the position of labels on the pins.

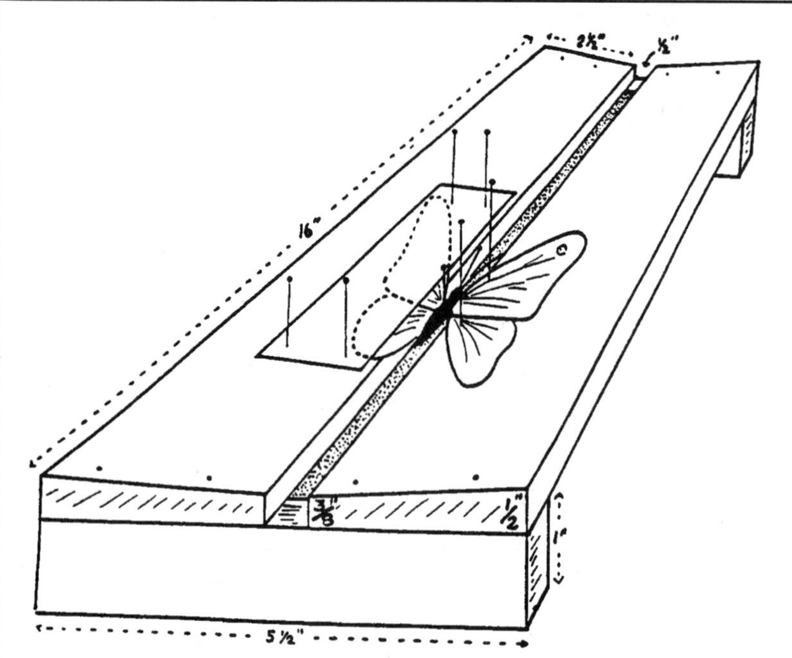

Figure 8

The spreading board showing dimensions. A pin is inserted through the body into the cork so the specimen rests in the groove. The wings are then pulled forward and held temporarily by pins, as shown on the right, while they are being permanently secured by a strip shown on the left.

How to Pin Small Insects

Figure 7 illustrates the card point method used to mount very small insects. Cut all points to a uniform size, 3/8 to 1/2 inch long and about 1/8-inch wide at the base. They are easily cut from a strip of filing card paper as wide as the points are to be long. Cut a large supply at one time, and keep them in a box for future use. This will save time and assure that the points will be uniform in size.

Note from Figure 7 that the pin is pushed through the base of the triangle and the specimen glued to the point. It is very important that the point be to the left of the pin and the specimen glued so that it will face away from the operator.

Mounting insects on card points is not difficult if you know the correct procedure. First, put the card point on the pin, and place a small amount of glue on the tip. Next, lay the specimen on its back on the edge of a table in such a manner that the pin and point can be turned upside down and pressed lightly against the insect. With a little practice you will learn to lay the specimen so that it will be in the correct position when glued to the point.

The Spreading Board

Butterflies, moths and frequently other insects are mounted with their wings spread. A spreading board is used for this purpose and is an important piece of equipment for the insect collector. Eventually, the collector should have different sized spreading boards to accommodate both large and small insects, but one board will do for the beginner. Adjustable spreading boards are available from entomological supply houses.

The complete spreading board (Figure 8) may be made at home, if desired, and is made of the following materials:

1. Two end blocks, 5-1/2 inches long and 1 inch square.
2. Two soft wood top pieces, 16 inches long, 2-1/2 inches wide and about 1/2 inch thick. These pieces should be planed down so that they are 3/8 inch thick on one edge.
3. One flat strip of corrugated box paper or cork, 14-inches long, 1 inch wide, and about 1/2 inch thick.

The two top pieces are nailed to the end blocks (Figure 8), leaving about 1/2 inch between the thin edges. The cork or corrugated paper is then tacked beneath the top pieces to cover the opening and provide soft material into which insect pins can be inserted.

The slope of the top pieces permits the wings to dry in a slight upward position. This allows for any sag that may occur after the specimen is removed from the board. Spreading boards with flat top pieces will do, but insects must remain upon such boards for a longer time.

The top pieces can also be sloped by carving the top sides of the end blocks into shallow "V's."

An inexpensive spreading board can be made from styrofoam. A grove to accommodate the body of the insect can be carved into a block of this material or pieces of stryofoam can be glued together to make a board similar in size and shape to the wooden one previously described. Boards of this kind do have some

➔

disadvantages. For example, they are more likely to rub the scales from the wings as they are being spread.

Spreading the Wings

Before attempting to spread an insect's wings, make sure that the insect is fresh or thoroughly relaxed. Pin the specimen in the usual manner; then thrust the pin through the cork, and push down until the body lies in such a way that the wings are flush with the top pieces. Now, with a fine pin or needle caught behind the heavy front margin of each wing, pull the fore wings forward until their hind margins form a straight line at right angles to the long axis of the body. Then hold the fore wings in place temporarily by pushing the pins into the wood, and work the hind wings forward in a similar manner until their front margins are concealed beneath the fore wings. After you are satisfied with the position of the wings, secure them permanently by pinning strips of paper lengthwise across them.

Most collectors notch these strips of holding paper so the strips will fit around the temporary pins and cover the entire wing surface. After the wings are secured, remove the temporary pins, and set the board aside for 10 days or 2 weeks, after which the specimens may be removed.

How to Label Specimens

To be of any scientific value, every specimen must be accompanied by information including the date and locality of its capture, and the name or initials of the collector. These data are printed on a small label that is placed on the pin beneath the specimen as shown in Figure 7. Collections for scientific purposes also have a second label on each pin showing the host or habitat of the specimen. The size of the pin labels should not be over 7/8-inch long and 5/16-inch wide. This is about the smallest size that can be written or printed on with ease. Labels used by entomologists, biologists, and college students are usually much smaller.

Homemade labels should be cut from stiff paper, such as filing card stock. It is essential that all labels be the same size; and collectors will find many advantages in cutting a large supply for future use. Those directing the activities of insect-collecting groups might want a printer to set up the locality labels in small type so that only the date and initials of the collector need be filled in by hand.

Always use a pinning block to place labels at a uniform height on the pins.

Display Boxes

Pinned insects cannot be kept in good condition unless placed in boxes to protect them from dust and damage. A standard display box is 18-inch x 24-inches x 2-3/4-inches outside measurements and has a glass top. Figure 9 shows a box that is simple and easy to make.

Precaution Against Pests

Several types of small dermestid beetles as well as other incidental pests readily feed upon dry insect specimens. To protect against those pests, it is necessary to use an insecticide or repellent in the display boxes. Naphthalene is a good repellent. If collections are infested, paradichlorobenzene flakes (PDB) can be used as a fumigant. Simply scatter a liberal amount of the flakes on the floor of each box, and close the lid.

Flat pieces of celotex or styrofoam provide a handy place for the temporary holding of pinned specimens while they are being labeled, identified, or arranged in display boxes. ■

Insect Collection

1. What are the two most essential pieces of equipment needed for insect collecting?
2. Why is an insect net supposed to be twice as long as it is wide?
3. What are the purposes of a pinning block and a spreading board?
4. What three types of information must accompany a pinned insect if it is to be of any scientific value?
5. Why are dermestid beetles of concern to insect collectors?

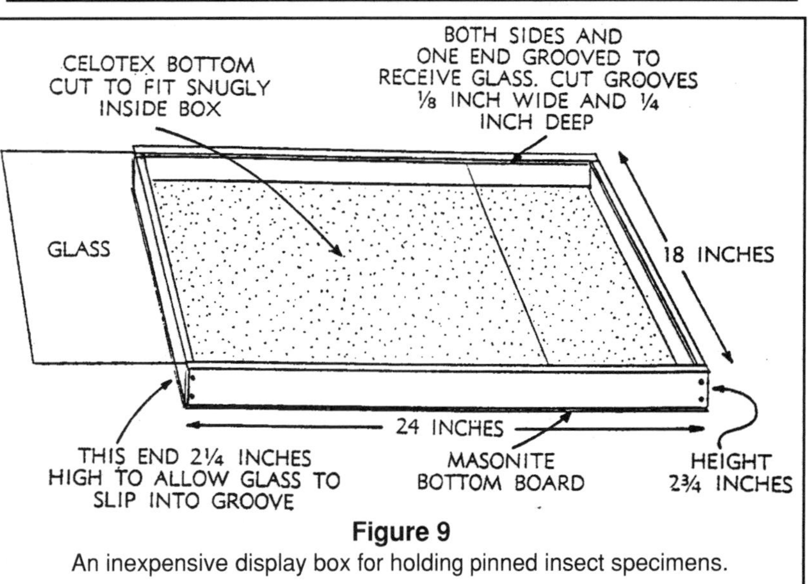

Figure 9

An inexpensive display box for holding pinned insect specimens.

Chapter 1

Classification, Nomenclature and Identification of Insects

Insects, like other animals, can be classified according to their phylogenetic (evolutionary history) relationships. This is the classification system used in biology today and it incorporates morphological (structure), physiological (processes of life) and ecological (relationship to environment) information about the organisms that are classified.

The classification system involves a hierarchy beginning with a broad category that includes one or more groups from the next lower level. This system is based on the system developed by Linnaeus, so it has been in use for more than 200 years. The hierarchy of categories used are as follows:

- Kingdom
  - Phylum
    - Class
      - Order
        - Family
          - Genus
            - Species

The use of this system to classify man and the housefly is illustrated in the table below.

Scientific Classification of the Housefly and the Human

Category	Housefly	Human
Kingdom	Animalia	Animalia
Phylum	Arthropoda	Chordata
Class	Insecta	Mammalia
Order	Diptera	Primates
Family	Muscidae	Hominidae
Genus	Musca	Homo
Species	domestica	sapiens

The system of naming species (Nomenclature) also originated with Linnaeus. Each species is given a name consisting of two words (binomen)— the first the genus, the second the species.

So named, we humans become *Homo sapiens* and the housefly *Musca domestica.* The names are Latin or Latinized and are either *printed in italics* or underlined if handwritten. The first word in the binominal nomenclature (the genus) is always CAPITALIZED, while the second (the species) is not.

The same Latin scientific names are used throughout the world. In fact that is the only part of a Chinese scientific publication that I can understand! The other names that organisms acquire are called common names. Common names can vary and some organisms might have several within a country or even a state. For instance the word gopher is used in parts of Arkansas as a name for a kind of tortoise. In Minnesota what people call a gopher is a kind of ground squirrel. In many parts of the U.S. a gopher is a nearly blind, grey fuzzy creature that tunnels underground devouring insects and earthworms as it goes and all the while creating unsightly mounds of soil on lawns. If someone uses the name gopher it is not possible to visualize the creature being discussed without knowing where the person is from. However, all the animals called gophers have scientific names that (if you knew the scientific names) would leave no doubt in your mind what creature was mentioned. That is the purpose of scientific names - to increase ease of understanding and eliminate confusion in the world of science.

Insects can be identified through the use of a key. A commonly used type of key has bits of information arranged in pairs - called couplets. The user of such a key must decide which description in the couplet best fits the specimen to be identified. The key will direct the user to another couplet. If the proper decisions are made the specimen will be identified by using such a procedure. No where is the old saying

→

"Practice makes perfect" more true than in using keys to identify insects.

A key to the adult stage of insects follows. This key is designed to identify the insect to order. Other keys are available that can be used to identify insects to genus and species. In using this key the first decision to be made would be whether or not the specimen has wings. If so the user is directed to couplet 2, if not the direction is to couplet 28. The user of the key continues going though the couplets until an identification is made.

Positive insect identifications are almost always made by using a key. Identifications can be made by using characteristics of the insect - such sight identification can be used only by learning what the insect looks like. However, many insects look alike and inexperienced (and sometimes experienced) insect identifiers can make mistakes by using sight identification. This is especially true if the identification needs to be genus and species levels.

■

Joint-Footed Creatures

Biologists classify all living things into groups. The broadest classification is either plant or animal. These groups are called kingdoms and each kingdom is divided into subgroups called phyla.

One such phyla of the animal kingdom is arthropoda. The word arthropod is based upon the Greek term "arthro," which means joint and "pod," which means a foot. We find the same combining of terms in arthritis, an inflammation of a joint, and podiatrist, a foot doctor.

Arthropods are nature's joint-footed animals that possess a hard outer skeleton. The most prominent of the arthropods are the insects. Insects have three body regions: The head, thorax, and abdomen. They also have six legs, two antennae and most have wings.

Crustaceans are also arthropods and include the water dwelling crabs, lobsters, crayfish and shrimp. Most have four antennae and appendages on segments of the abdomen.

Some arthropods are identified because they have many legs. The slow-moving millipedes are worm-like creatures that have four legs on each body segment. They don't have to be fast afoot because they feed on dead organic matter. Pillbugs, sometimes called sowbugs or roly-polies, are a type of millipede. Centipedes, on the other hand, move very fast. They are predators and must catch up to the other arthropods on which they feed. Centipedes have only two legs on each body segment.

The last major group of the arthropods is arachnida. Arachnids include the spiders, granddaddy longlegs, ticks and mites. All have eight legs, no antennae or wings, and only two body regions. Because of this, some folks say that spiders appear to have lost their heads. Spiders and granddaddy longlegs, also called harvestmen, are predators on other arthropods.

So there you have it, the family of insects. You might say that mites, ticks, crayfish, millipedes, centipedes and insects are cousins. Some people don't worry about the relationship and lump all of the arthropods together under one heading. They call all of nature's joint-footed creatures "creepy crawlies!" And I don't think it could be considered a term of endearment.

■

Key to Insect Orders

Key to the Adult Stage of Insect Orders

1. **(A)** Insect with wings 2
   (B) Insect without wings 28

2. **(A)** Front wings hardened, leathery or parchment-like, at least at the base 3
   (B) Front wings membranous 8

3. **(A)** Chewing mouthparts .... 4 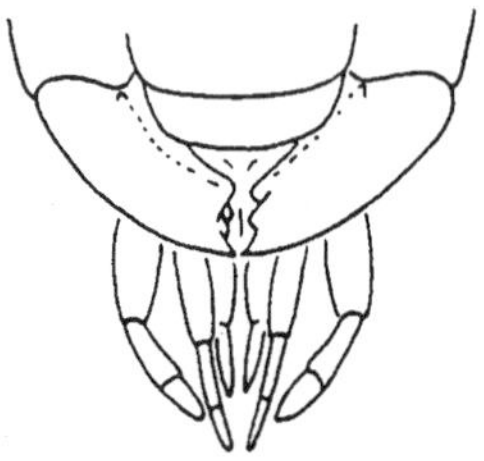
   (B) Sucking mouthparts 7

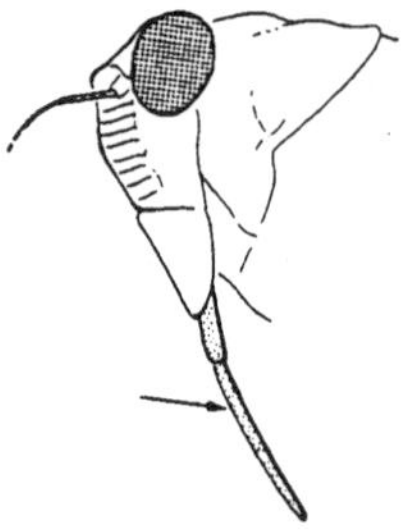

4. **(A)** Without pincer-like cerci 5
   (B) With pincer-like cerci (earwigs) ... DERMAPTERA

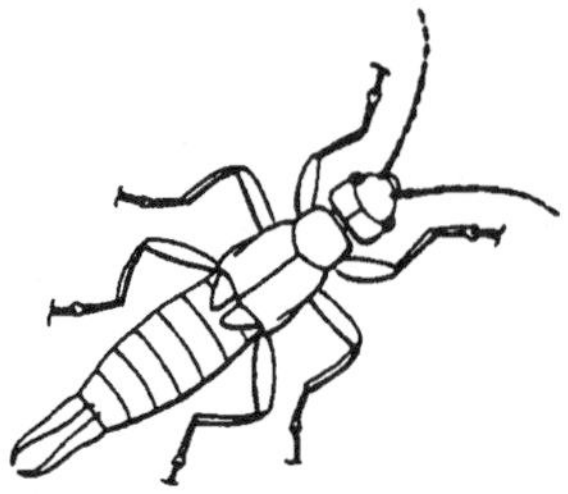

5. **(A)** Front wings with branched veins .... 6 
   (B) Front wings hard, without veins (beetles) .... COLEOPTERA

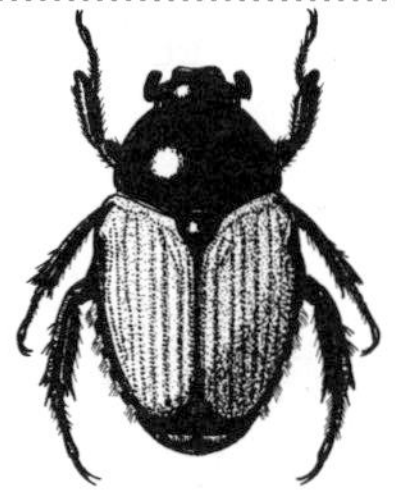

6. **(A)** Jumping insects; hind femur enlarged; tarsi with four or fewer segments (crickets, katydids, grasshoppers) .... ORTHOPTERA 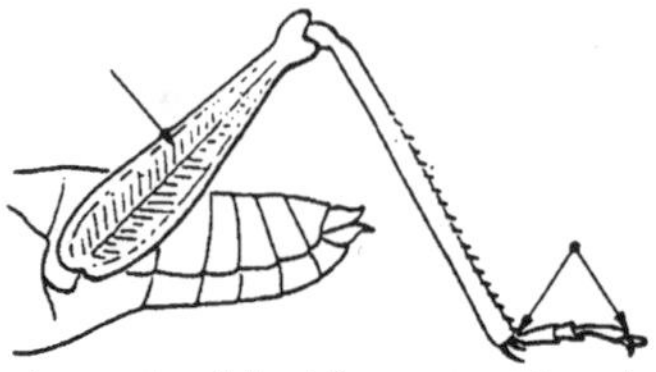
   (B) Walking insects; hind femur not enlarged; tarsi with five segments (roaches, mantids, walking sticks) .... DICTYOPTERA

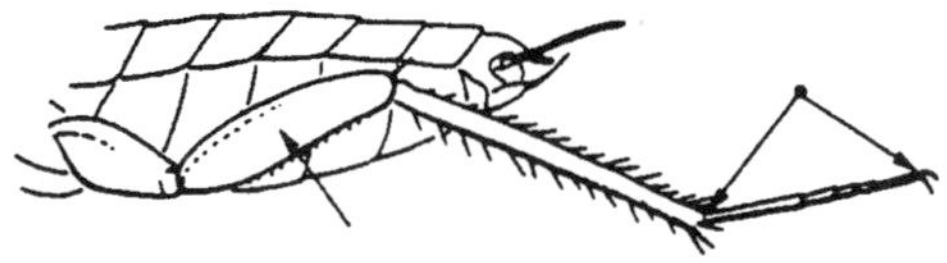

7. **(A)** Front wings leathery at base, membranous at end (true bugs) .... HEMIPTERA 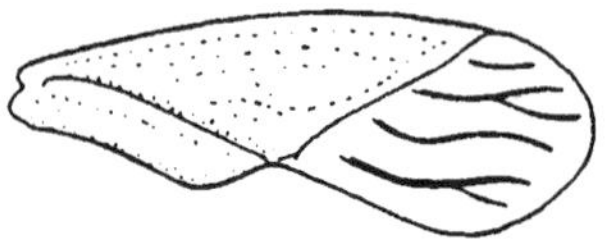 
   (B) Front wings of uniform texture (leafhoppers, treehoppers, spittlebugs, cicadas, aphids) .... HOMOPTERA

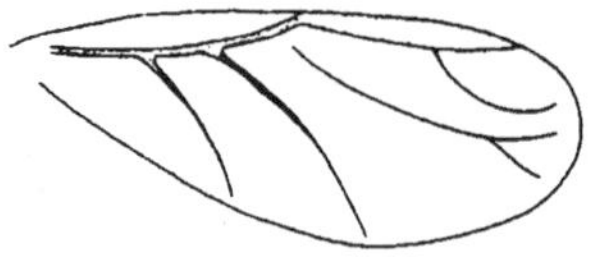

8. **(A)** Two wings 9
   (B) Four wings 13

9. **(A)** Pronotum extending over abdomen (pigmy grasshoppers) .... ORTHOPTERA 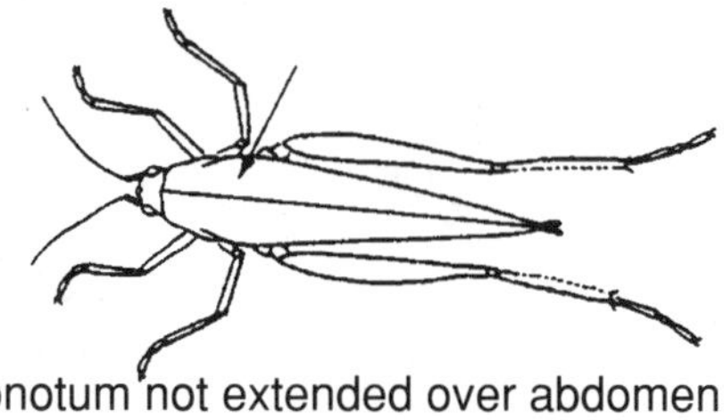
   (B) Pronotum not extended over abdomen 10

10. **(A)** End of abdomen without noticeable appendages 12
    (B) End of abdomen with style or thread-like tails . 11

→

11. (A) Style-like tail (male scales) .... HOMOPTERA

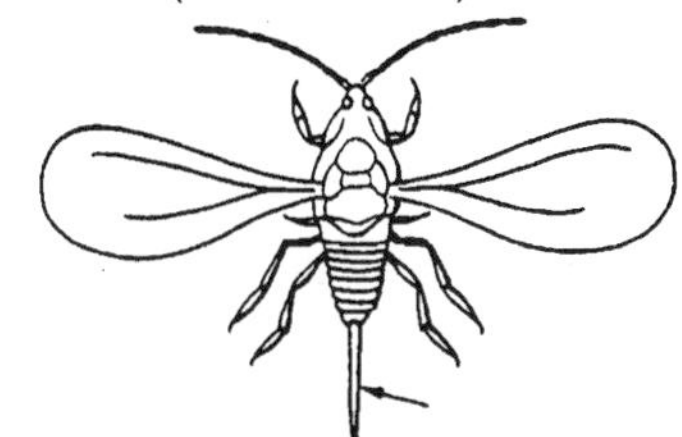

(B) Two or three thread-like tails (mayflies) .... EPHEMEROPTERA

12. (A) With haltere-like organs in front of wings (male stylopids) .... STREPSIPTERA

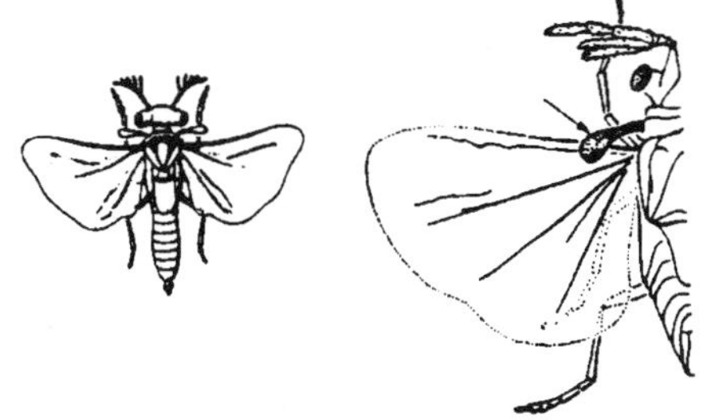

(B) With halteres behind wings (mosquitoes, flies, gnats, midges) .... DIPTERA

13. (A) Wings usually covered with scales; mouthparts consist of a coiled proboscis (butterflies, moths) . ... LEPIDOPTERA

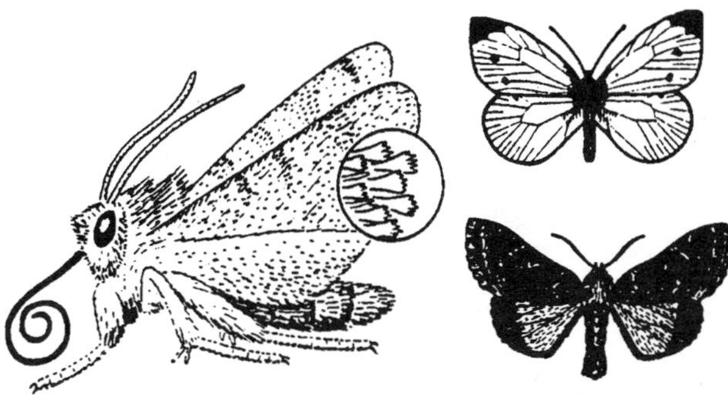

(B) Wings with few or no scales; without coiled proboscis 14

14. (A) Very slender wing with fringe of hairs as long as wing is wide (thrips) .... THYSANOPTERA

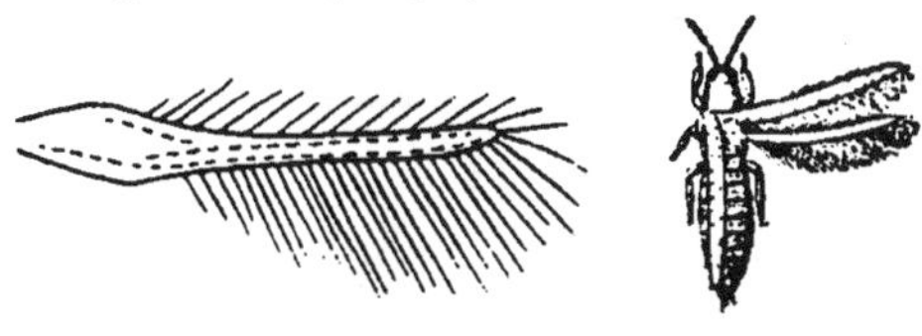

(B) No fringe of hairs, or if present, not as long as wing is wide 15

15. (A) Hind wings equal to, or larger than front wings 21

(B) Hind wings smaller than front wings 16

16. (A) No long abdominal tail-like appendages 17

(B) Abdomen with two or three thread-like tails (mayflies) .... EPHEMEROPTERA

17. (A) Tarsi two or three segmented 18

(B) Tarsi with more than three segments (usually 5) 20

18. (A) Piercing-sucking mouthparts (leafhoppers, plant hoppers, spittlebugs, aphids, cicadas) .... HOMOPTERA

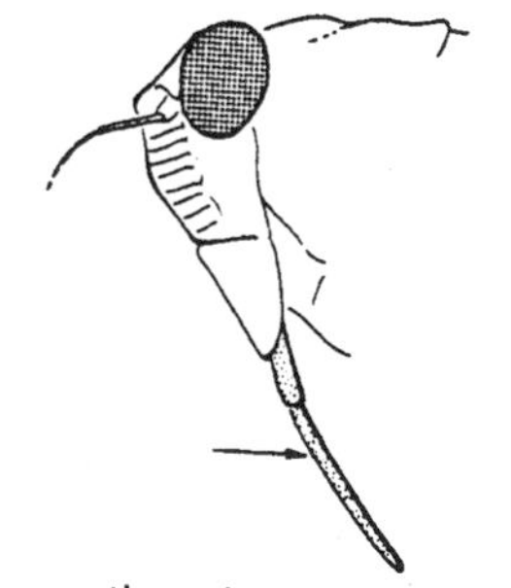

(B) Chewing mouthparts 19

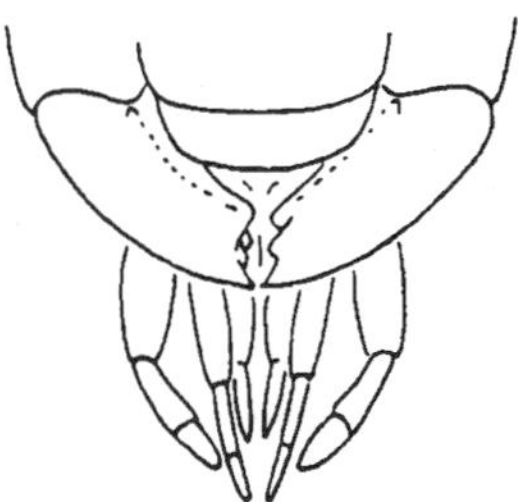

→

19. (A) Cerci present (zorapterans) .... ZORAPTERA

(B) Cerci absent (booklice, barklice) PSOCOPTERA

20. (A) Antennae shorter than body, not noticeable scales (bees, wasps, ichneumons) .... HYMENOPTERA

(B) Antennae as long as body; wings and body often with hairs (caddisflies) .... TRICHOPTERA

21. (A) Mouthparts close to eye 22

(B) Mouthparts at end of beak-like structure some distance from the eye (scorpionflies) .... MECOPTERA

22. (A) Wings never held flat over abdomen 23
(B) Wings held flat over abdomen 25

23. (A) Bristle-like inconspicuous antennae (dragonflies, damselflies) .... ODONATA

(B) Antennae apparently with several segments ... 24

24. (A) Hind wings with enlarged anal area folded fan-like; wings tend to curl around the body lengthwise (dobsonflies, fishflies, alderflies) .... MEGALOPTERA

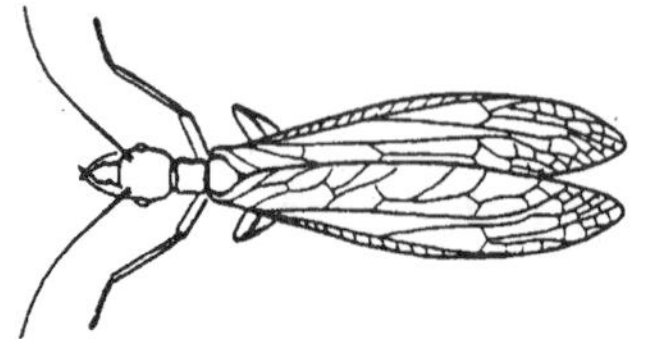

(B) Hind wings without enlarged, folded area; wings do not tend to curl around body lengthwise (lacewings, mantispids, ant lions, owl flies) .... NEUROPTERA

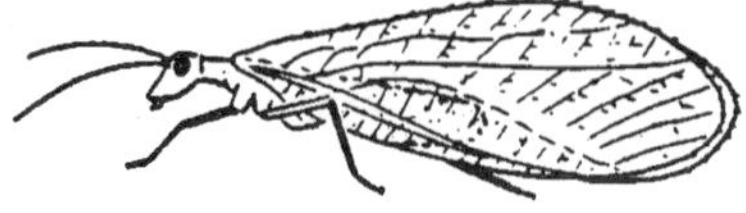

25. (A) All legs of walking type 26

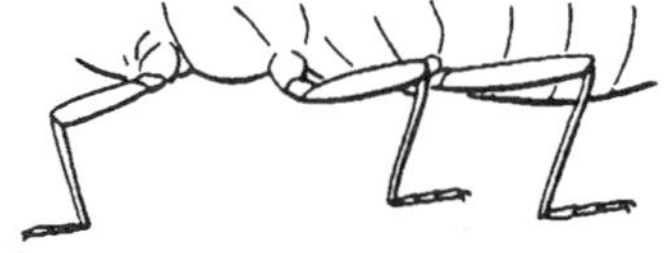

(B) Hind legs modified for jumping (tree crickets) .... ORTHOPTERA

26. (A) Basal segment of front tarsus has swollen appearance (webspinners) .... EMBIOPTERA

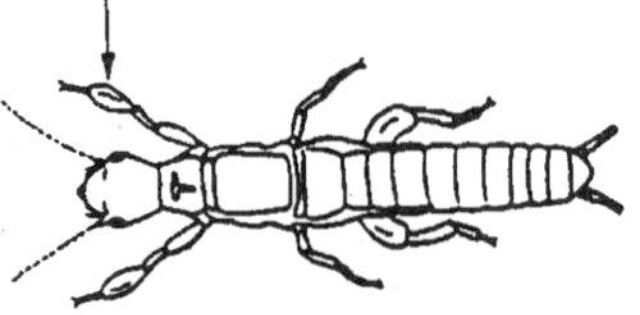

(B) All tarsal segments approximately equal in size 27

→

27. (A) Cerci usually long; more than 8 segments (stoneflies) .... PLECOPTERA

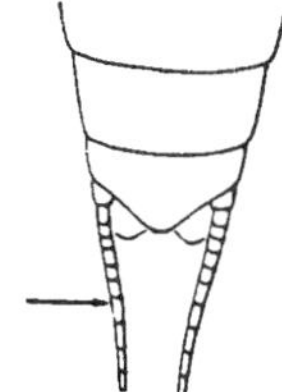
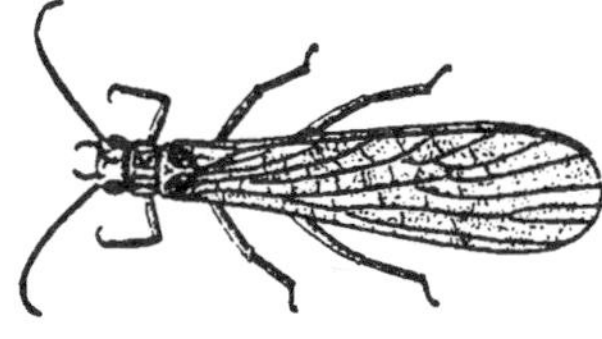

(B) Cerci short; with 2 to 8 segments or absent (termites) .... ISOPTERA

28. (A) Antennae present 29
(B) Antennae absent 39

29. (A) Mouthparts usually withdrawn or enclosed in the head and not apparent 30
(B) Mouthparts usually distinctly apparent 31

30. (A) Collophore present; spring-like organ usually present (springtails) .... COLLEMBOLA

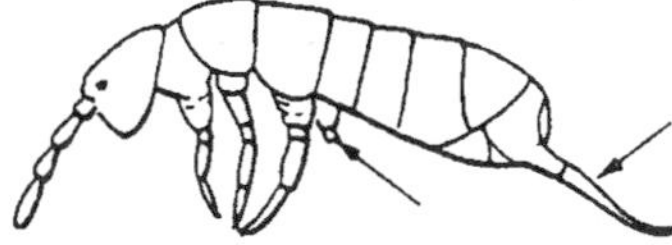

(B) Both collophore and spring-like organ absent; distinct cerci present .... DIPLURA

31. (A) Long tail-like appendages absent 32
(B) Three tail-like appendages present (silverfish, firebrats) .... THYSANURA

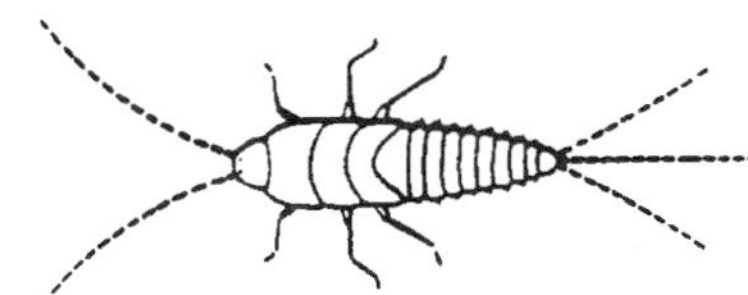

32. (A) Body flattened laterally or dorsoventrally 33

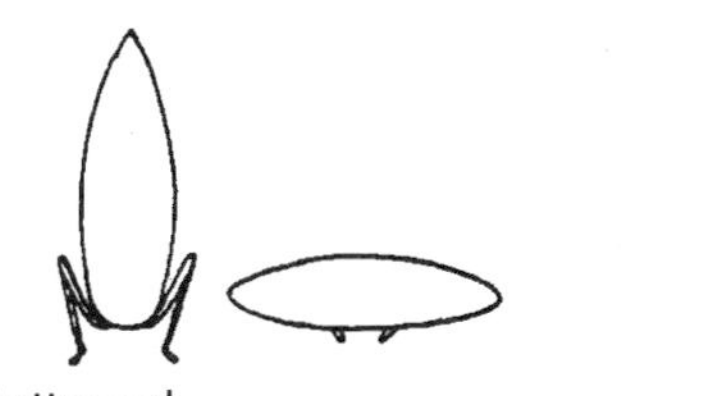

(B) Body not flattened 43

33. (A) Body flattened laterally (fleas) . SIPHONAPTERA

(B) Body flattened dorsoventrally 34

34. (A) Sucking mouthparts externally visible 35
(B) No sucking mouthparts externally visible 36

35. (A) Antennae longer than head (true bugs) .... HEMIPTERA

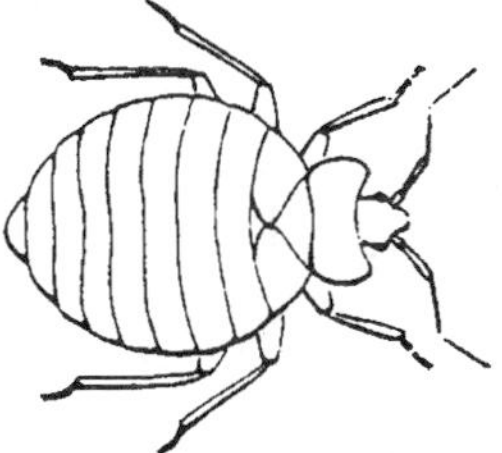

(B) Antennae shorter than head (louse flies, bat flies) .... DIPTERA

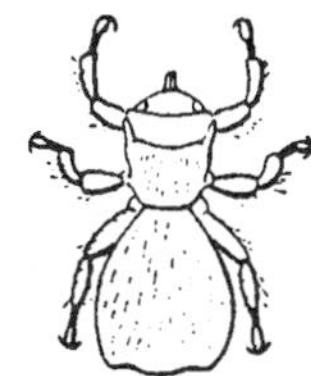

36. (A) Antennae longer than head 37
(B) Antennae shorter than head 39

37. (A) Basal segment of front tarsus swollen (web spinners) .... EMBIOPTERA

(B) Basal segment of front tarsus not swollen 38

➔

38. (A) Tiny insects; tarsi 2 to 3 segmented (booklice, barklice) .... PSOCOPTERA

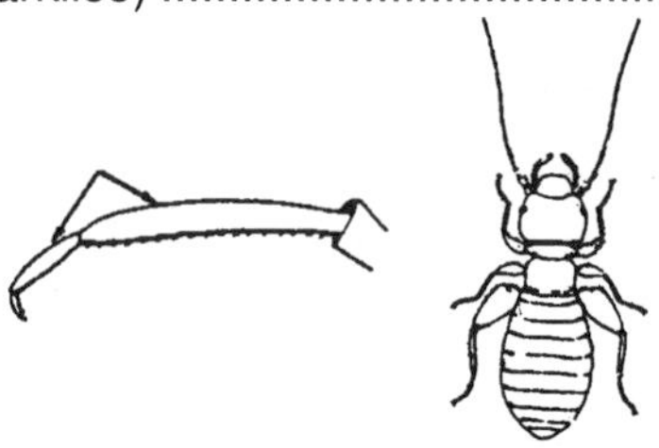

(B) Large insects; tarsi five segmented (cockroaches) .... DICTYOPTERA

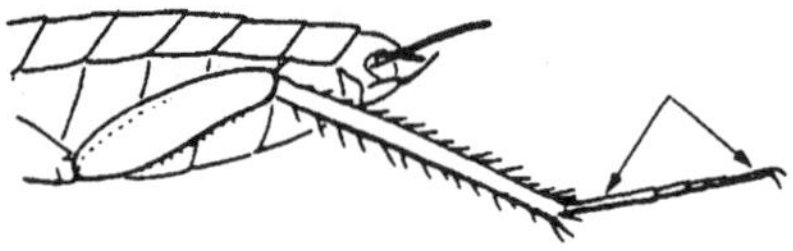

39. (A) Head wider than thorax at point of attachment to thorax (chewing lice) .... MALLOPHAGA

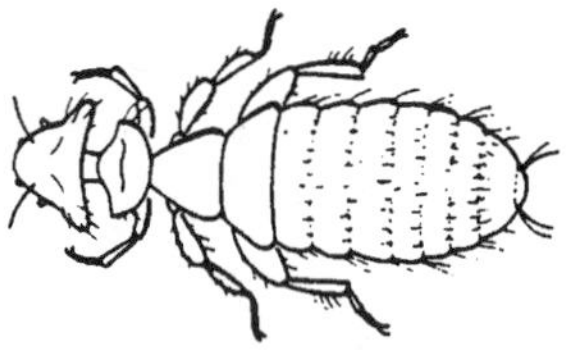

(B) Head narrower than thorax at point of attachment to thorax (sucking lice) .. ANOPLURA

40. (A) Legs present 41
(B) Legs absent 42

41. (A) Fewer than 12 abdominal segments (bat flies, louse flies) .... DIPTERA

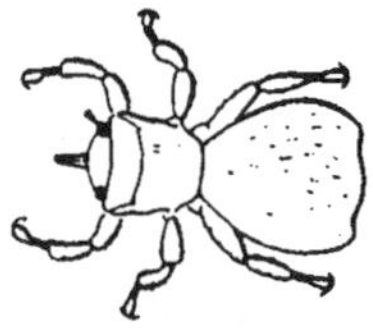

(B) Twelve abdominal segments (proturans) .... PROTURA

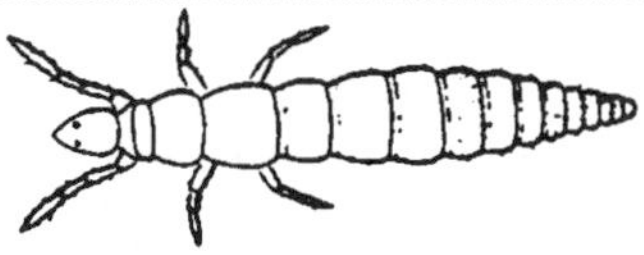

42. (A) Head and thorax separate (scale insects) .... HOMOPTERA

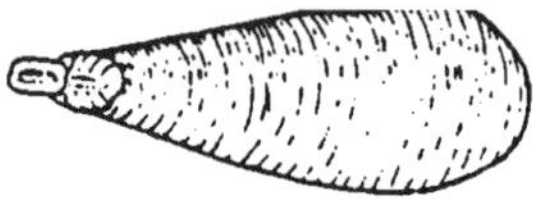

(B) Head and thorax fused (female stylopids) .... STREPISIPTERA

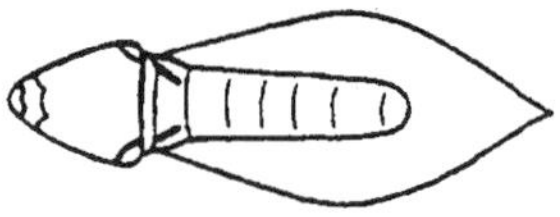

43. (A) Abdomen and thorax narrowly joined together (ants) .... HYMENOPTERA

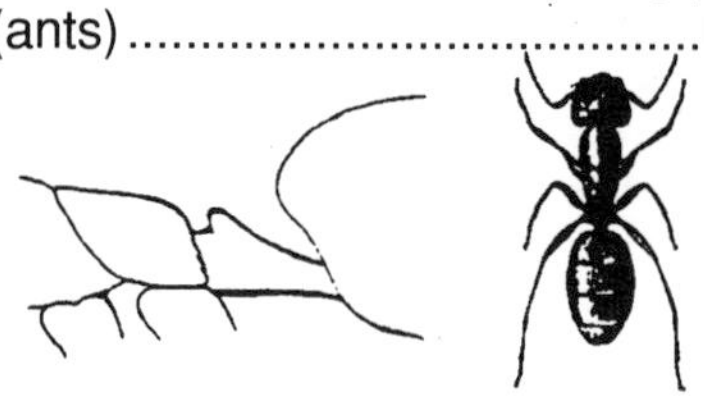

(B) Abdomen and thorax broadly joined together 44

44. (A) Body covered with scales (female cankerworms) .... LEPIDOPTERA

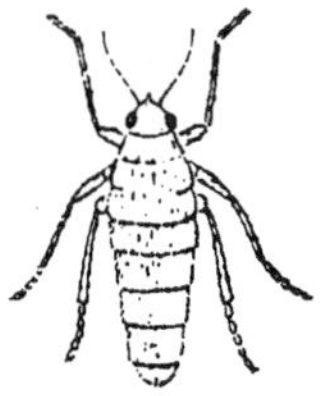

(B) Body not covered with scales 45

45. (A) Tarsal claws absent (thrips) ... THYSANOPTERA

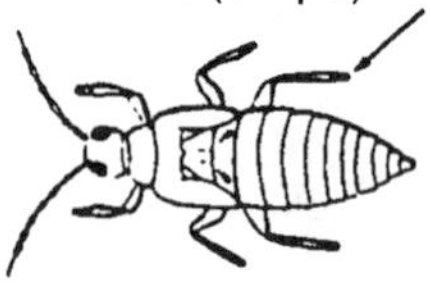

(B) Tarsal claws present 46

46. (A) Piercing-sucking mouthparts 47
(B) Chewing mouthparts 49

47. (A) Cornicles usually present (aphids or plant lice) ... . HOMOPTERA

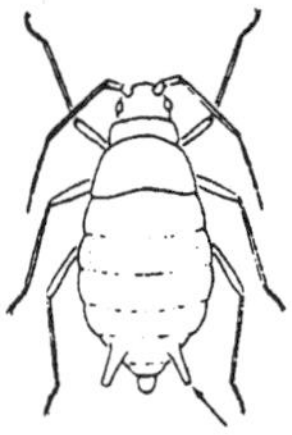

(B) Cornicles absent 48

➔

48. (A) With distinct head and eyes (bed bugs) .... HEMIPTERA

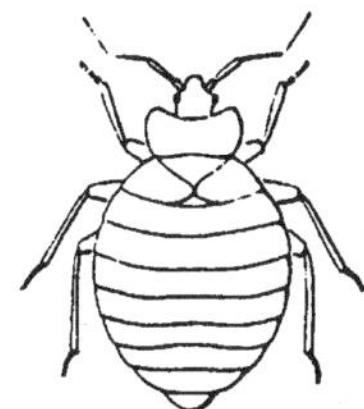

(B) Without distinct head and eyes (female scales) .... HOMOPTERA

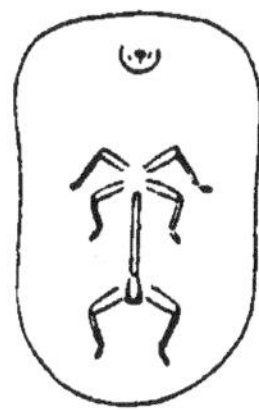

49. (A) Abdominal forceps present (earwigs) .... DERMAPTERA

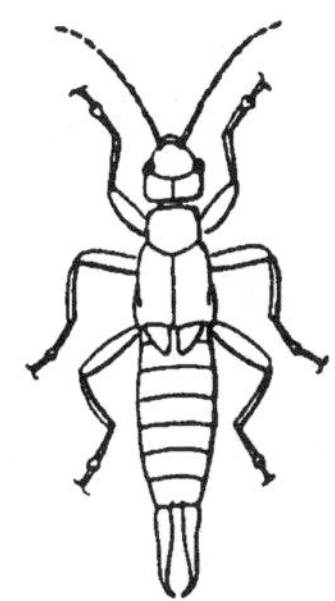

(B) Abdominal forceps absent 50

50. (A) Mouthparts at end of beak like structure some distance from eye (scorpionflies) .. MECOPTERA

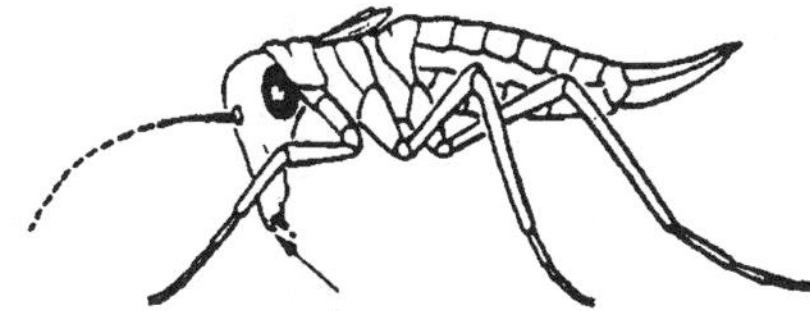

(B) Mouthparts not elongated, close to eyes 51

51. (A) Cerci present 53
(B) Cerci absent 52

52. (A) Antennae longer than one-third of body length (booklice, barklice) .... PSOCOPTERA

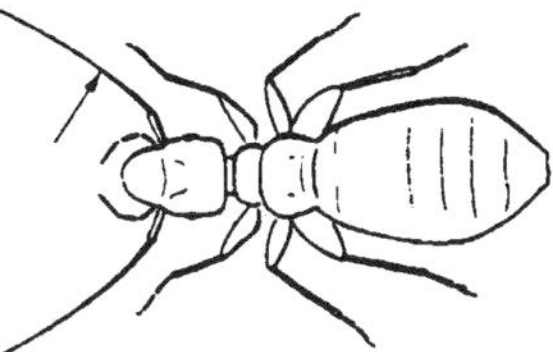

(B) Antennae shorter than one-fourth of body length (female stylopids) .... STREPSIPTERA

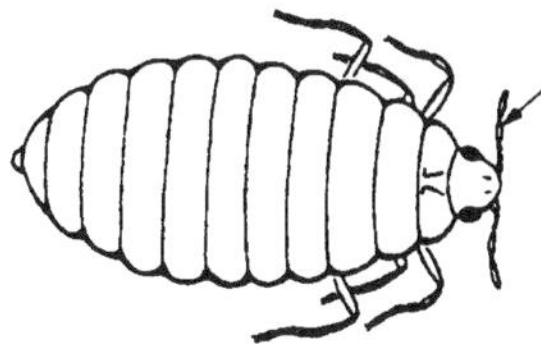

53. (A) Body leathery and usually grey or dark colored 54
(B) Body soft and pale colored 57

54. (A) Hind legs adapted for jumping .... ORTHOPTERA

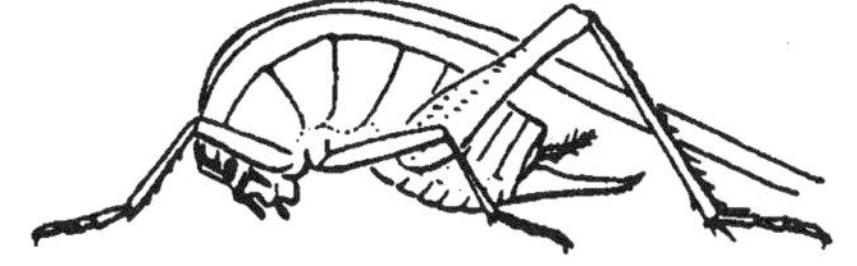

(B) Hind legs not adapted for jumping 55

55. (A) Pronotum narrow, body pencil-like or stick-like ... . PHASMIDA

(B) Body not elongated and stick-like 56

56. (A) Front legs enlarged grasping type (mantid) .... DICTYOPTERA

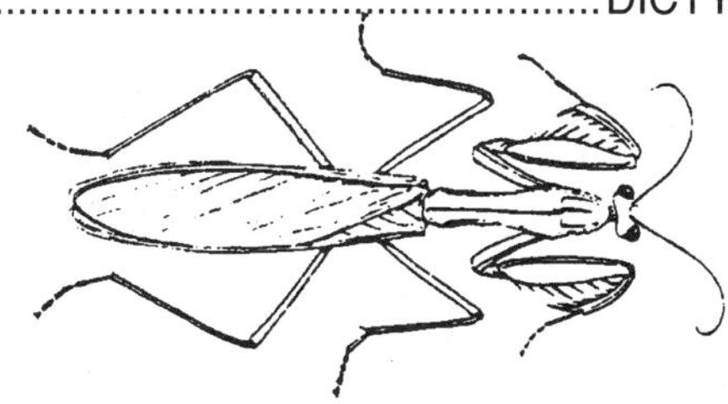

(B) Front legs not enlarged, pronotum broad and flattened, frequently pronotum covers head (cockroach) .... DICTYOPTERA

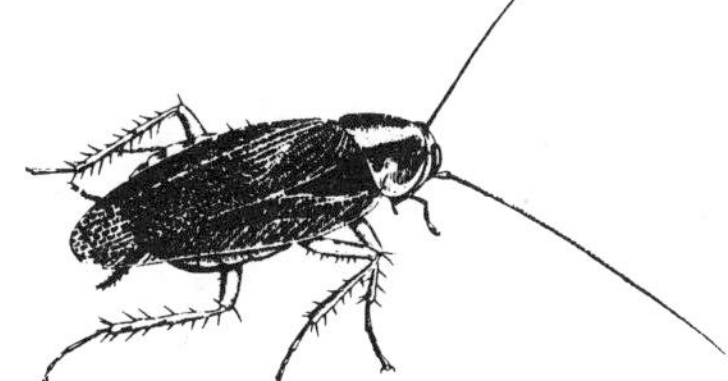

→

57. (A) Two tarsal segments (zorapterans) ....ZORAPTERA

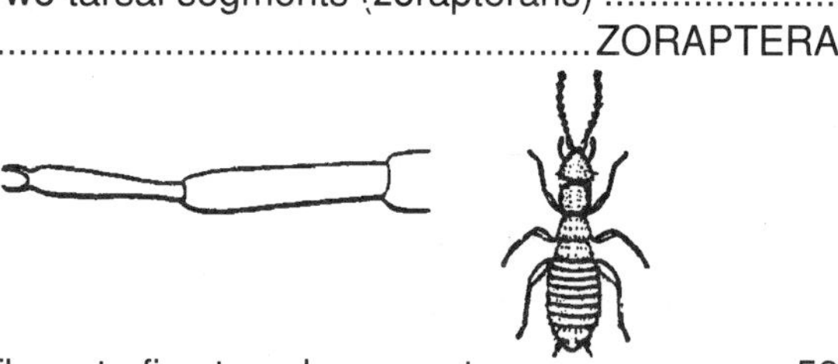

(B) Three to five tarsal segments 58

58. (A) Basal segment of front tarsai with swollen appearance (webspinners) ....EMBIOPTERA

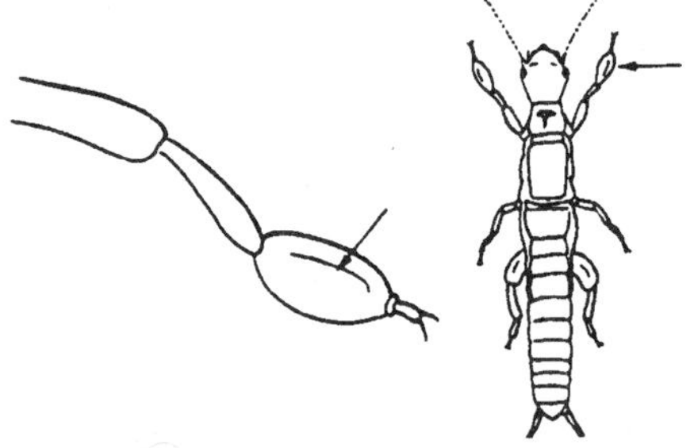

(B) Basal segment of front tarsi about same size as ones immediately following (termites) ....ISOPTERA

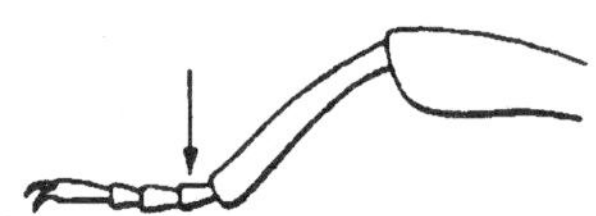

References

Blackwelder, R.E. 1967. Taxonomy; a text and reference book. J. Wiley and Sons, New York. 698 pp.

Borror, D.J., D.M. DeLong, and C.A. Triplehorn. 1981. An introduction to the study of insects. Saunders College Publishing, Chicago. 827 pp.

Brues, C.T., A.L. Melander, and F.M. Carpenter. 1954. Classification of insects. Harvard Univ. Mus. Compar. Zool. Bull. 73. 917 pp.

Comstock, J.H. 1964. An introduction to entomology. Comstock Publ. Assoc., Ithaca. 1064 pp.

Imms, A.D. 1957. A general textbook of entomology. Methuen and Co., London. 886 pp.

McCafferty, W.P. 1981. Aquatic entomology. Sci. Books Internat., Inc., Boston. 448 pp.

Usinger, R.L., Ed. 1956. Aquatic insects of California with keys to North American genera and California species. Univ. of California Press, Berkeley. 508 pp.

What's In a Name?

Entomologists, like other scientists, name living things according to a two-name system called binominal nomenclature. For instance, in this scientific lingo humans are called *Homo sapiens,* our official genus and species. Scientific names are Greek to some people. And for good reason. Most scientific names are based on Greek and Latin roots.

Scientific names serve a very useful purpose. They are universally recognized across all languages. However, most people do not use scientific notation in their daily language. As a result, most living things are known by common names. So it is with the insects.

What's in a name? Some say quite a bit about their owners. Insect common names sometimes reflect a geographical location. We have Chinese mantids, Carolina grasshoppers, California harvester ants, European hornets, German cockroaches, Hawaiian carpenter ants, and the Tahitian coconut weevil.

Some names are such that you might want to use them to describe your worst enemy. For instance, tropical rat louse, western treehole mosquito, twig pruner, vagabond crambus, uglynest caterpillar, goat sucking louse or even corn sap beetle.

Names sometimes reflect the food that an insect uses. We have coconut scales, corn leaf aphids, cranberry weevils, onion maggots, yucca moths, raspberry sawflies, and cotton borers.

A few insects lay claim to noble birth. We have Monarch butterflies and regal moths. Other insects are of more humble ancestry. Those insects include the common cattle grub, the common green lacewing and the common malaria mosquito.

Some insects apparently behave in ways that entomologists thought unusual. The crazy ant, the confused flour beetle, the gloomy and greedy scales, and the thief ant all fall into this category.

Other insects, it appears, could use some grooming tips. The crinkled flannel moth might need an iron, a shower could benefit the rough stink bug, and perhaps the roughskinned cutworm just needs a little lotion. The resplendent shield bearer, however, is fine as it is.

If imitation is the sincerest form of flattery, then toad bugs, rhinoceros beetles and crab lice have paid their compliments. In addition to borrowing their names, they also bear some resemblance to their namesakes.

Some insects are small, like the small milkweed bug. Others are smaller, such as the smaller yellow ant. As might be suspected, we also have a large milkweed bug and a larger yellow ant.

If all of this seems a bit confusing, well it is. You see, that is the purpose for those scientific names. For instance, take that famous insect called the small pigeon louse. It's not really clear if it is a small louse that attacks pigeons or if it is a louse that attacks small pigeons.

A Bee or Not a Bee?

Millions of insects inhabit planet Earth. To keep track of these six-legged creatures, scientists divide insects into groupings called orders. Beetles belong to the order Coleoptera. The order Orthoptera includes grasshoppers and crickets, while bees, ants and wasps are Hymenoptera.

Nearly 900,000 insects have been given a scientific name. Each scientific name includes at least two parts: a genus and a species name. The genus corresponds to a human family name, and the species is equivalent to a human first or given name. This method of naming organisms is known as bionominal nomenclature — a two-name system.

Scientific names are normally Latinized words, which makes them somewhat cumbersome for use by the general public. For instance, everyone would recognize the Musca domestica, but almost everyone calls that insect by its common name: house fly.

But even insect common names can be a bit confusing. For example, many insects fly, but all insects that fly are not flies — insects technically of the order Diptera. Thus, the common dragonfly is not a fly at all, even though it is an accomplished flyer.

To avoid this confusion when using common names, most entomologists use the following rule: If an insect is not technically a member of the order for which it is named, then its common name is written as one word.

Take, for instance, our friend, the dragonfly. Also the dobsonfly, damselfly and lanternfly. True flies, such as the house fly, the horse fly, the deer fly and the bot fly, have their common names written — or, rather, written properly, — as two words. (Some dictionaries disagree, leaving them etymologically correct, perhaps, but not entomologically correct!)

The same is true for insects called bugs. All bugs — members of the insect order Hemiptera — are insects, but all insects are not bugs. For example, the ladybug is not a bug at all but a beetle. So ladybug should be written as one word. If, however, this insect is called a lady beetle, two words are correct. The same is true of the insect called a Junebug; it's really a beetle and is sometimes more correctly called a May beetle. The lightningbug is frequently called a firefly, but it is neither a bug nor a fly, it is a beetle.

Some insects look like insects of another order, but their common names — when written in proper entomological fashion — can betray their charade. To wit, the bee fly and the bee moth. These imposters should not be confused with the real McCoy, such as the honey bee and the bumble bee.

So, if the question is, "A bee or not a bee?" the answer would be found in the way it's written. ■

Classification, Nomenclature and Identification of Insects

1. What is meant by classification according to phylogenetic relationships?
2. What classification category do humans and insects share?
3. What is binominal nomenclature?
4. What are common names of animals?
5. What is the correct method of writing genus and species names?
6. How can you tell if an insect with the name fly in its name is a true fly (a member of the insect order Diptera)?

The Insect

Insect Structure and Function

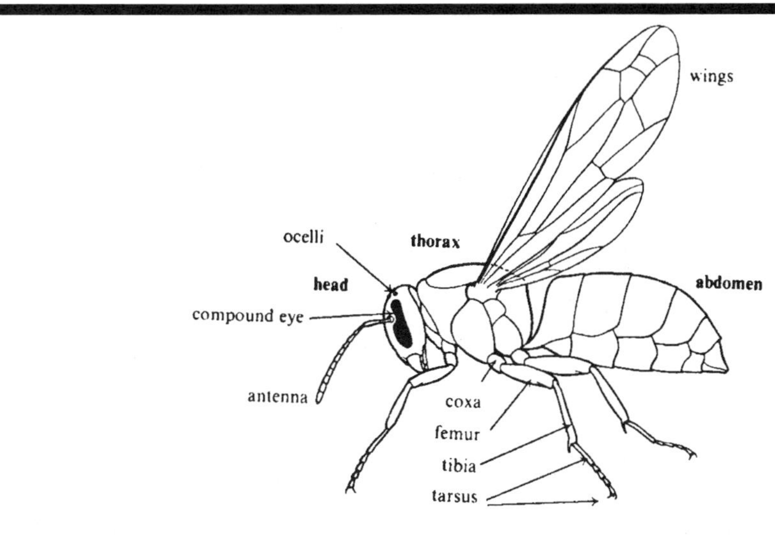

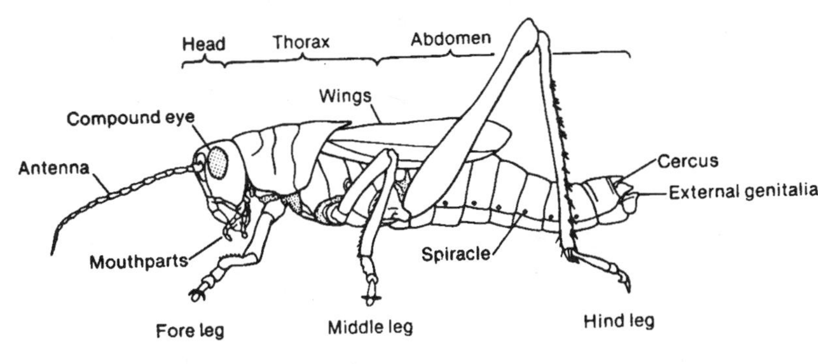

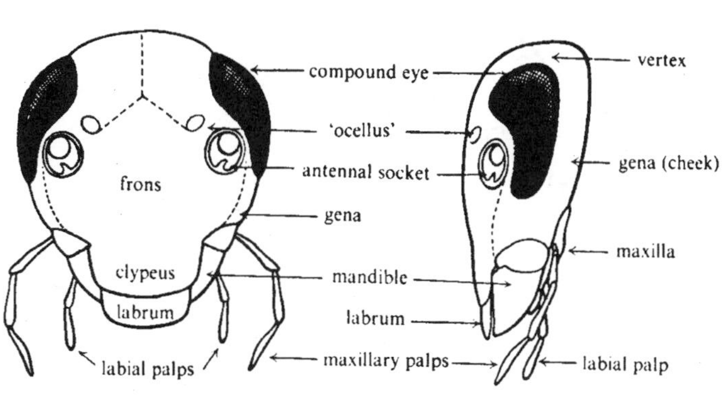

Adult insects typically have three distinct parts to the body. The parts are the head, thorax and abdomen. The insect body is basically composed of 20 segments although some of the segments are fused and it is not possible to count them. The head is composed of six segments. There are three segments in the thorax and 11 in the abdomen. Each of the parts of the insect body is adorned with protrusions — wings, legs and other things.

HEAD

The head of the insect functions primarily in a **food acquisition** and **sensory** role. The insect head is adorned with a pair of **compound eyes** (compound because they have more than one lens - the better to see you move) and a pair of **ocelli** (eye spots). Two **antennae** - to feel and smell. And a mouth. The mouth, in a typical chewing insect (cockroaches, crickets and grasshoppers), is a box-like structure with a lid called a labrum. On each side of the mouth are two chewing devices the mandible and the maxilla. The maxilla typically has an antenna-like structure called the palp. The floor of the mouth is the labium which may also have a pair of palps. The structures forming insect mouths are believed to have developed from the legs on the segments of some insect ancestor that looked a bit like a centipede with a pair of legs on each segment.

The mouth structure varies widely among insects. In houseflies the mouth is a sponging-sucking apparatus. Mosquitoes and bugs are equipped with piercing-sucking mouth parts. Butterflies and moths have a coiled tube for sipping nectar. Honey bees have chewing lapping mouths.

THORAX

The middle part of the insect body is specialized for **locomotion**. On the thorax we find the wings and legs. There are three pairs

of legs, two on each segment of the thorax. Like the mouthparts the legs differ among insects. They can function for running (cockroaches), jumping (crickets), holding onto hairs (lice), swimming (water bugs), grasping (preying mantids) or digging (mole crickets). Some insect legs may be modified to provide a device for noise-making as is the case in some grasshoppers.

Wings are very important to insects as a method of locomotion. Wings are also widely used by entomologists as a method of classifying insects. Many insect orders can be based on wing characteristics. The Greek word "**pterum**" meant a wing, feather or fin. That Greek word has become the root of many insect orders. For example Hemi**ptera** the true bugs which literally means half-wing, a reference to the fact that the wing is half leathery and half membranous. Not all adult insects are winged, lice, fleas, and some ants for example. Wingless insects are called apterous - a (without) and ptero (wings). Most winged insects have four wings - two on each of the second and third segments of the thorax. However the flies (Di**ptera**) have only two (di = two) wings - the back pair having been modified into balancing organs called halteres.

Insect wings are not thought to be modified legs because each segment of the thorax already has a pair of legs. Wings seem to have developed separately as extensions of the cuticle. Wings, like legs, are greatly diversified among the insects. Some wings are shell-like (beetles), others are covered with scales (butterflies and moths), or leathery (grasshoppers and cockroaches) or clear (cicadas).

ABDOMEN

The function of the abdomen is **breathing, excretion**, and **reproduction**. Along each side of the insect abdomen can be found spiracles. **Spiracles** are holes in the cuticle that connect to the insect breathing tubes called **trachae**. While insect breathing tends to be passive some insects, at times, telescope the abdomen to force air into and out of the spiracles.

The end of the abdomen (which is also the end of the insect) is the location of the end of the digestive system, the **anus**. **External reproductive organs** are also found at the end

The Wings Have It

Wings have made insects the most successful animals on earth. Yes, it's true that most birds have mastered the art, and one mammal, the bat, is considered an accomplished flyer. But insects, in terms of numbers that have taken up flying, are the masters of the air.

Insect wings are as diverse as insects themselves. In fact, many of the insect orders used to classify insects are based on wing characteristics. Most order names include the Greek "ptera" which means wing. The ancient Greek philosopher Aristotle even classified insects according to their wing structure.

The typical number of wings for insects is four. However, the flies have only two wings. They are classified as Diptera which literally means two wings. The back pair of wings in the Diptera are modified into knob-like structures called halteres. Halteres function as balancing organs when flies are in flight.

The butterflies and moths, Lepidoptera, are known as the scale wings, because their wings are covered with scales. These scales provide the beautiful color patterns that make butterflies among the most recognized insects.

Some insects like the cicadas, dragonflies, bees and wasps have four transparent wings. In the case of the cicada, the transparent wing allows the surface under the insect to show providing camouflage from potential predators.

Beetles have forewings that are hardened structures called elytra. These structures cover and protect the membraneous hind wings of these insects. It is the elytra that provide the look of "beetleness" that most of us readily recognize. It is that shape that has resulted in a well-known vehicle called the "beetle."

Some insects, the true bugs, like squash bugs, boxelder bugs and stink bugs have forewings that are part leathery and part membraneous. When these bugs fold their wings, the membraneous part is overlapped to cover the abdomen of the insect. Bugs are either right winged or left winged depending on which wing is placed on top of the other when they fold them.

Not all insects have wings. Fleas, lice and bedbugs have no wings at all. The lack of wings really hasn't hindered the ability of these little creatures to get around. They have taken to hitch-hiking as a preferred mode of transportation. However, there are far more insects using wings than hoofing it.

Flight is indeed the preferred means of transportation in most adult insects. "Have wings - will fly" seems to be the motto of the insect world. ■

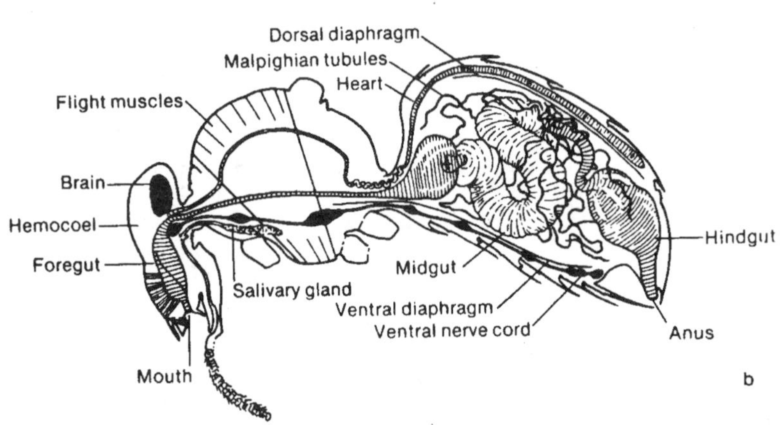

➔

Chapter 2

Cold-Blooded Insects

When you hear the words "cold blooded," what comes to your mind? Someone who gets cold easily? Or someone who is unfeeling, uncaring or ruthless? Of course, some of you more hip readers may think of Paula Abdul's song "Cold-Hearted Snake." But most of you probably don't think of insects.

Biologically, humans are not cold-blooded creatures. We maintain our body temperature near 98.6 degrees Fahrenheit winter or summer. But not so for snakes, salamanders, frogs, earthworms and insects. These animals are part of nature's "cold blooded" approach to life. Their body temperatures are near that of their environment.

Such a lifestyle does have its disadvantages, but insects manage to cope. Everything happens more quickly in insects as the temperature increases. They move faster, eat faster and even grow faster. This means that insects complete their life cycles in less time when the temperature is warm than when it is cool.

When temperatures are too low for activity, some insects rely on the sun for help. They sunbathe, soaking up a few rays to increase their body temperature. These insect sunbathers are called baskers. Like human sunbathers, some insect baskers bathe with their backs in the sun. These are called dorsal baskers. Others prefer the rays on their sides — the lateral baskers.

Some other insects increase their body temperature by vibrating their wings. Moths and bees can frequently be seen with their wings quivering in the cool morning air or in autumn. Such activity is akin to warming up an aircraft engine prior to flight. But with the insect, as soon as the body temperature is high enough, it's off into the wild blue yonder.

Honeybees have a sustained flight temperature threshold of about 54 degrees Fahrenheit. When the air temperature drops below 54 degrees, honeybees may not be able to fly. It is for that reason that some honeybees will be found away from the hive during the cool evening hours of spring or fall. These bees leave the hive when temperatures are suitable for flight, but are unable to return when temperatures drop below threshold. Such is the risk that a cold-blooded insect takes when flying near flight threshold temperatures.

Of course in human terms, if the insect is really cold blooded, it won't matter anyway. ■

of the abdomen in most insects (dragonflies are an exception). The most conspicuous reproductive organs are the ovipositors of the females. Some ovipositors hard not to notice are those which are modified into stingers such as in female bees and wasps. Some insects also have antennae-like sensory organs called **cerci** on their abdomen.

Insects, compared to humans, are said to be inside out. That's because their skeleton is on the outside instead of the inside like ours. The insect **exoskeleton** thus serves not only for support but is also the outer covering of the insect body. The exoskeleton of the insect is composed of several layers. The outer layer (called the cuticula) contains pigment and a nitrogenous polysaccharide called **chitin**. Chitin is insoluble in water and along with a wax layer provides the insect with protection against water loss. Chitin is very similar to another complex organic compound found in plants — cellulose.

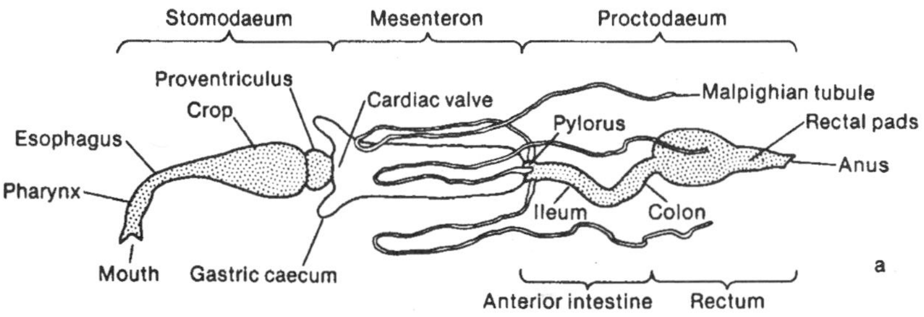

The outer layer rests on a cellular layer called the basement membrane. When an insect sheds its exoskeleton, which it must do to grow, the basement membrane digests the lower portion of the cuticula and forms a new cuticula under the outer portion of the old skin. That old skin is then shed. The cast skin is called the **exuviae**.

The process of an insect (or other arthropod) shedding its skin is known as **molting.** The time following emergence from its old skin is a dangerous time for an insect. It takes a while for the new cuticle to harden, a process called tanning. During this time the skin is soft and the insect is a target for predators.

The internal systems of the insect, as in the human, can be described in terms of five primary functions. However the system in the insects is somewhat different than in humans.

Nutrient procurement and processing. Both insects and humans have a mouth and esophagus that leads to a stomach. Both have salivary glands that begin the digestive process in the mouth. In an insect before the food gets to the stomach it enters first the **crop** and then the **proventriculus** (or gizzard), two organs

→

insects have in common with birds. As food enters the insect stomach it is encased in a sac called the **peritrophic membrane**. From the stomach in both humans and insects food enters the intestines and then goes to the rectum and leaves through the anus. In insects the remainder of the digestive process is called frass — a fancy way to say insect manure!

Internal transport. Both insects and humans have an internal transport fluid. Both fluids are pumped by a heart but in the human the fluid is contained in a closed system (our veins and arteries). In insects the system is an open one. The fluid in humans is called blood and it carries oxygen from the lungs and nutrients to and waste products away from the cells. The internal transport fluid in insects is called **hemolymph** and it flows from the tube-like heart and bathes the tissues before it returns to the opening of the heart. The insect system is a bit like a pump submerged in a sac of liquid — the sac being the insect and the liquid the hemolymph.

Regulation of body fluids. Insects and humans both have fluid filtering devices. We humans have kidneys. Blood flows through the kidneys where the nitrogenous wastes are removed and excreted in urine through what is called the urinary system. The insect kidney is called the **Malpighian tubules**. Named after an old time Italian scientist the Malpighian tubules remove the nitrogenous wastes, but since the insect does not have a separate urinary system the waste is excreted through the intestine (same as in birds).

Gas exchange. Gas exchange in fine folks everywhere is achieved through the lungs (that's why you shouldn't smoke). In the lungs the blood is oxygenated and it carries the oxygen to the cells. Insects lack lungs. Oxygen is supplied to cells by **diffusion through the trachae**. This requires that all cells be within diffusion distance of air. This means that insects have to be small for the system to work.

Nervous system. In both insects and humans the basis for the nervous system is the nerve cell and synapse. The chemical and physical nature of both systems is identical. That is why insecticides that attack the nerves work equally well on humans and insects.

Both insects and humans have a brain and a central nerve cord. The major difference in the nervous system of the two organisms is where the central nerve cord is located in the body. In humans the central nerve cord (the spinal cord) is located on our back or dorsal side. In insects the central nerve cord is located on the ventral side. Relative to the heart the position is reversed in humans and insects. Compared to humans the insect is built upside down.

Insect Structure and Function

1. Name the three major parts of the insect body. What is the primary function(s) of these body parts?

2. What does the Greek word pterum mean? Where in the study of entomology do you commonly find the use of this Greek root?

3. What name is used for the breathing holes of insects?

4. The cerci that are found on the south end of an insect headed north are analagous (correspond in some respects) to what other insect structures?

5. Are insect wings modified legs?

6. What are apterous insects? Name some.

■

Chapter 2

Insect Movement

When it comes to "gittin' along" insects rank right up there with "little doggies!" Insects walk, crawl, fly and some even hitch a ride, but they manage to get there just the same. Insect movement can be classified into three general categories: seeking something good, avoiding something bad, or moving to new habitat. How this is done varies from insect to insect and between development stages of the same insect.

In insects as in humans crawling precedes walking. Most immature insects do an insect version of the crawl. Maggots, larvae of flies, are legless so they have to wiggle and writhe through their habitat. Bee and wasp larvae are also legless but they normally don't have to go anywhere since their sisters bring food to them. Many grubs have legs, but some don't use them effectively because of the shape of their bodies. Indeed one soil-dwelling grub uses its legs to sort of swim through the soil using a back stroke.

Caterpillars are the most interesting of the immature insect walkers. Caterpillars have six legs — the same number as the adult insect — on body segments very near the head. However the caterpillar has some extra leg-like structures further back. These of course can't be legs since insects can only possess six (otherwise they would be spiders, crayfish, or centipedes). So entomologists have overcome this obvious contradiction by calling the extra legs prolegs! The last two prolegs on caterpillars are used for clasping — hanging onto sticks and the like. In general caterpillars walk by enlarging and contracting body segments and sort of pushing segments along in the general direction of the head.

➔

Have Wings, Will Fly

Birds do it. But so do the bees. In fact, most insects are real experts at it. They've been cruising the airways of planet Earth for 350 million years or so.

Insects have so mastered the art of flight that it is one of the reasons for their success. Indeed, in honor of their winged proficiency, we call some of them "flies."

As landlubbers, we humans stand in awe of the aerial gymnastics performed by insects. Scientists have studied insect flight and even counted the number of beats of an insect wing. A swallowtail butterfly, for instance, will flap its wings about nine times a second. A honey bee has a wingbeat frequency of 250 beats per second; the old housefly, about 190; and the Culex mosquito, a little over 300. It is the frequency of the wingbeat that produces the mosquito's all-too-familiar humming sound.

House flies cruise along at nearly 5 miles per hour. Some sphinx moths are the fastest insect fliers, reaching a top speed of over 33 miles per hour. The honey bee can fly about 8 miles per hour, and the bumble bee can buzz along at 11 miles per hour, a respectable number considering that a scientist once calculated that a bumblebee couldn't fly at all.

It seems that the surface area of the bumble bee wing was too small to carry that fuzzy, yellow- and black-striped body aloft. Of course, folks who have been dive-bombed by a bee intent on causing bodily harm have experienced the error of that calculation firsthand!

Insects use the power of flight for many purposes, including finding mates, avoiding enemies and moving to a new territory. Some insects travel many miles on the wing. The champion traveler in this regard is the Monarch butterfly. This insect travels each year from its breeding grounds in Canada to overwintering sites in the mountains of Mexico—a trip of over 2,000 miles.

Of the teeming billions of insects, not all use flight as a preferred form of locomotion. Some prefer to hoof it, as this old poem tells:

The Junebug hath a gaudy wing,
The lightingbug a flame,
The bedbug hath no wing at all,
But he gets there just the same!

■

Insect Movement

1. What name is used for the "excess" legs of caterpillars?

2. What geometric shape is the basis for adult insect walking?

3. What insect is reported to be the fastest flyer among all insects?

4. What insect travels further under its own power than any other?

5. Why was it said that a bumblebee should not be able to fly?

One of the modifications of this push scheme to caterpillar walking is with a group of lepidoptera larvae called loopers. Loopers are so called because they grasp the terra firma with their true legs (they have six of those you know) and then loop their body forward. This brings their terminal pair of prolegs along side the real things. At this point the caterpillar hangs on with the prolegs and propels the rest of the beast forward. This produces a looping motion hence the name. Some loopers are called measuring worms because the worms appear to be taking a measurement as they loop forward.

Walking, in adult insects, requires coordination of six legs. The common method used by insects to keep from getting tangled up is the tripod method. In this case, the insect uses the middle leg on one side with the outside legs of the other to move forward using the single leg as a pivot for the tripod. However if the insect needs to move quickly it sometimes uses a system where all three legs on one side move forward at the same time. In the military this would be something like: your left, left, left, your right, right, right!

Flight is the real accomplishment of insects. This is accomplished by direct muscle contraction in dragonflies, grasshoppers and butterflies. In which case the maximum wing beat frequency is about 30 beats/second. Other insect groups use indirect flight muscles where the muscles are used to contract the sides of the thorax in a spring-like fashion. Such a system can produce frequencies of up to 1000 beats/second in some of the flies. How fast can a fly fly? Some horse flies can go 9 mph. Bumble bees can do better, 11.2 mph. But the hawk moth has been clocked doing 33.7 mph — hopefully not in a school zone.

Other insects hitch a ride, especially when moving to a new habitat. This is always true of fleas and lice. They just ride on the host. Some insects catch a ride on the wind. Winds bring more than rain when they come into an area. It is not a free ride since most insects have to flap their wings to keep aloft in a moving air mass. When they get tired or stop flapping for whatever reason they drop out like rain. Hopefully to find a great place to live.

■

Chapter 2

Metamorphosis

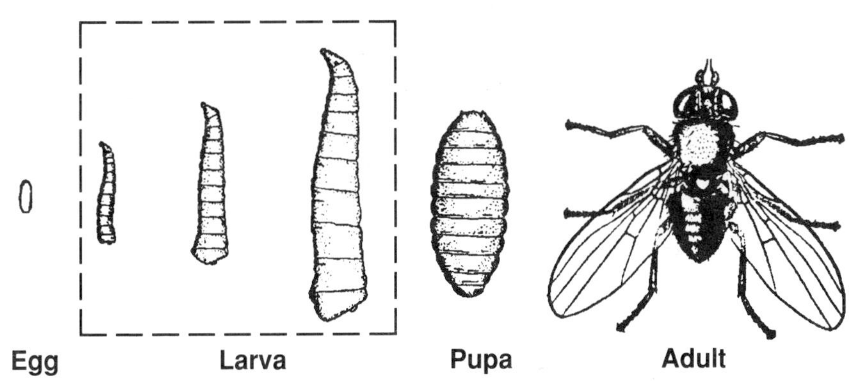

Complete Metamorphosis

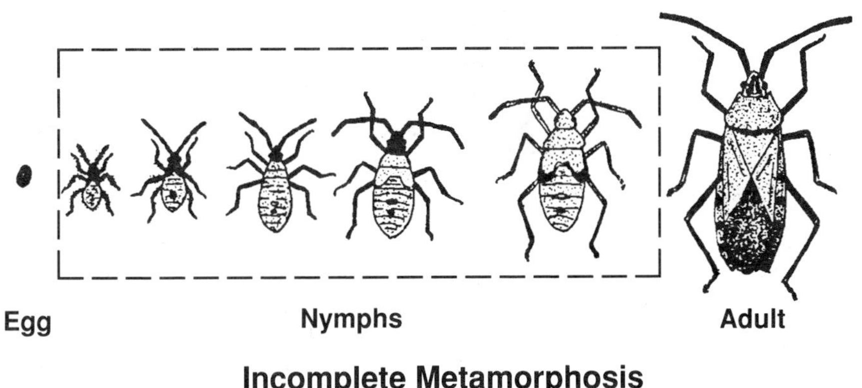

Incomplete Metamorphosis

Stage	Egg	Larva	Pupa	Adult
Function		Feeding	Transformation	Reproduction
Characteristics	Inactive	Active	Wiggle	Active
Growth	Yes	Yes	No	No
Names	Nit	Grub Maggot Caterpillar	Chrysalis Puparium Cocoon	Imago

The life cycles of insects involve a process called metamorphosis which is a change from one life form to another. Insects are not the only animals that practice metamorphosis. Frogs, toads and salamanders change from water breathing tadpoles into the adult form that breathes air. The process of metamophosis is widespread among the insects. The process is said to benefit the insect because the juvenile does not compete with the adult for the same food resource. For example the immature form of a butterfly, a caterpiller, feeds on leaves, the adult on nectar. The larvae of mosquitoes feed on microscopic plant and animal life in water, the adult on nectar and blood.

Insect life cycles can generally be divided into two groups. Those with a complete life cycle go through four stages of development — egg, larva, pupa and adult. In most instances, unless you have studied the larval stage of an insect, it would be impossible to know what kind of an adult insect it would become. Because of this mystery the ancient Latin word for this stage was larva (meaning ghost or mask) — the stage covered up or masked what it was going to be, what it would look like in the adult stage.

The table on the left presents a summary of the stages included in the life cycle of an insect with complete metamorphosis.

Insects that do not go through all four stages during development are said to exhibit incomplete metamorphosis (get it - not complete!) because they do not have a pupal stage. In this insect there are three stages — egg, nymph and adult. The nymph (from the Greek meaning bride) looks much like the adult but is not sexually mature and has no wings or only partially developed wings. In this case, such as with many plant bugs, both the immature and adult feed on the same food.

➔

Presto Chango!

Long before Dr. Jekyll transformed into Mr. Hyde, some insects had already mastered the ability to change their personalities.

These insects use a unique biological process called metamorphosis to change from one life form to another. By this process, a "Mr. Hyde," or a larva that can damage plants by its feeding, can become a Dr. Jekyll, or a usually harmless and sometimes beautiful adult insect.

Franz Kafka addressed the concept of metamorphosis in his work of fiction by the same name. A popular movie of more recent times, "Cocoon," also drew parts of its theme from the process of metamorphosis. Even Yuppies have noted the parallel between a quiet time in their own hurried lives and the apparent quiet of an insect undergoing pupation. In Yuppie lingo, a lazy day of lounging at home is known as "cocooning."

Changes in the insect during metamorphosis are miraculous. The tissues and organs of the larva are broken down and reassembled. The result is to produce a winged, adult insect, completely different from the wingless eating machine of its youth.

The insect stage that harbors these changes is the pupa, from the Latin word for doll. Apparently, ancient people saw in that insect form a likeness to the inanimate toy for a child. The same Latin root is used to form the word "puppet."

Insects protect their pupae in a variety of ways. Some, like the common housefly, are thrifty, using their last larval skin to form a protective cover for the pupae. Other insects, like that pest of lawns — the white grub — industriously form a nice chamber in the soil at pupation time. Still others follow the Boy Scouts' lead and make a tent-like structure by tying the edges of leaves together.

Some insects spare no expense or trouble to make their cocoons. Probably the most famous of this group is the silkworm, which spins a cocoon of silk for pupation. Centuries ago, it was discovered that the silken thread used by silkworm larvae to construct pupation chambers could be unwound and used for human purposes. Since that time, uncounted silkworms have spun up cocoons with the biological intent of becoming an adult. However, humans have interceded to claim the silk for their own uses.

And then there are those insects that choose the no-frills method. Most butterflies — unlike their close relatives the moths — have pupae that are naked. As larvae, these streakers among the insect pupae normally attach their tail end to a leaf or twig before pupating. Then while the butterfly pupa, called a chrysalis, hangs upside down, Mother Nature gives the creature a makeover.

Of course, this is absolutely necessary. How else would an ugly caterpillar turn into a beautiful butterfly?

■

Chapter 2

Strip Teasing — Insect Style

Insects and their arthropod relatives — shrimp, crabs, and lobsters — possess exoskeletons, a combination skin and skeleton which protects them against crushing, scratching, invasion by microorganisms, and water loss. A hard, durable exoskeleton is a great protective device, but it is a real problem as the insect grows — it won't stretch.

Knights of olde who covered themselves with suits of armor had a similar problem at times. Indeed, the knight who forgot to mind his waistline discovered the need for a new suit. Insects face a similar problem several times during their life cycles, and like the ancient knights, they acquire new suits of armor.

Before an insect grows a new exoskeleton, it sheds the old one, a process called molting. Most people are familiar with the shed skins of insects. For instance, what youngster hasn't gathered the conspicuous shells of cicadas? When the immature cicada nymph emerges from its underground home, it immediately molts to the winged adult stage. The old exoskeleton can be found fastened to a tree, shrub or fence post. Aphids also molt, and sometimes the only evidence of these pest insects on a plant will be hundreds of white, ghost-like skins.

Insect molting has long fascinated scientists, who have worked hard to describe the chemical nature of the process. Even poets have noticed — and described — the magic of an insect shedding its skin. In Tennyson's "The Two Voices," we read about a dragonfly molting:

An inner impulse rent the veil
Of his old husk; from head to tail
Came out clear plates of sapphire mail.

The ancient Greeks were aware of the molting process and had a word to describe it — ecdysis (eck DEE sis). It was from this word that H.L. Mencken coined his humorous term for a stripteaser — an ecdysiast!

The practical nature of an insect molting might not hold the same attraction to most people as the dance of a stripteaser. However, the result is the same; both the insect and the ecdysiast end up removing their outer clothing. ■

Autumn Wanderers

These autumn days are made for wandering. The air, so recently laden with the heat and humidity of the summer, acquires a refreshing crispness. The coolness of fall is a blessing and a curse. It relieves us of the summer swelter, but reminds us of the cold to come.

"As you go a wandering," you might even be moved to sing. However, if a "Val-de ri-val-de ra" fails to escape your vocal chords in an oral celebration of the season, you are not alone. Many of nature's finest songsters — insects and birds — have grown silent with the onset of fall.

The fall is a time when birds and insects prepare for winter. Some birds follow the sun and wander far from their summer homes. One North American insect, the Monarch butterfly heads south to Mexico. Most insects just prepare to wait the winter out.

For some insect caterpillars, winter preparation means looking for a suitable place to face the cold. The insects go "a wandering" and are appropriately called wanderers. Many wandering caterpillars, but not all, go unnoticed by humans. Caterpillars of the giant silkworm moths are large, showy insects. Since they primarily feed on trees, they are not noticed by casual observers during the summer. As fall approaches, they leave their food plants and seek a sheltered site to spin a cocoon. This brings them down to our level, where they are found crawling across sidewalks, on porches and into garages.

Another group of highly noticeable insect wanderers includes the small, fuzzy caterpillars. These moths-to-be overwinter in some protected site. They seem to have difficulty finding just the right place to spend the winter, so they frequently wander about looking for another site. One group of caterpillars — the wooly bears with black and brown stripes — is famous for predicting the severity of winter. Its fame is probably enhanced by the fact that it wanders on most sunny days late into the fall, long after much other insect activity has ceased.

A little wandering on a fall day is good for humans and insects. "Val-de-ri-val-de ra!" ■

Metamorphosis

1. Why is metamorphosis said to be a benefit to insects?
2. What are the four life stages of insects that have complete metamorphosis?
3. What is the primary biological function of insect larvae?
4. What Greek word meaning bride is used to describe a form of immature insect?
5. The word "puppet" has the same Latin root as what insect stage?
6. Which group of the Lepidoptera have naked pupae?
7. What two terms used for the process whereby an insect sheds its exoskeleton?

Chapter 2

Velvet Wings

Butterflies and Springtime

The signs of spring. Little frogs, called spring peepers, croaking at the top of their amphibian lungs. Redbirds singing from the highest branch of the tallest tree. Bursting buds on the maple tree. Daffodils, tulips and violets. And butterflies.

There's nothing like the sight of a butterfly to indicate springtime. For many centuries, people everywhere have noticed the first butterfly of the new season.

The term butterfly probably was derived from the common yellow cabbage butterfly because it is first seen in the early spring season. Early spring has been called the butter season because milk production tends to increase then. In Anglo-Saxon language, these insects were called "butter-fleage," — meaning butter fly. A German name for these insects is "Schmeterling," — from cream, — suggesting a similar derivation from the English term.

In most temperate regions of the world, butterflies overwinter as mature larvae or pupae. So when spring rolls around, they are ready to pupate and emerge as butterflies.

Butterflies are well-known seasonal travelers. The Monarch butterfly goes north in the spring and south each fall across North America. In South America, travelers in the jungles can sometimes determine the points on the compass by observing the direction of the flight of butterflies.

Whether as newly emerged adults or as migrants headed to summer breeding grounds, the presence of butterflies is a sure sign of spring in North America.

Many folk sayings are associated with the first butterfly of the season. In Devonshire, England, people are admonished to "Kill the first butterfly you see each year, or you will have bad luck all through the year." This may be a reflection on the pest nature of the cabbage butterfly; its larvae feed on and damage many plants of the cabbage family.

In some areas of the world, good luck is said to follow when a butterfly lands on a person. That saying was known to a Congressman who, while in attendance at a Washington political rally in the late 1800s, noticed that a butterfly had alighted on his hat. The fellow stated that his luck was going to be good. However, another Congressman of the opposition party commented that he wouldn't be so sure. It was a cabbage butterfly that was on the hat. The insect, the observer noted, had recognized a cabbage head when it saw one!

■

Tenting on the Old Campground

For many folks, spring means the return of the camping season. It's time to retrieve the musty-smelling tent from the basement or attic. But before most human campers make their first spring foray into the great out-of-doors, the insect tents are already in place.

The most conspicuous of the insect tentmakers is the eastern tent caterpillar. This insect, a hairy brown caterpillar that grows to about 2 inches in length, has been observed making tents in America's trees since 1646.

The insect passes the winter in the egg stage. In early spring, the eggs hatch. Young larvae band together and produce a large thick web, called a tent. The tent is normally located in the fork of a tree.

Larvae do not feed within the tent. They use the tent for protection from the weather, and possibly, from predators. Hungry larvae leave the tent where they feed on the newly forming leaves of their host trees. Favorite trees are wild cherry, apple, peach, and plum, although other trees are sometimes attacked.

By midsummer, the larvae pupate and turn into yellowish brown moths. The moths mate and lay clusters of eggs which will hatch the next spring to start the cycle over again.

Some people, it seems, do not like the sight of a group of happy campers — at least of the insect variety — so they try to dispose of the little beasts. If the tree under attack is small, one approach is to prune the limb with the web and worms and destroy it. Several insecticides can also be used to kill the caterpillars. However, treating large trees with insecticide requires specialized equipment, so it may be necessary to hire a professional.

In general, the feeding of tent caterpillars will not cause permanent harm to a tree. Usually the tree will have time to leaf out following the feeding. However, defoliation by tent caterpillars in two or more consecutive years could stress the plant and warrant control.

So the damage caused is more to the aesthetics of the tree and the pride of the owner. However, some people take the approach that a few insect tents in a tree are an interesting biological event — especially if they can't be reached with the pruning shears.

■

Chapter 2

Cutworms Everywhere

Gardeners hate them, and the farmers live in fear of them. They are cutworms, larvae of moths that are named after their habit of cutting plants as they feed.

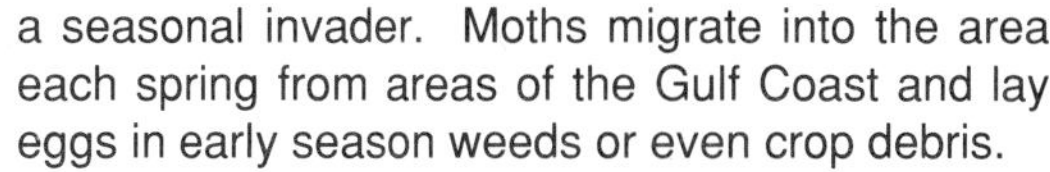

There are many species of cutworms, and their numbers vary greatly from year to year.

Some cutworms are described in terms of their lifestyles. There are climbing cutworms, solitary cutworms, army cutworms and subterranean cutworms. Some cutworm names are descriptive of their appearance, such as spotted, black, dingy, yellow-striped, white, glassy, or bronzed cutworms. But generally, cutworm moths are rather nondescript, drab-colored insects. The moths are normally grey and brown with few distinct markings.

Most cutworms spend the winter in the larval stage in temperate regions. In the spring, the larvae pupate and emerge as moths, which then lay eggs in areas of vegetation. There, newly hatched larvae begin to feed on the closest plants.

One of the most widespread cutworms is the black cutworm, which is found worldwide. In the heartland of the United States, the black cutworm is a seasonal invader. Moths migrate into the area each spring from areas of the Gulf Coast and lay eggs in early season weeds or even crop debris.

When a new crop is planted, the hungry larvae begin to feed on those plants. These young larvae feed on foliage for a week or so, then their feeding habits change. Black cutworm larvae become light-sensitive and go underground. The insect, which is now termed a subterranean cutworm, emerges from its soil hideaway during the nighttime hours to feast upon tender stems of all kinds of plants.

If the target of cutworm feeding just happens to belong to a gardener, an irresistible force has met a self-proclaimed immovable object. The gardener cherishes each plant. The cutworm looks at all plants as mere food items and proceeds to do what it does best: eat! What's more, the cutworm adds insult to injury by cutting more plants than it really needs for a food supply. Much to the dismay of the gardener, this results in dead and damaged plants, so chemical warfare begins.

It's a timeless battle between cutworm and gardener, and one thing is for sure: gardeners will, at some time, get caught with their plants down!

■

Ugly Worms

True silkworm moths are not native to North America. However, the largest and most-attractive moths on this continent are called giant silk moths.

The giant silk moths vary in size with wing spans from 3.5 to 6.5 inches. These moths include the Cecropia, the Promethea and the Polyphemus, named after Greek mythology gods.

Adults of the giant silk moths do not feed. Their mouths are barely developed and not capable of sucking up nectar as is done by most moths. Their immature forms, however, make up for the lack of feeding on the part of their parents. Larvae of giant silk moths are voracious eaters, feeding on leaves of trees and shrubs. These large larvae are spectacular insects. Most are green and ornately armed with brightly-colored tubercles and spines. Some folks think these larvae are down right ugly!

During the summer months, the larvae are small and generally go unnoticed by the public. However, they grow quickly and as fall approaches, the small worms have turned into big worms. Some are 5 to 6 inches in length, and are quite visible as they wander around looking for a suitable site to spin a pupal case.

These "wanderers" are sometimes discovered crawling across sidewalks or up the sides of houses. Such encounters between humans and giant silk moth larvae elicit less than appreciative responses from most folks. Many people are inclined to describe these large, spine-bedecked larvae as gross, disgusting or worse.

"Ugly is as ugly does." In this case, being ugly discourages most predators from attempting to make a meal of the creatures. But the worm's appearance only fascinates little boys, who frequently carry them home for pets. Whereupon, long suffering mothers will come up with a make-shift cage for the new pet. The worm responds by spinning a cocoon. There, snug as can be in its silken case, the worm waits for spring. When spring comes, the ugly worm is miraculously transformed into a beautiful moth. Could it be that the "ugly duckling" was really the larvae of a beautiful, large moth?

■

Chapter 2

Caterpillars

It's the time of year when mother nature evicts old man winter from the seasonal driver's seat and hands the reigns to spring. A season of renewal — birds sing, flowers bloom, and butterflies and moths lay eggs.

These butterfly and moth eggs will hatch into creatures called caterpillars, which have a very important biological function — eating. Their most common food is the green tissue of plants. For this reason springtime, when all the leaves and trees are green, is a great time to be a hungry caterpillar.

The word "caterpillar" is based on the Latin catta pilosa which means hairy cat. The exact origin of the term is unknown, however, hairy does apply to some caterpillars. Immatures of moths are generally covered with hair and include such familiar insects as the wooly bear. The majority of butterfly larvae are naked — without hair — but are still called caterpillars. Most caterpillars move using a creeping motion, therefore, ancient Romans may have related it to the stalking motion of a cat.

Caterpillars, of the insect type, are familiar creatures. Some folks find them chowing down on their favorite plants and become hostile to the little creatures. To other folks, a caterpillar is something to admire, or in the case of little boys, something to collect and take home in the pocket of a shirt.

Such admiration is expressed by Christina Rossetti in her poem "The Caterpillar."

Brown and furry
Caterpillar in a hurry
Take your walk
To the shady leaf or stalk
Or what not,
Which may be the chosen spot.
No toad spy you,
Hovering bird of prey pass by you;
Spin and die,
To live again a butterfly.

To most people the caterpillar is of the insect variety, but to others it is a yellow crawler tractor manufactured by the Caterpillar Corporation. Why such a name for a tractor? It seems that the early crawler tractors brought to mind the insect version, thus, the name of the company and its products. Whether it's a tractor or an insect larva, the caterpillar can frequently be seen working in the green fields of summer. ■

The Death's-Head Moth

Remember the old saying "if looks could kill, you'd be dead?" Well, the death's-head moth has the look — the pattern of a human skull is well-defined on its back.

But don't be afraid, this insect is not some dastardly devious member of the insect world. It can't bite or sting, nor does it possess a sinister threat to humans. Unlike some moths, the death's-head moth isn't interested in destroying our possessions.

This large moth has a wingspan of 4 inches and is found throughout Europe. Technically, the death's-head is one of a family of moths known as Sphinx or Hawk moths. They are swift fliers and are found around flowers in the evening. Because of this behavior, they are sometimes called hummingbird moths.

Larvae of these moths are known as hornworms because they have a conspicuous horn protruding from their posterior. The familiar green worm that feasts from time to time upon tomatoes is a hornworm, the tomato hornworm to be exact.

Because of its name, the death's-head hawk moth is a well-known insect. Hood used the insect in his poem "Haunted House." More recently this insect has been featured in the movie "Silence of the Lambs." In the movie's advertisement, the death's-head moth is shown across the mouth of the film's star, Jodi Foster. The insect plays an important role in the movie. In fact, it lives up to its name although through no fault of its own. The movie makers, however, while acknowledging the foreign nature of the real death's-head moth, appeared to have used its entomological cousin, a tobacco or tomato hornworm as a stand in for the real thing. No matter, the real thing still gets the bum rap.

So how does the death's-head moth live? In its immature stage, it feeds on potatoes, and in its adult stage, it hangs around honey bee hives, perhaps hoping for a little sip of honey.

Unlike other moths, the death's-head squeaks like a mouse. A hired killer this insect is not. Its reputation is due entirely to the clothes it wears. ■

Hawk Moths

One of the spectacles of summer occurs during the evening hours in many backyards across America. The hawk moths come out as nature soothes the transition of a hot, bright day to a cool, dark night by casting the mantle of dusk across her handiwork.

These fast-flying moths leave their daytime retreats to seek the sweet nectar provided by flower blossoms that open after dark, such as the evening primrose.

Hawk moths are well-equipped for the job of sipping nectar through a straw. They have a long, coiled proboscis, a tubular sucking organ, similar in structure to a paper party horn. They hover in front of the plant and use the uncoiled proboscis to reach the nectaries of the flowers.

Hawk moths feed in a similar fashion to hummingbirds, and because of it are sometimes called hummingbird moths. Like their namesakes, these moths can fly backward, which helps them retreat when the flower is empty.

It is hard to imagine a more idyllic life than that of a hawk moth — flying around flowers at dusk sipping nectar. However, like a lot of insects, hawk moths are a bit like Dr. Jeckyll and Mr. Hyde. As larvae, they are leaf feeders and are called hornworms because of the horn that protrudes from their south end when they are headed north.

These insects aren't normally pests, however, the tomato hornworm is. It is a prolific consumer of tomato foliage. In no time at all, a large hornworm can turn a tomato plant into an unsightly batch of stems. Because hornworms are easy to find, some gardeners use the shoe leather approach for control. They merely extract the hornworm from the plant, toss it to the ground, and do their version of the barnyard stomp!

That's the way it is with the tomato hornworm, as a larva it is hated. Then through the power of metamorphosis, it becomes an adult, a hawk moth, which is greatly admired for its power of flight and food habits.

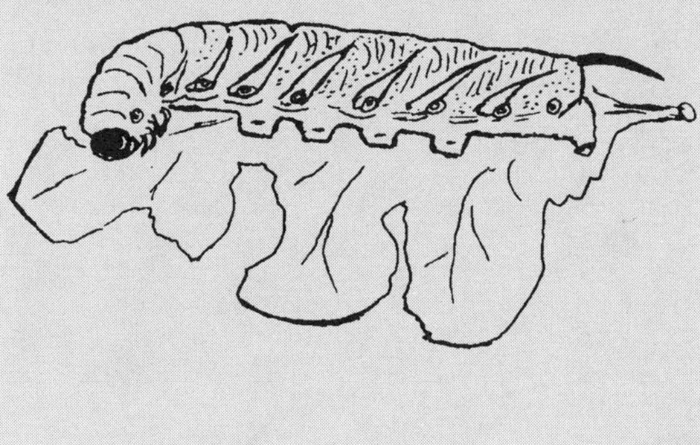

■

Corn Borer Murder

If murdering a corn borer moth were a crime, all nighttime motorists would be in jail. Those cream-colored moths fluttering in snow storm-like density in the glow of headlights are corn borers. They are the victims that end up on radiators, in grills, or as unsightly grease spots on windshields and headlights.

In their immature or larval stage, corn borers are major pests of corn. As worms, they bore in the corn stalk - - that's the basis for their name. Such activity weakens the plants and can result in yield reduction. Those borers become moths, and the moths in turn lay eggs that hatch into borers, so the cycle goes.

In most years, the borers are still chomping on corn plants during late summer and fall in preparation for winter. However, the unusually warm summer of 1991 has accelerated development of many insects, including corn borers. The moths that were flying in August normally do not emerge until the following June. The early emergence coupled with high numbers have created the nightly "storm of moths."

Corn borer moths spend their days lounging around in grassy areas such as roadsides and creekbanks. When the sun goes down, these moths take to flight, seeking suitable plants on which to lay eggs.

Corn borer moths, like many other night-flying insects, are attracted to lights. Consequently, moths are frequently found congregating around porch lights and windows far from their home cornfields.

However, drivers traveling through areas of high corn density are most likely to encounter the fluttering masses of moths. These insects are going about their "mothly" business when the auto invades their airspace. The stream of air flowing over the auto sucks the hapless insects into an unexpected death.

If the car is moving at 40 mph or slower, most insects safely flow over it. However, at higher vehicle speeds, they are unable to control their destiny and end up in a fatal crash landing. As a result, windshields are messy as well as hazardous to the motorist who is trying to peer down the road.

The next morning, one can assess the mess, but be wary. The corn borer's misfortune is a boon to another insect. In many cases, yellow jackets have arrived on the scene and are busy extracting the moth carcasses as food for their larvae.

In nature nothing is wasted. Of course, to most folks having yellow jackets swarming around the corn borer carnage on their auto is just adding insult to injury.

■

Chapter 2

Twilight Beckons Insect Jeckyl and Hyde

The best thing about some hot summer days is that they turn into cooler summer evenings. That's when the accumulated heat of day slowly begins to escape the clutches of the earth. It's a time of day when humans appear in backyards to lounge in lengthening shadows, courtesy of the decaying rays of the westbound sun.

Twilight is also the time of day when hawk moths descend on flower beds to sip nectar from awaiting blossoms. Hawk moths are medium to large moths that are strong fliers. It is because of their speed of flight and rapid wing beat that they are named after that bird of prey, the hawk.

These moths also are called hummingbird moths. Most feed from flowers like hummingbirds and, in some cases, are about the same size as these diminutive birds. They even hover in front of flowers like these birds and use their proboscis to extract nectar from the blossoms.

In addition to being called hawk or hummingbird moths, these insects also are called hornworms or sphinx moths. These latter names are based on the immature form. Larvae have a conspicuous horn protruding from the top of their last segment and are appropriately called hornworms. Hornworms sometimes rear up when disturbed, and this makes them look a little like the Egyptian Sphinx. Thus, some people have called them sphinx moths.

Larvae of hawk moths feed on plants. The most commonly observed of the hawk moths consumes tomato foliage as a larva and is called the tomato hornworm. Most gardeners recognize this insect as a serious pest of tomato because of the amount of leaf tissue that it can consume before it crawls from the plant to form a pupa. The insect then emerges from the pupa as a moth and begins to spend its evenings looking for flowers in search of a little sip of nectar.

The tomato hornworm is truly one of the Dr. Jeckyl and Mr. Hyde insects in this world. As a larva, it feeds on and damages our tomato plants, so we consider it a pest and try to get rid of it. As an adult, it is a beautiful and graceful moth that is fun to watch as it gathers nectar from our flower beds.

Most children have at one time or another tried to catch a hawk moth as it hovered in front of flowers in the early evening hours. Most are not successful. After all, in the adult stage a hawk moth is one of the fastest insects known, reaching speeds of nearly 30 mph.

Velvet Wings

1. What was the probable origin of the term butterfly?
2. What is the function of the tent produced by larvae of the tent caterpillar?
3. Why are cutworms called cutworms? What is the common name of the adult cutworm?
4. What is the food of the giant silkworm moths?
5. How is the term wanderer used in reference to insects?
6. In general how would you distinguish the larva of a moth from the larva of a butterfly based on their hair covering?
7. Why are hornworms so called? What is the common name of the adult hornworms?
8. What moth is said to squeak like a mouse?

Chapter 2

Insects in Armor

Flies of Fire

They are one of the true wonders of the insect world: fireflies. To some folks, no warm, summer evening would be complete without the flickering aerial gymnastics of these beetle pyromaniacs.

Many a youngster has spent countless evening hours pursuing the elusive creatures. Much of the fun is in the chase and capture. However, like any big-game trophy hunter, the quarry must come home. Filled with firelies, a jar provides a barrage of flickering light. A miniature aurora borealis on the windowsill. The intensity of the insect-generated lightning flashes can even keep the successful hunters from falling asleep.

But fireflies don't fly around flashing just to become a prisoner in an empty peanut butter jar. They are flashers with a purpose. Their goal is to electrify one of the opposite sex — to find a mate.

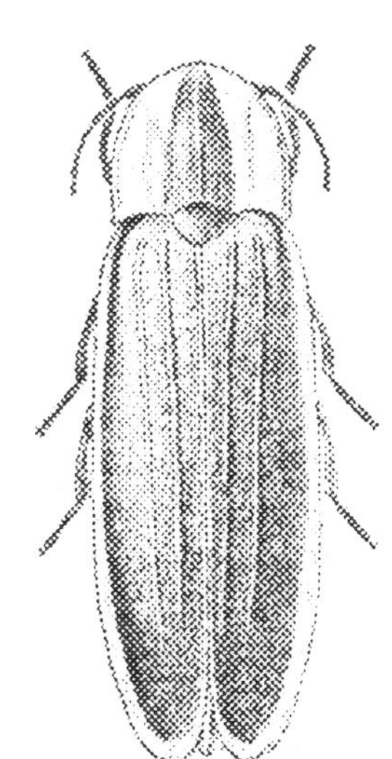

The romantic purpose of firefly activity has not been ignored by the human population. Indeed, the imagination of many a poet has been stirred by fireflies. One of the most interesting poems is that of James Montgomery, who explains the purpose of the firefly's beacon:

When Evening closes Nature's eye,
The glowworm lights her little spark
To captivate her favorite fly,
And Tempt the rover through the dark.

Conducted by a sweeter star
Than all that deck the fields above,
He fondly hastens from afar,
To sooth her solitude with love.

While Montgomery cites the glowworm as his main character, he is actually describing firefly activity. The term glowworm is used most commonly for the larvae of fireflies. These larvae are found in the fall of the year in the vicinity of streams. They do not flash their neon lights but instead produce a constant glow — a real sight on a cool fall evening along some gently flowing brook.

The firefly has been immortalized in the Mills Brothers song "Glowworm." Who among us, young or old, cannot help feeling a spark of romanticism when hearing the lilting strains of this classic:

Glow little glowworm, turn the key on,
You are equipped with a taillight neon.
You've got a cute vest, sparkin' master,
Which you can make both slow and faster,
I don't know who you took the shine to,
I've got a gal that I love so.
Glow little glowworm, glow.

Once again, the insect in the song is not technically a glowworm, but a firefly. But hey, when you're in love, who cares? ■

The Age of Beetles

We live in the age of beetles. This idea may puzzle some people, but the truth is beetles are the most common animal present on the surface of the earth. There are well over one quarter million species of beetles. One animal in every four is a beetle!

Beetles tend to keep a low profile, so they're not frequently observed. To be sure, most of us notice the ladybird beetle feeding on aphids on our rosebushes. We may even take note of the sound of May beetles crashing into lighted window panes in the spring and summer. And, on occasion, we fleetingly admire the black beetles that manage to wander into our basements—that is, before we step on them. But unlike their showier cousins, the butterflies and moths, beetles generally go unnoticed.

Beetles are equipped to avoid the limelight. The hard shell that beetles wear as protection allows them the freedom to inhabit the underground of nature. Beetles are often found under things such as leaf litter, tree bark, rocks, boards, and carpets. That hard shell will even allow them to withstand the footfall of a hefty human, at least if the soil is soft.

The name beetle comes from the Old English word meaning "to bite," an early recognition of the rather fearsome biting mouthparts of many beetles. The word beetle is also used to describe a heavy hammer and something that projects, such as a beetle-browed person.

The look of beetles, that indescribable beetleness of this group of insects, was simulated in the shape of that now-famous automobile — the Volkswagen beetle. Some folks have been known to call the Volkswagen version a bug—an entomological error. Real beetles are not bugs, but they are insects.

Of course, any discussion of beetles brings to mind the British rock group of the same name. It is not entirely clear how the four lads from Liverpool arrived at the name the Beatles. However, it has been suggested that they so admired Buddy Holly and the Crickets that they too wanted a name with an entomological connection. They may have changed the spelling to Beatles to reflect the style of music they played, known then in England as "beat" music.

In the early days of the British rock invasion, some people who saw the Beatles and their haircuts — or lack thereof — were probably reminded of beetles of the insect variety. To some their music may have conjured up thoughts of a band of insects. But then life was never meant to be easy, for beetles or Beatles. The success of both groups speaks for itself. ■

Waste Disposal Experts

The ancient Egyptians worshiped them as a god. Barefoot farm boys in denim overalls have admired them for decades. Scientists have studied them. My teenage daughter thinks they're gross!

They are popularly known as dung beetles, tumble beetles, or tumble bugs. Technically known as scarab beetles, these insects feed on manure. Not any old manure, mind you, but mammal droppings left in pasture areas. They are specialists in cow-pie disposal procedures.

Mated pairs of tumble beetles dig burrows in the soil, a home for their prospective offspring. Following construction, the tumble beetles begin to provision the home. The food chosen is mammal excrement, frequently cow manure. Once a cow-pie — the fresher the better — is discovered, the beetles must package the food. They make it into a ball — a very convenient shape for transporting — and roll the food home.

It is this habit of rolling the dung ball that gives the insects their common names. Normally, one beetle pushes the ball with its hind feet while its mate pulls while walking backwards. This procedure results in uncertain progress at best. The journey is punctuated with frequent falls and tumbles. But where there's a will, there's a way, and the two dedicated travelers usually make it home.

Once the manure ball is safely in the underground home, the female lays eggs on it. The young larvae hatch and begin to feed on the manure and possibly the fungus that grows there. Dedicated mother that she is, the female beetle frequently remains in the burrow to tend to the brood.

It was the ball-rolling habit of the tumble bugs that no doubt attracted the attention of the ancient Egyptians. In fact, the scarab became the most popular insect in Egypt. The scarab beetle common in Egypt has five terminal segments on each of its six legs. To the ancient Egyptians, this symbolized the 30 days of each month.

The ancient Egyptians adopted the scarab as the symbol for their sun god, Khepera. It is said that they believed that the beetle rolling the dung ball across the earth symbolized Khepera rolling the sun across the sky. Because the sun was "reborn" each day, the beetle became the symbol of rebirth and was associated with the idea of the soul.

Scarab beetles were frequently put in tombs in an effort to ensure the immortality of the soul of the departed. Nearly 3,000 years later, Roman soldiers adorned necklaces with a scarab form and wore them into battle. This tradition was apparently based on the same idea of immortality that had been accepted by the Egyptians. Necklaces with the scarab design can still be found today.

Dung beetles serve a very practical function, in ancient times and today, that of keeping our pastures free of animal manure. The Australians learned this when large mammals were introduced to their country. You see, Australian dung beetles had not adapted to dealing with manure other than that of the kangaroo, so the Australians had a problem piling up. They solved it by importing "foreign" dung beetles.

Maybe the ancient Egyptians were correct. If dung beetles aren't magical, they are surely essential! ■

Tigers of the Insect World

To most people, the tiger is a ferocious animal, a blood-thirsty carnivore. So it is in the insect world. Tiger beetles are aptly named. They are among the most vicious of insects.

Tiger beetles feed on other insects. They have large sharply-pointed jaws and large eyes, the better to spot their prey.

They capture most of their prey by running. Tiger beetles can run at speeds of up to 60 centimeters in a second, or nearly 1.5 miles per hour. Not so great, you say? Well think about that speed in terms of body length. A tiger beetle is about 1/2 inch long. A race horse about 8 feet long would have to run about 250 miles per hour to cover its body length as speedily as does a tiger beetle!

Tiger beetles like to hunt in open spaces, where speed is useful. Once a tiger beetle catches an insect, its eating habits live up to its name. Tiger beetles seize the prey in their jaws and bang the unfortunate victim against the ground until dead. Then the tiger beetle sucks the juices from its prey. For dessert the tiger beetle may just proceed to chew some of the parts of the insect's shell.

The young of tiger beetles are at least as proficient as their parents in procuring food. However, lacking the wings and feet of the adults, the larvae resort to trickery.

Tiger beetle larvae live in the soil where they construct a burrow. A larva climbs to the mouth of the burrow and places its head, which is mostly jaws, out through the opening. When a potential meal passes close by, the larva rushes out, captures the prey and pulls it back into the burrow. Once inside the burrow, the juvenile tiger beetle may retreat to the deep dark depths of the innersanctum to dine.

Tiger beetles are not often observed. Primarily because they frequently fly away when people approach. Apparently we are too large to qualify as a potential meal. However, many tiger beetles have beautiful iridescent green and blue colors and are quite showy.

Next time you are walking in an area without vegetation, such as on a dirt path, a sandy beach or even near a log in a sunny spot in the woods, keep an eye open. A few feet ahead you might spy a tiger beetle. With a little patience you might even observe a tiger beetle stalk and capture prey. You will then appreciate why these insects are called tiger beetles. ■

Chapter 2

Insect Flashers

No warm July evening would be complete without the flickering lights of fireflies. Sometimes called lightning bugs, these insects are neither flies nor bugs. They are beetles that have long amazed scientists and amused children with their ability to produce light.

Although scientists have studied the lighting mechanism of fireflies, it is not completely understood. However, the idea has been incorporated in the development of chemical light sticks, such as emergency flares. The light produced by the firefly is a cold light with efficiency in excess of 90 percent. By comparison an incandescent lamp is about 10 percent efficient, which means about 90 percent of its energy is used for heat. Sunlight is about 25 percent light and 75 percent heat.

Fireflies produce light from a substance called luciferin. When luciferin is mixed with oxygen in the presence of an enzyme called luciferase, light is produced. Both luciferin and luciferase are based on the Latin word Lucifer, meaning "to bring light." The same name was given to the angel of light, who fell from grace and became Satan.

Scientific names of fireflies also show an association with light. For example, one genus is called *Lampyris*. Photo is found in the common genus name *Photouris* and *Photinus*. A species within the genus *Photinus* is named *pyralis*, which is drawn from the Greek root pyr, meaning "fire."

Fireflies flash their lights in various patterns — sort of the Morse Code of the insect world. The flashing has one purpose: to attract a mate. The males fly overhead, advertising with their mobile neon lights for a mate. Females commonly remain on the vegetation but respond to an attractive male with similar flashing. When both sexes agree that they are the light of each other's lives, the male lands near the female. Then they "turn out the lights" and proceed with the firefly mating game.

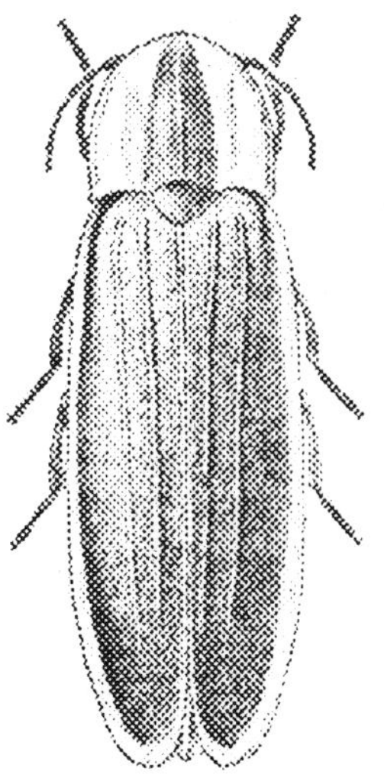

Most of the flashing activity of fireflies occurs in the early evening hours, beginning at dusk. By midnight, most of the outbursts of miniature lightning have subsided for another day.

Fireflies are predators, both in the immature and the adult stages. They consume slugs, snails and other insects. This food-procuring activity takes a strange twist in one firefly species. The female mimics the flashing pattern of males of other species of fireflies. When the lovestruck male lands by the female, he becomes not a mate, but a meal. This firefly is known as the "femme fatale" of the insect world.

Could it be that even among the beautiful and graceful fireflies there is a need for truth in advertising? ■

Ladybug, Ladybug, Fly Away Home

Some people know them as ladybugs. They're also known as ladybird beetles or lady beetles, which are more appropriate names because these insects are beetles. Lady beetles are bright orange or red in color and frequently have black spots.

There are about 370 species of lady beetles in North America. Most lady beetles are beneficial because they feed on a group of pest insects called aphids. Aphids feed on plants — our garden plants, our crop plants, even our decorator plants. Because of their appetites, the lady beetles can "eat up" an aphid problem. A larvae of a lady beetle will consume 200-300 aphids before it becomes an adult. Some lady beetles will lunch on over 500 aphids before laying eggs. That's 15 to 20 aphids per day.

Farmers in the Middle Ages recognized that aphids could destroy their crops. To help with the aphid problem, the ancient farmers sometimes prayed to the Virgin Mary, who is also known as Our Lady. The aphid-eating beetles frequently saved the crop and gained the name of "Our Lady" bug.

Ancient reverence for the insect and the season-ending practice of burning crop stubble led to the familiar nursery rhyme about the lady bug.

Lady bug, lady bug, fly away home,
Your house is on fire, your children will burn!

The lady bug is admonished to fly away home to save her wingless youngsters before they perish in the fire. The rhyme probably also reflects that lady bugs migrate during the fall season. They seek protected places to spend the winter and, at the time, could be found far from "home."

We still recognize the beneficial aspect of lady beetles — a process called biological control — in our gardens and crops. Some gardeners purchase lady beetles by the quart for release. It is important for homeowners considering such a practice to make sure that aphids, which are the food source for the beetles, are present at the time of release. If food is not present, a modern version of the nursery rhyme will occur, and the beetles will "fly away, fly away" to some other home! ■

Fly-By-Night Beetles

Each year, thousands of beetles arrive in the spring to attend Mother Nature's annual "coming out" party for insects. Appropriately, these debutantes are called May or June beetles.

June beetles are well-known to most homeowners and gardeners. In the adult stage, these beetles feed on the foliage of broadleaf plants. In their larval stage, called white grubs, they feed on the roots of grass. In either case they can cause severe damage to the plants attacked.

So what's a person to do when faced with white grubs in the lawn? Some rely on natural control measures, such as moles and skunks, which feed on the white grubs. Most people, preferring instead to prevent further damage to their lawns, choose to use insecticides. However, chemical control of white grubs is only effective when applied to lawns in early spring or late summer.

These insects have an interesting life cycle. Most species overwinter as mature adults in the soil. In the spring, the adults burrow from the soil and fly about, feed on leaves, mate and lay eggs. Larvae feed on organic matter in the soil. During the winter or under dry conditions, the larvae burrow deeper in the soil. They return to the surface as soil temperature or moisture content increases.

Some June beetles, like the Japanese beetle, spend only one year feeding as a larva. Other species spend two or three years in the larval stage.

Adult June beetles are night fliers. The fact that they fly at all is a minor miracle of the world of nature. These beetles are compactly built, sort of the sumo wrestlers of the insect world. Like all beetles, their front wings are modified into elytra. These shell-like covers protect the insect's body and conceal the hind wings. When a beetle takes flight, it must move the elytra forward and unfold the membraneous hind wings.

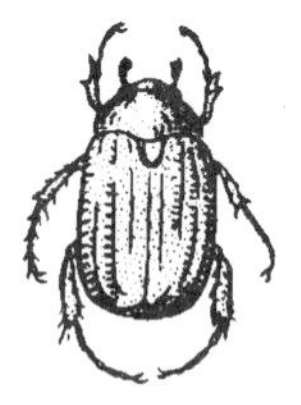

June beetles look awkward in flight. However, their takeoffs and flight are almost graceful compared to their landings, which fit nicely into the category of "crash!" Beetles just fold up their wings and drop in. In fact, the poet James Whitcomb Riley once described the flight of June beetles as "bumping along the dusk."

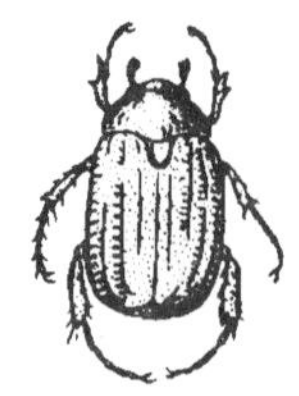

June beetles are attracted to lights. Frequently during spring and early summer months, quiet evenings are punctuated with the sounds of June beetles crashing into lighted window panes. Such grounded beetles, apparently no worse for the wear, repack their wings under the elytra and proceed on foot.

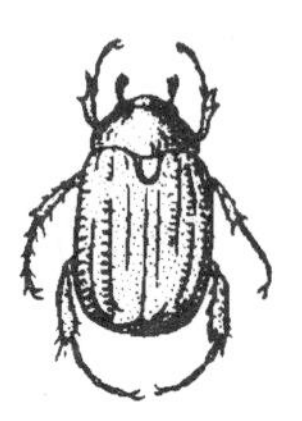

Prowling neighborhood cats have discovered that the ground below lighted windows provides a veritable smorgasbord of crunchy morsels, especially during heavy flights of Junebugs. At least June beetles are good for something.

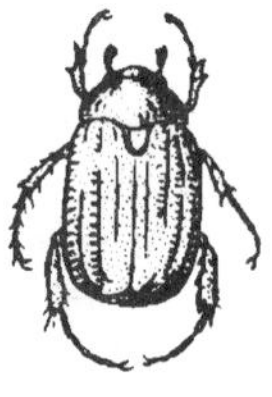

Here a Grubworm, There a Grubworm

Editors Note: In the fourth paragraph, the reference to "Junebugs" is correct as is, even though it may not match your dictionary. Scientifically speaking, since a Junebug is NOT a true bug, the words "June" and "bug" are combined into one word. Most dictionaries list this reference as two words. A future column will address this subject in more detail.

Most lawn owners and home gardeners are eternal optimists, at least in the springtime. During the first warm days of spring, these creatures emerge from their domiciles armed with rakes, spray cans and fertilizer bags. With the accumulated energy of winter relentlessly driving these people onward, they prepare to battle Mother Nature over the appearance of a bit of real estate called the lawn. The eternal springtime dream of an insect-free lawn is quickly shattered through the specter of a grubworm infestation.

Grubworms, sometimes just called white grubs, are the scourge of the green-lawn enthusiast. These insects are the larvae of beetles known as Junebugs or May beetles. Japanese beetle larvae are also called white grubs.

These insects deserve to be called grubs. They spend their life underground grubbing around for food. Some, including an insect called the masked chafer and the Japanese beetle, spend only one year in the larval, or grub, stage. Other grubs may spend two or three years underground.

Grubs feed on plant roots, especially the roots of grasses, such as those found in lawns. Most feeding occurs during the warm months of the year. During cold or dry periods, the grubs burrow deeper in the soil and stay there until the soil returns to desirable temperatures or moisture.

Grub feeding does horrible things to the grass plant. They deprive the plant of its ability to procure water and nutrients, so it dies. This, of course, results in brown spots in the lawn.

Neighbors have the uncanny ability to notice grub-induced brown spots in lawns and immediately begin to talk: "Guess who has grubs?" Of course, the social disgrace of having grubs is more than most lawn owners can take, so they do what they can to solve the problem.

Chapter 2

Just Looking for a Home

People in the cotton industry wish the boll weevil would look for a home somewhere away from the cotton belt. The destructive, little pest causes enormous losses in the production of cotton fiber and cottonseed each year.

The boll weevil invaded Texas from it's original home in Mexico, and now is residing wherever cotton is grown in the United States except for California, New Mexico and Arizona.

The boll weevil name is widely recognized in America. It was popularized in *The Boll Weevil* song. The first verse of the song says:

Oh the boll weevil is a little black bug,
Come from Mexico, they say.
Come all the way to Texas,
Just looking for a place to stay.

Technically, this insect is not a bug, weevils are beetles, sometimes called snout beetles, because they have mouthparts on the end of a snout. Boll weevils use the snout to feed on the cotton bolls which causes the boll, the fruiting part of the plant, to fall and reduce the yield.

The second verse of the song is:

The first time I seen the boll weevil,
He was sitting on the square.
The next time I seen the boll weevil,
He had all his family there . . .

How true it is. The square is the flower of the cotton plant and is a favorite feeding site for the weevil. The boll weevil female lays eggs in the feeding punctures, up to 250 per female. The young grubs then feed in the developing boll.

The rest of the song deals with the damage caused by the boll weevil and the economic straits of the affected farmers. According to the song:

The merchant got half the cotton,
The boll weevil got the rest.
Didn't leave the farmer's wife
But one old cotton dress,
And it's full of holes, and it's full of holes.

In spite of the damage caused by the boll weevil, the insect is a hero in Enterprise, Alabama. So much so that in the center of town stands the *The Boll Weevil Monument*. The monument was erected in recognition of the role that the boll weevil played in causing crop diversification in the area. Peanut production was introduced, and the economic climate of the area became more stable.

Even major pest insects, like the boll weevil, sometimes provide opportunities for folks other than entomologists. ■

Where there are grubs, there are also grub eaters. Moles, blackbirds and skunks are grub eaters of the first order.

While moles and skunks can rid a lawn of grubs, the solution might be worse than the problem. Indeed, no one is certain how many skunks per lawn it takes to eliminate white grubs. In addition, this control method carries with it the risk of exceeding the clean air standards of some cities.

Insecticides are useful tools in dealing with the grubs. But applications need to be properly timed, which is tricky. Also, the use of insecticides carries with it some environmental hazard.

There are other methods. Some folks have tried walking around on the lawn with spiked-shoe, lawn "aerators" attempting to spike the grubs. No one is sure if this method is effective, but it gives the owner the satisfaction of having gotten even with at least one grubworm. ■

Bombardier Beetles

Bombardier beetles are fittingly named. Historically, bombardiers were people who waged war by lobbing a variety of objects at their foes. Bombardier beetles don't drop bombs, but they have mastered the art of chemical warfare.

When these insects are attacked or disturbed they live up to their name. The bombardier beetle ejects a secretion composed primarily of chemicals known as quinones. The quinones are not stored in the insect. They are produced as needed in a complex reaction that would make any chemistry teacher proud.

The reaction, which takes less than a second, produces heat and gaseous oxygen. The gas propels the mixture from the insect with a popping sound. The temperature of the explosion has been shown to reach 100 degrees Celsius, the boiling point of water. Consequently, any creature unlucky enough to raise the ire of a bombardier beetle is sprayed with a hot chemical mixture.

Bombardier beetles are not just mad bombers. They are excellent marksmen – or should we say "marksbeetles?" – who direct the spray precisely. The gland that produces the defensive chemicals is located at the tip of the abdomen. The abdomen works like a movable turret that is pointed in the direction of the attack. If an ant attacks a beetle's leg, for example, the beetle "bombards" in that direction.

The chemicals in the beetles' spray are very effective. A toad attempting to make a meal out of a bombardier beetle is rewarded with a mouth full of hot chemicals. The amphibian spends the next few moments doing a toad's version of "Yuk," probably thinking seriously about a life devoted to eating insects.

Bombardier beetles really are pacificists in their little insect hearts and will only live up to their name as a last resort. When disturbed, they try to avoid trouble by running away. If such an evasive technique does not work, they pull out all the stops and employ their chemical weapons. For these beetles "Bombs Away!" is not just a cute saying, it is a matter of survival. ■

Sexton Beetles

Years ago every church had a sexton. As underofficers of the church, sextons had several jobs. They rang the church bell; took care of church property, including the graveyard; and dug graves.

There are a group of beetles called sexton beetles, who like their church namesake are gravediggers par excellence. Also known as scavenger beetles or burying beetles, sexton beetles make their ecological living by burying the carcasses of small animals as a food resource for their young. They are carrion eaters.

The rather grisly life of the sexton beetles also is reflected in the scientific name of one species. *Necrophorus marginatus* has a name that can be roughly translated as "the body carrier." The sexton beetles are attracted to a carcass by the odor of death. If the dead animal happens to be on soft earth, the beetles bury it where they find it.

A dead mouse on a hard surface, however, presents a challenge to these six-legged gravediggers. The solution is simple, just move the carcass to a place where digging is easy. Doing it is another matter, at least if the insect is moving a dead weight several times heavier than it is.

Sexton beetles have solved the problem, they crawl under a carcass and do the insect equivalent of standing on tiptoes. This process scoots the carcass forward millimeter by millimeter. After every to or three shoves, a beetle will merge from under his prize carcass and scurry around to survey the progress being made. It then scampers back to continue the working frenzy.

To sexton beetles, speed is of the essence in burying a carcass once it has been discovered. They need to cover it up before other carrion-eating insects, such as flies, get a chance to share in the feast. And what a feast it will be! Once the carcass is buried, the sexton beetles will lay eggs on it. The eggs hatch quickly, and the young larva that emerge will dine to their hearts content on the repast provided by their parents.

Historically, humanity has looked down on the job of gravedigger. Most of us also tend to put the life of the sexton beetle under the heading of "yuk." Theirs may be dirty little jobs, but ecologically speaking someone or some insect has to do it!

Eating Beetles is No Picnic

Let's have a picnic! Eating in the great out-of-doors ranks right up there with swimming and going to the ball game as things to do in the summer. We even have special equipment named for the occasion – picnic baskets and picnic tables.

You can't have a picnic unless someone shows up with the food. The food attracts not only ants but another insect named especially for the event, the picnic beetle. This uninvited picnic crasher is a black beetle with four yellow dots. It's about the same size as a house fly and is sometimes called a fungus beetle or sap beetle.

These common names all reflect the food habits of the picnic beetle. The insect in both the adult and immature stages feeds on decaying plant material or the fungus that grows in such situations. It commonly can be found around plants that have been damaged. Some entomologists have suggested that the insect may be more common in years when corn is badly damaged by corn borer. The damage to the plants provides breeding sites for the beetles.

In fact, picnics are frequently smorgasbords of damaged and fermenting plant material. Potato salads, cole slaw, cucumbers and relish trays must seem like heaven to hungry picnic beetles. So when these beetles discover our picnic they drop in for a bite.

These beetles drop in literally. As they fly about searching for food, the odors from the picnic dishes are a signal that dinner is served. The beetles then fold their wings and fall from the sky. Sometimes they are on target and fall right into the dish of choice – theirs not ours. Sometimes they crawl around to find it.

Always, their presence is disconcerting to picnic-goers who want to eat outdoors but don't want to share their food with outdoor creatures; or worse yet, who shudder at the thought of inadvertently devouring one of the little creatures in a spoonful of potato salad.

It's not easy to keep picnic beetles from crashing a picnic. Some people have been known to place jar lids of beer laced with a dash of insecticide in the vicinity of the picnic-to-be a day prior to the event. The picnic beetles are attracted to the fermented plant sap known as beer and get a dose of insecticide.

Most of us have just learned to live with picnic beetles. We, of course, eat more carefully when they are around. After all, sharing your picnic with an insect is one thing, but eating an insect in your potato salad is, shall we say, "no picnic!"

Insects in Armor

1. What American music group is said to have inspired the Beatles to choose an insect name for their group?
2. According to the Old English language the word which is the basis for beetle had what meaning? Why is this appropriate for this group of insects?
3. What is the name of the substrate and enzyme used by fireflies in light production?
4. What is the ecological role of scarab beetles?
5. What is the femme fatale of the insect world?
6. How would the food habits of the tiger beetles be described?
7. Where did the ladybug get its name? What is the food of this creature?
8. What is the food of immature Junebugs? What are they called?
9. What was the original home of the boll weevil?

Chapter 2

Flies, Flies, Flies

Doggers of Civilization

Of the world's pest insects, none are more prominent than flies. These "two-winged" insects have been called "doggers of civilization." And for good reason.

Of the 10 plagues of ancient Egypt, two were flies. Fly-borne diseases are said to have hastened the decline of ancient Athens and Rome. Sleeping sickness, a disease transmitted by the tsetse fly, long delayed the civilizing of Africa.

Ancient Semitic people recognized a deity known as Beelzebub, Lord of the Flies. It might have been wishful thinking, but these people thought that Beelzebub would defend them against flies. The Philistines of the era apparently couldn't depend on Beelzebub. They appointed a fly control officer. No one knows how this first government-sponsored program for insect control worked out.

Songwriters have recognized the importance of flies as pests. "The Blue Tail Fly" is about a species of horsefly that has a vicious bite. The song became so popular that it was number one on radio's hit parade of songs in the late 1940s.

Many folk sayings exist that relate to flies and fly behavior. Most people prefer not to have "A fly in the soup," but other lessons can be learned through the less common sayings of our ancestors. For example, a lesson on the value of even the smallest thing, "Every fly has its shadow," on hard work, "Flies are busiest about lean horses," on common sense, "Even flies won't light on a boiling pot," on overdoing it, "Cover yourself with honey, and the flies will have at you," on watching what you say, "No fly gets into a shut mouth," and on watching your step, "If the fly flies, the frog goes not supperless to bed. "

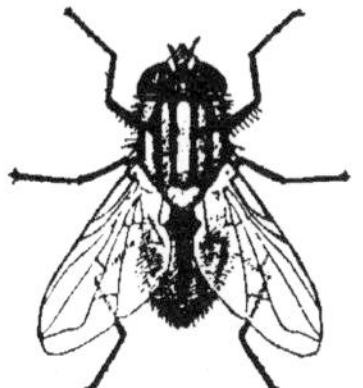

Flies also have a reputation as weather predictors. Flies collect on the screen door just before a storm. Flies, it is said, "bite sore when there is a good chance for rain."

Modern civilization is still fighting flies. Flies are annoying us and stealing our blood and that of our animals and we can't entirely stop them. To be sure, we have window screens, flypaper, and flyswatters. We even have insecticides, but we still have flies.

The most common of all flies is the housefly. Even its scientific name — *Musca domestica* — indicates how closely it lives with mankind. While the housefly can't bite with its sponging mouthparts, it has been implicated in disease transmission. These flies can carry germs that cause dysentery, diarrhea, and food poisoning.

The housefly, in spite of all its imperfections, appears polite. The little beast always cleans every one of its six feet before tromping around in the mashed potatoes and gravy on your plate. ■

Justice and the Blue-Tail Fly

The Southern folk song "Jim Crack Corn" relates a mystery of sorts. The song recounts a death plot suitable for the popular TV show "Murder She Wrote."

In case you've forgotten, the song chronicles the demise of "master." He was rather unceremoniously unseated from the saddle of his pony and tumbled in the ditch. He died. A jury deliberated the crime, and the verdict was that, not the butler, but the blue-tail fly was the guilty party.

Blue-tail fly is a common name for one group of insects also known as horse flies. Adult horse flies and their insect cousins, the deer flies, are blood feeders. Neither insect feeds exclusively on the animal for which it is named. Almost any mammal is fair game for these bloodthirsty flies.

These insects are known for their painful bites and their persistence in obtaining a meal. Anyone who has been bitten or repeatedly dive-bombed by a horse fly or deer fly will attest to those attributes. Fear of the insect's bite and buzzing causes threatened animals to behave erratically. Fly nets were probably developed for use on draft horses to protect them from this group of flies.

Horse flies and deer flies are frequently found in the vicinity of wetlands. Larvae of these insects live in saturated soil. However, adults are strong fliers and are frequently found far away from breeding sites.

Farm kids have always been fascinated by horse flies and have been known to capture the pesky insects. Of course, a horse fly doesn't make a great pet, but they can be used for other purposes. For example, children have been known to "research" the behavior of a headless horse fly. Such decapitated insects will, with proper provocation, fly. Flights of these unguided insect missiles usually end with spectacular collisions with immovable objects, such as trees, fence posts and, best of all, barns.

Such apparently barbaric behavior on the part of kids toward horse flies likely arose as an act of revenge — for having been bitten while skinny-dipping in the creek or pond.

Once again, the jury has convicted a habitual offender — the blue-tail fly. ■

Chapter 2

Seeing Cluster Flies? It Must Be Spring!

Ah, the signs of spring. Robins hopping on the lawn, crocuses emerging from the ground, and spring peepers singing in water-filled ditches along the roadside. An even better harbinger of spring, though, is flies bouncing off window panes.

In the poem "Spring," Oliver Windell Holmes penned these lines:

"The housefly, stealing from his narrow grave,
Drugged with the opiate that November gave,
Beats with faint wing against the sunny pane,
Or crawls, tenacious, o'ver its lucid plain."

The fly that Holmes describes is not the house fly, but a similar-looking fly known as the cluster fly. Cluster flies are parasites. In their immature stages, cluster flies feed on earthworms. In the adult stage, they hibernate to while away the long, winter hours in temperate regions of North America.

Cluster flies prefer a nice, cozy place in which to hibernate. So each fall, millions of the little buzzers invade buildings, barns, garages and houses. Now most people don't mind sharing their barns or garages with a few flies, but it's a different story when it comes to houses.

The cluster flies normally find their way under eaves and into chimney chases and attics, where they settle down for a little serious hibernation. However, the increasing minutes of sunlight associated with late winter days frequently results in warm attics.

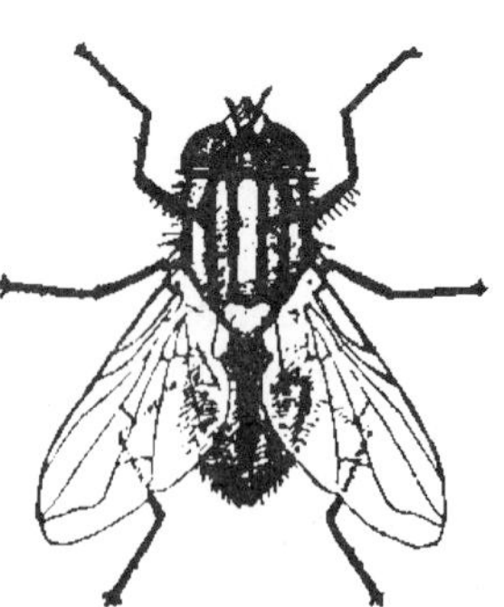

The increased temperatures do not go unnoticed by our slumbering parasitic fly. It assumes that spring has sprung and begins to search for some earthworm on which to lay eggs. However, the return journey to the great out-of-doors frequently results in a slight detour into the interior of the house.

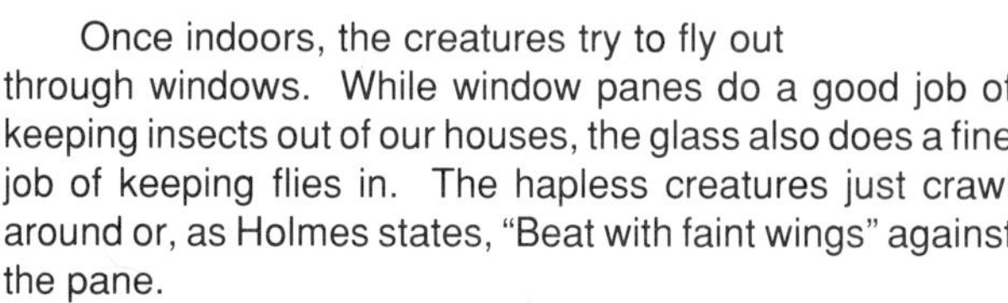

Once indoors, the creatures try to fly out through windows. While window panes do a good job of keeping insects out of our houses, the glass also does a fine job of keeping flies in. The hapless creatures just crawl around or, as Holmes states, "Beat with faint wings" against the pane.

Of course, the presence of flies makes most homeowners a bit fidgety. Some run for the good ol' insecticide spray can. Others just fire up the vacuum cleaner. A few engage in hand-to-tarsal combat with the unwelcome invaders. Regardless of the elimination approach, there always seem to be more. In fact, hibernating flies can sometimes be several inches deep in corners of attics.

Let's hope that most of the cluster flies can find their way out as easily as they found their way in! ■

Gnats, Gnats and More Gnats

When you come within a gnats eyelash, you're close. In fact you can't come much closer, short of winning.

How close is a gnat's eyelash? Well it's so close that it's not measurable, because gnats don't have eyelashes! But if these little insects did have eyelashes, they would be too small to see and that is the basis for comparison.

Gnats are small flies, and some of those babies bite. They even take their name from their biting habit. The word "gnat" is based on the Greek word "gnathos" or "jaw."

There are many kinds of gnats. Buffalo gnats, also called black flies, are definitely worth swatting since the females are blood-suckers and vicious biters. Anyone in the northern areas of the United States during the summer can understand the problems these insects cause. Both humans and livestock are tormented by female black flies as they attempt to obtain a blood meal. Immatures of these insects occur in streams. The adults swarm in groups, hence the name, buffalo gnats. Bicyclists and joggers can attest that running or riding through a swarm of buffalo gnats is something that should not be done with a wide-open mouth!

Fungus gnats are slender mosquito-like insects. They are found in damp places where decaying vegetation abounds. These insects frequently occur in mushroom cellars and sometimes emerge from the soil of potted plants. The presence of fungus gnats in a home normally receives less than rave reviews from homeowners who suddenly discover these insects flying around the living room.

There are also root gnats, gall gnats and wood gnats. And there is a small fly sometimes referred to as an eye gnat. This insect seems to be attracted to animal secretions and is particularly attracted to eyes. Because they are attracted to eyes, they are sometimes vectors of the disease pinkeye of humans and animals.

To most people, a gnat is a gnat, and something to be avoided. Indeed gnats swarming around your face is a bit disconcerting at best. The next time you see a gnat try and spy its eyelashes. Then and only then will you truly appreciate the closeness of the event that was won "by a gnats eyelash." ■

Chapter 2

Flying Syringes

Mosquitoes have been called living, flying syringes. A fitting description.

Technically a kind of fly, the mosquito has long been famous for its bite. The ancient Greek philosopher Aristotle, a student of insects, concluded that, "Four-winged insects have the sting in the tail, and the two-winged ones have the sting in the head." Aristotle was, of course, talking about bees and biting flies, probably mosquitoes.

Mosquitoes need to obtain blood for egg production. Therefore, only female mosquitoes bite. The males are nectar feeders. Because of their need for a blood meal, female mosquitoes are notorious carriers of disease. Diseases transmitted by mosquitoes include malaria, yellow fever, dengue fever, elephantiasis and encephalitis.

The relationship between mosquitoes and disease transmission has been an important area of study. Walter Reed, a U.S. army surgeon, gained fame by leading the effort to control the yellow fever mosquito in Panama. This effort allowed the construction of the Panama Canal. Yellow fever was one of the reasons the French were unable to complete construction of the canal.

The American poet Longfellow suggested a relationship between mosquitoes and malaria in "Hiawatha." And the relationship between swamps and the disease was noted also in the line:

He, the mightiest of magicians,
Sends the fever from the marshes.

This was written some 40 years before it had been established scientifically that the mosquito was a vector of malaria.

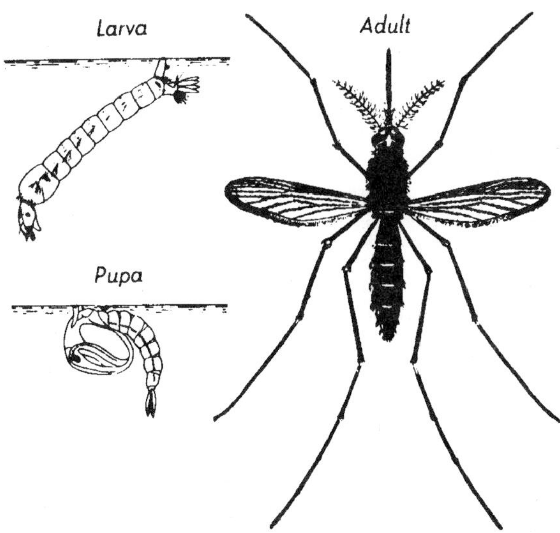

Mosquito larvae live in stagnant water. Thus the relationship between swamps and mosquito-borne diseases. Many common names of mosquitoes, such as tree-hole mosquito and rain-barrel mosquito, suggest the location of their larvae. One of the most common methods of mosquito control is removing possible larval breeding sites, including the draining of swamps.

Of course, the very best and most modern of mosquito control activities will not be completely successful. So the next time you are being pursued by a hungry mosquito, watch what you say. That mosquito is bound to be a lady! ■

Flies, Flies, Flies

1. What is the adult food of horse flies and deer flies?
2. Why do mosquitoes need a blood meal?
3. What disease, transmitted by mosquitoes, delayed the construction of the Panama Canal?
4. What is the larval food of cluster flies? How do cluster flies overwinter?
5. What word based on the Greek word meaning jaw is used to describe a group of small flies?

Chapter 2

The Socializers

Spring Hive-Cleaning

As days begin to grow longer during late winter and early spring, housekeepers everywhere begin to think of that annual ritual of tidiness called spring cleaning. So it is with honey bees.

Honey bees should certainly win the Good Housekeeping Seal of Approval for their efforts in keeping their hive spotless. However, their early spring efforts might draw the ire of environmentalists who are concerned about airborne pollution.

Honey bees clean their home and empty their digestive tracts by flying from the hive and releasing the refuse while on the wing. What goes up must come down, but the bees are less concerned about the landing site of their airborne sewage than with the tidiness of their home. Consequently, bees' cleaning efforts sometimes result in spots on houses or automobiles. This, of course, does not go unnoticed by the human owners of such items.

With bees, as with people, the call of nature is sometimes a pressing proposition. Bees, like all insects, are cold blooded. Thus, cleansing flights are confined to times when air temperatures will allow. Sustained flights of honey bees occur when the temperature exceeds 50 degrees Fahrenheit. So during cold periods, waste material begins to build up in the bees and in their hive.

When the first warm period comes around, the bees leave the hive like planes launched on a bombing run from an aircraft carrier, but in this case, the mission is not secret. As temperatures rise, they also remove other trash from the hive. Dead bees, for instance, are rather unceremoniously pitched from the mouth of the hive — the insect equivalent of burial at sea.

Many people try to avoid having their possessions bombed by bees on a cleansing flight. When dealing with bees and their unauthorized deposits, an ounce of prevention is required. It is easiest to move the prized possession out of the line of fire, especially on the first warm day following a cold spell.

However, if bees get to the car before you do, prompting a trip to the local car wash, just be thankful that honey bees are smaller than elephants. ■

Hornet Artisans

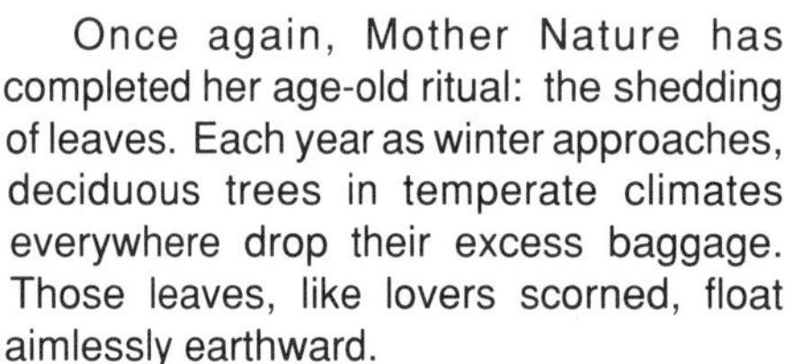

Once again, Mother Nature has completed her age-old ritual: the shedding of leaves. Each year as winter approaches, deciduous trees in temperate climates everywhere drop their excess baggage. Those leaves, like lovers scorned, float aimlessly earthward.

But the annual departure of the leaves reveals more than just bare, nurturing limbs. Hornet's nests, hidden from view by summer foliage, suddenly stand naked against the winter sky. Hornet artisans build and maintain their homes for months. Then in the fall, like the leaves that had concealed it, the hornet's nest is left to the wiles of nature. It will soon be gone.

Bald-faced hornets — their name comes from the white spot between their eyes — are engineers of the highest order. They construct their globe-shaped nests from a paper-like material. The hornets collect wood from any available source, and by chewing and mixing it with saliva, they produce the nest material. Because these insects frequently use different sources of wood, the nest may appear multicolored.

As the summer progresses, the nest is enlarged to accommodate a growing family. By summer's end, many nests are basketball-sized or larger.

Bald-faced hornets pack a powerful sting, and few things are madder than a mad hornet! However, most hornets are quite docile, at least wnen away from their nests. However, they are willing, even anxious, to sting in defense of the home.

Hornets feed protein to their young. They are active hunters and can frequently be found around homes in pursuit of flies. They have even been known to land on people after mistaking a button or spot on clothing for a food item.

Hornets are beneficial because they prey on pest insects, but some people might say the greatest benefit of bald-faced hornets is the decorative value of their nests. Indeed, many hornet nests have ended up hanging over the mantel of a fireplace. Procuring such a decoration from the wild carries with it the inherent risk of introducing a few hornets into the house.

Each fall bald-faced hornet queens mate and seek shelter in woods to overwinter. The next spring, the queen starts the process over. The remaining workers stay with the nest until they are killed by freezing temperatures.

Of course, the rather fragile nest must be maintained constantly, and a nest will not last long when exposed to seasonal winds and marauding animals. Therefore, a good nest for decoration must be procured after the tenants are deceased but before it is blown to pieces. That, my friends, is where the rub — or rather the sting — comes in. ■

Chapter 2

The Wisdom of Ants

Ants can be a nuisance. Especially at picnics, in kitchens or even "in someone's pants." In spite of the problems ants cause, we humans have come to admire the little creatures. It's their work ethic that we so revere.

The industry of ants, their widespread distribution and large population have provided ample interaction with humans. Such encounters provide fodder for writers and poets. Indeed, it is a rare wordsmith that has not taken a pen in hand to wax eloquently about the virtues of ants.

Aesop used the lowly ant to extol the virtues of hard work and planning in his well-known fable, "The Ant and the Grasshopper." Who can forget the moral of that story: It is thrifty to prepare today for the wants of tomorrow.

Folklore includes many references to ants, especially to their small size: "A coconut shell full of water is an ocean to an ant," and "Even an ant is eight spans long as measured by its own hand." But folklore also speculates on the potential of ants if their size were equal to their might: "What would the ant do if she but had the head of a bull?"

But while they are small in stature, their wisdom looms large. "Ants never bend their course to an empty granary," according to folklore. And the Bible includes references to the wisdom of ants. In Proverbs 30:25 we read: "The ants are a people not strong, yet they prepare their meat in the summer." In Proverbs 6:6 we are admonished: "Go to the ant thou sluggard; consider her ways and be wise."

Odgen Nash penned a few well-chosen words about ants.

The ant has made himself illustrious,
By constant industry industrious.
So what. Would you be calm and placid,
If you were filled with formic acid?

Nash refers to formic acid, a chemical commonly found in ants that is used by many to communicate with each other. "The word goes out in formic," as penned by Robert Frost, provides another account of the chemical communication used by ants. Frost describes the regimented structure of these social insects in his aptly named poem, "Departmental."

We can all learn a few things from ants. In fact, ants are great teachers. Such is communicated by this proverb: "None teaches better than the ant, and she says nothing."

'Nuff said!

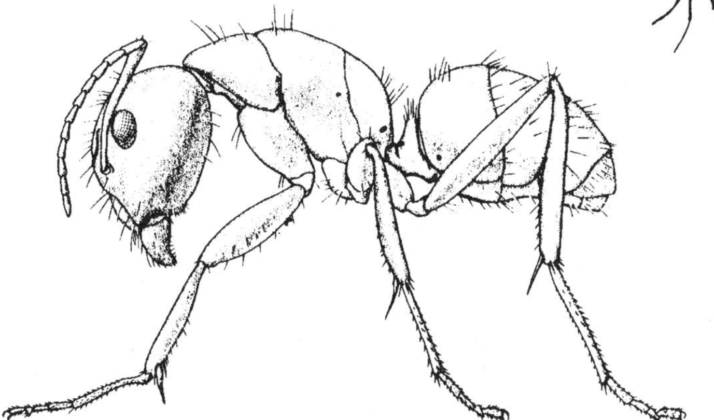

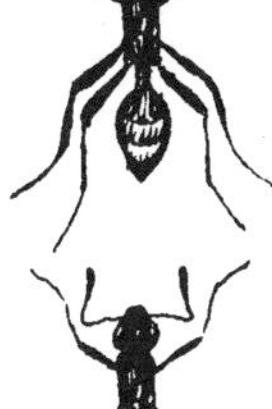

Ants in Your Pants

Ants. They're everywhere, they're everywhere! Or so it seems. Ants can be found from the Arctic regions to the tropics. From the mountain peaks to the seashore. From the kitchen counter to the backwoods picnic, they'll be there.

Ants are one of the most recognizable of insects. It is no wonder. There are over 10,000 species of ants and everyone, at some time, has encountered an ant or two.

There are black ants and red ants. There are carpenter ants and fire ants. Some ants are predators, feeding on other animals — primarily insects. Some ants are scavengers, including the fire ants. Others harvest seeds and some tend aphids and use the aphids excreta, called honeydew, as a food resource.

Often in the spring and summer large numbers of winged ants can be seen swarming about. Winged ants are the sexual forms. They possess wings for only a short time and use them to disperse from old nests in an effort to establish new colonies.

Many of us are familiar with ants because we consider them pests — whether in the sugar bowl, lawn or field. Ants also are beneficial and have even been used in medicine. In early medical literature it is noted that black ants could be used to close incisions. This was accomplished by placing an ant so that its wide open jaws snap shut across the incision. The ant's head is then pinched from its body and the jaws remain closed until the wound heals.

However, humans have long admired ants, primarily because of their industry. An old proverb admonishes us, "Go to the ant thou sluggard, consider her ways and be wise." Another proverb says, "None preaches better than the ant, and she says nothing." Even Aesop recognized the industry of the ant in the fable of the grasshopper and the ant.

Formic acid is the chemical commonly found in ants that they use in their sting and as a trail-marking substance. It is also included in the family name of ants, Formicidae.

No doubt, the potential bite and sting of ants combined with their presence in the most unlikely of places has given rise to the time-honored description of a fidgety person. Indeed everyone can imagine what it would be like to "have ants in their pants!"

Killer on the Loose

There's a killer on the loose! But neither the FBI nor the local police departments are concerned. You see, this killer is of the insect kind. It's a cicada killer.

Some people are frightened by these wasps, quite understandably. Cicada killers are one of the largest wasps in North America. These rusty-brown insects with yellow stripes range from 1 to 1-1/2 inches in length. That size wasp, one is to assume, has a good-sized stinger! Indeed, the female is said to have one of the most severe stings of any insect.

For the most part, people's fear of cicada killers is unfounded. These wasps reserve most of their stinging activity for—you guessed it—cicadas. The adult wasps catch cicadas. Often the catch is made while both are on the wing. The cicada killer then stings its victim, a process that paralyzes the cicada. Before the cicada is paralyzed, it squeals loudly. It makes quite a sight — this B-52 of the wasp world headed toward home with a squealing cicada in its legs.

The cicada killer uses the cicada to feed its young. The wasp first digs a hole in the ground. At the end of the hole, 6 inches or more in depth, the mother-to-be places one or more cicadas. She then lays an egg, which hatches in two to three days.

The newly hatched larvae begin to feed. The adult wasp has guaranteed a fresh food supply for her young by paralyzing the cicada. Not just any cicada, mind you, but a particular species, the dog-day cicada. The cicada is immobilized, but remains alive. The larvae keep the cicada alive by selective feeding. They destroy nonessential parts of the host first, leaving the vital organs until the final stages of feeding.

By fall the larvae have completed development. They then pupate and hibernate until the following summer, when a new crop of cicada killers begin to ply their trade.

It is the wasp's behavior in the vicinity of the nesting sites that frightens people. The wasp buzzes around, hovering menacingly, as it checks out intruders. Fortunately, it seldom resorts to warfare as a means of protecting the nest.

When in the vicinity of the nesting grounds of cicada killers, the best approach is to keep your cool. And it might be prudent to minimize noises similar to those made by a cicada! ■

Aphids and Ants: Another Dynamic Duo

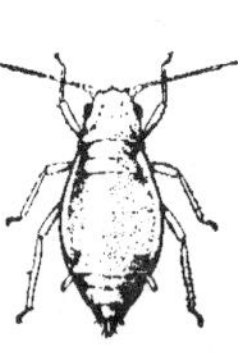

Throughout the ages, mankind has had its share of dynamic duos — Adam and Eve, Samson and Delilah, Anthony and Cleopatra, Bonnie and Clyde, and Batman and Robin to name a few.

Insects also have their duos. Ants and aphids are often found together. To many gardeners and homeowners neither ants nor aphids are favorite insects. Both can be pests, and when they show up together, some gardeners panic.

Aphids, sometimes called plant lice, and ants have a mutually beneficial relationship. The aphids provide a food resource for the ants, and the ants provide protection for the aphids. Some say that ants are farmers and aphids are their cows.

Ants feed on the honeydew produced by the aphids. Aphids feed on the sap of plants, filtering out the portions they need and excreting the rest. The excreted, sticky liquid, known as honeydew, includes a high concentration of sugar, which is highly prized by the ants.

It is the sticky honeydew that sometimes gums up automobiles parked under an aphid-infested tree. The sugar concentration of the honeydew also provides an ideal place for fungi to grow. Sooty mold growing on aphid honeydew frequently turns aphid-infested plants black. This adds an unsightly insult to gardeners' prized plants.

Since the ants are harvesting the honeydew produced by the aphids, they become quite possessive of their cows. The ants protect the aphids from predators, like ladybird beetles and lacewings, and parasites. Ants even carry aphids to uninfested plants to provide fresh pastures for their herd.

That famous duo of song composers, Rogers and Hammerstein, once noted that love and marriage go together like a horse and carriage — at least in Oklahoma. Maybe they also could have included aphids and ants in the song. After all, in love and marriage and between aphids and ants, sweetness is the tie that binds. ■

Chapter 2

Insect Carpenters

Carpenter bees and carpenter ants. These insects don't carry hammers or saws, or belong to a local carpenter's union. However, their wood work creates few friends in the human world.

Bee and ant carpenters build their homes by hollowing out wood. This is accomplished by using their strong mandibles. They literally chew out a new dwelling. In the woods this home-building activity is largely unnoticed by humans. However, when either of these insects decides to make their home in our homes, we are less than hospitable.

These insect carpenters can weaken the structure of a house by building their domiciles. So we call them pests and try to get rid of them.

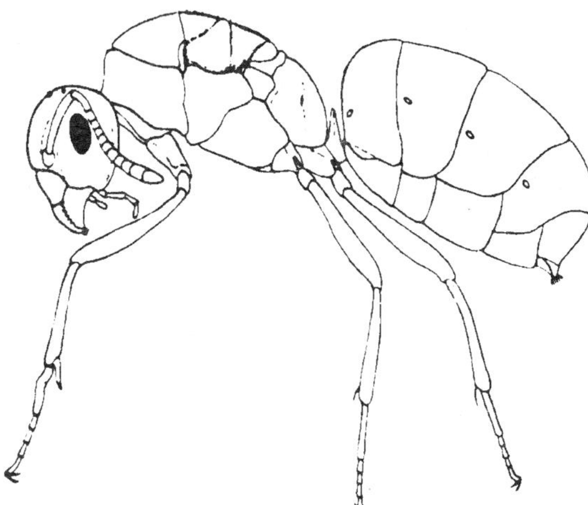

Carpenter bees resemble bumble bees. However, the carpenter bee is nearly black, while the bumble bee has yellow markings. Also, bumble bees are fuzzy, while carpenter bees are slick. They excavate a nesting burrow in exposed timbers like rafters and porch railings. The entry hole to the burrow is normally upward into the wood for about an inch. The burrow then turns and runs with the grain of the wood. The female bee makes cells which are filled with pollen and nectar and separated with wood pulp. One larva lives in each cell.

Much of the concern about carpenter bees is due to the habit of the males flying around the nest area. Males cannot sting, and females, unlike bumble bees, will not defend their nest. They only will sting if mishandled.

Carpenter ants are large and black. They can be either winged or wingless. The presence of carpenter ants in a home does not mean they are nesting there. These ants will look for food away from their nest and will often search a human dwelling for something to eat.

Carpenter ants, like human carpenters, leave sawdust as evidence of their work. A pile of sawdust on the carpet may indicate that these insect carpenters have constructed their new home in yours. If this is the case, it is probably wise to do something about the ants. Their nests can weaken the structure of our homes.

Most homeowners find it necessary from time to time to have carpentry work done. But not the kind provided by carpenter bees or carpenter ants. ■

The Socializers

1. What is a bee cleansing flight?
2. What is the larval food of bald-faced hornets?
3. Robert Frost's poem, "Departmental" is about which group of insects?
4. What substance is utilized by ants for trail marking and as a sting?
5. Where would the larvae of cicada killers be found?
6. What is another name for plant lice?
7. What insects have been said to be cows for ants?

Their Names are Mud . . . . Daubers

Their names may be mud, but you won't see them slinging any. In fact, the mothers-to-be mud daubers carefully construct cozy nests for their young.

The adult female wasp frequents creek banks or puddles, gathering mud in her mouthparts and carrying it to the nest site. There she fashions the mud into a nest characteristic of her species.

The pipe-organ mud dauber forms nests in series of 3 to 4 inch tubes constructed side by side in a way that resembles the pipes of a church organ. Each pipe of the nest contains cells which are provisioned with food such as spiders and caterpillars.

For those mud daubers choosing small spiders as meals for their young, as many as 20 can be placed in a cell. Each spider is stung by the wasp and paralyzed. Once the food is in place, the wasp lays an egg and the cell is sealed.

The newly-hatched wasp larva feeds on the spiders until it is fully developed. Then the larva forms a pupal cell and changes into a wasp. The following spring, the new wasp chews a hole through the mud walls of the nest and emerges. Once out, the adult wasp begins the age-old ritual of "mud daubing" a new nest.

While mud daubers sometimes act as if they might sting humans, they seldom do. They are peaceful neighbors who build their nests in our attics, garages and barns. Mud daubers even have been known to build nests in unused items such as sleds, boots, and picnic baskets.

By the time the young emerge, the parent will be dead — a victim of old age, hard work or the first freeze. Mud daubers work very had to provide for their offspring even though they will never live long enough to see them. For mud daubers, the words "generation gap" are appropriate. ■

Chapter 2

Bugs

So What's Bugging You?

Little boys have been known to "bug" older sisters and sometimes parents. Operatives of secret organizations fear "bugged" meeting rooms. Gossips have sometimes put a "bug" in a willing listener's ear. And we have all slept "snug as a bug in a rug" on a cold winter's night.

The word bug conjures up all kinds of ideas in people's minds. For instance, mentally ill people are sometimes incarcerated in a "bug house," and society has come to regard such folks as "buggy." Most of us have at some time in our lives committed a bug-a-boo, to the dismay of our colleagues. But what do children look like when they are "cute as a bug's ear?"

We may never know the answer to that question, since bugs don't have real ears, but most of our current uses of the word bug reflect an ancient meaning similar to the Celtic word "bwg," (pronounced BOOG), which meant ghost or spirit. Such an idea, and the word, is incorporated into the thought of the bogeyman — that mystical spirit of darkness sometimes used by parents to keep children in line.

The word bwg was probably first used to describe the bed bug. This pest of humans is rather reclusive in its habits. It hides in cracks and crevices of houses during the day. It emerges at night and, under the cover of darkness, attacks sleeping humans. To the ancient Celts who fell victim to this insect, it must surely have seemed that they were victims of a ghost or spirit. Thus, the name bwg. We call the shy creature a bed bug and, to this day, admonish, "Good night, sleep tight, and don't let the bed bugs bite."

Scientifically, bug is used to describe members of the insect order Hemiptera, the true bugs of the insect world. Bugs include such aquatic insects as the giant water bug, water striders and backswimmers. And on our plants, we sometimes find squash bugs, stink bugs, and boxelder bugs. Ambush bugs and assassin bugs are, as their names suggest, predators — mostly on other insects. Kissing bugs, like the bed bugs, are pests of humans. They get their name from the habit of biting folks around the mouth.

Regardless of its scientific merit, the word bug is frequently used in reference to any insect. An entomological error! You see, all bugs are insects, but not all insects are bugs.

Such a mistake was made by the computer folks who discovered that an insect had short-circuited their computer. The insect was a moth — not a bug — but after its removal, they coined the term "debug" to describe the process of fixing a nonfunctioning computer.

Oh well, most entomologists don't worry about the misuse of the term bug. ■

Leafhoppers by the Zillions

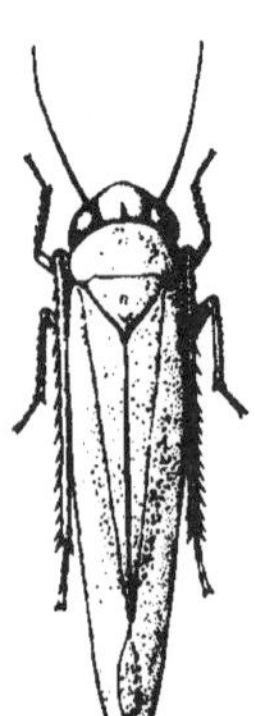

Leafhoppers seem to be everywhere during the summer. These small insects, measuring only millimeters in length, can be found on almost all types of plants.

They feed by taking sap from leaves. Their feeding pattern plus their habit of jumping when disturbed has given them the name "leafhoppers."

Many leafhoppers have a single generation a year and spend the winter in the adult or the egg stage. Some are seasonal invaders, coming into the midwestern states in the spring as passengers on a spring weather system.

Leafhoppers are important pests of plants. Damage is caused in several ways, including stress due to removing sap. Some species injure plants by laying eggs in twigs. Other species are vectors of important plant diseases, including potato yellow dwarf and corn stunt.

One of the most common pests, of this group of insects, is the potato leafhopper. Though it is a pest of potatoes, it also feeds on alfalfa and soybeans. When the potato leafhopper attacks alfalfa, its saliva produces a toxic effect, causing the leaves to turn yellow in a V-shaped pattern.

You don't have to grow potatoes or alfalfa to consider the potato leafhopper a pest. This insect invades our homes much too frequently. The potato leafhopper really doesn't want to be a house guest. It just happens to be an insect that cannot stay away from lighted windows.

The potato leafhopper is so small that it can go through window screens in search of the nearest light fixture. By the next morning, leafhopper carcasses are strewn like fallen infantrymen across counter tops, in light fixtures and on window sills.

Home owners who have enlisted bug zappers in their personal battle-of-the-bugs will find that their prized device has claimed leafhoppers by the buckets full. Still, many leafhoppers manage to find their way into the house. In the battle with insects, we humans have come to realize that numbers can sometimes overcome the most modern devices.

■

Chapter 2

Plant Lice

Springtime. That time of the year when plant fanciers' thoughts turn to green growing things — and to insects! Indeed, each spring, growers of ornamental and food plants prepare to assist their leafy-green wards in the "Battle of the Bugs."

About half of all insects feed on plants. It's a natural ecological process; the plant is the producer, and the insect, a consumer. Most plant owners, however, take a dim view of such insect activity.

Almost all plants are associated with one or more species of aphids. Sometimes called plant lice, aphids are small insects about the size of the head of a pin. Some have wings and some are wingless, even within the same species.

Aphids are one of the suckers of the insect world. They get their food by sucking sap from the leaves and stems of plants. In doing so, they can weaken the plant, cause abnormal tissue growth, and even transmit disease organisms. That's enough to send even the most seasoned plant grower looking for the spray can.

How can a little insect provoke such fear? It has to do with numbers. You see, aphid populations can grow very rapidly. As Erasmus Darwin, grandfather of Charles, once wrote:

> *The countless aphides, prolific tribe,*
> *with greedy trunks the honey's sap imbibe;*
> *swarm on each leaf with eggs or embryons big,*
> *and pendant nations tenant every twig.*

Many aphids give birth to live young. Some of these young can themselves become mothers in about a week. To help speed the process, some species have cut out the middle man — they reproduce without mating. No need to slow down the process by taking time to find a mate.

Aphids aren't despised by all creatures. For example, ants use the aphids' waste material, called honeydew because it is sweet, as a food resource. So attached are some ants to honeydew that they protect the aphids that produce it. This has prompted some scientists to call aphids "ants' cows." Ants are even known to move aphids from one plant to another as they manage their herd.

A few insects see the aphids themselves as the meal. Ladybird beetles are famous as predators on aphids. So are lacewings. Because the predators eat so many aphids, gardeners love these beneficial insects. Some people even purchase ladybird beetles for release to help in aphid control. However, it is important to make sure that aphids are present before turning the ladybird beetles loose. If aphids aren't present at the time of release, the ladybird beetles won't have food to eat and will leave.

In addition to causing plant stress, aphids sometimes create other problems by their presence. As aphids feed on trees, their honeydew can drift downward and leave rather unsightly spots on automobiles. Honeydew on plants provides a great place for sooty mold to grow, which results in a black layer on the surface of the plant. It is not a pretty sight to the plant owner.

All of this from a little insect called an aphid. It's no wonder that they are called plant lice. The very thought of having them makes most gardeners get itchy! ■

Insect Groupies

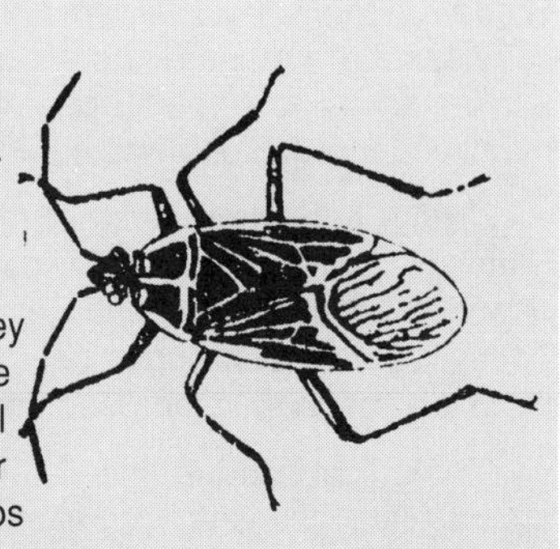

Every rock and movie star has groupies. So do athletes. On the golf links Arnie Palmer had his army. These human hangers-on are common around the rich and famous.

Even insects have groupies — at least they hang around in groups. One such insect groupie is the boxelder bug. No famous individual attracts these bugs. They just hang around for the warmth of it. You see, they gather in groups to absorb the rays of the sun.

Each fall as the season turns cooler, boxelder bugs begin to congregate in great numbers. These groups of strikingly marked red and black insects can be found everywhere. On trunks of trees, on porches, on walls and even on sidewalks. Often the presence of large numbers of boxelder bugs causes a great deal of concern among humans in the vicinity.

Such concern is unwarranted. Boxelder bugs can neither sting nor bite. They do not harm food or clothing. However, they do seek protection during the winter months in sheltered places. Sometimes these places are our homes. However, most homeowners take a fairly dim view of sharing their domicile with a bunch of insect groupies.

Because of such concern, homeowners have been known to take drastic measures to eliminate boxelder bugs. One such method is to attempt to burn the bugs. This approach generally involves a homemade torch on a pole. But there are secondary effects of such an effort. For instance, singed hair — from falling pieces of disintegrating torch. And we cannot forget the possibility of an emergency run by the fire department if the fire gets a little out of hand!

A better approach is to spray a common insecticide. Another way to reduce the problem is to eliminate boxelder trees in the vicinity of the house. These insects feed primarily on the seeds of the boxelder tree, but they also consume seeds of ash trees. Removal of the food source — in this case, the trees — will reduce the population to low levels.

Boxelder bugs characteristically have a disagreeable odor and taste. This is well known to people who have accidentally encountered this insect. Such a bad taste — a fact advertised by its bright color — keeps the insect from being eaten by insect predators.

Boxelder bugs aren't called boxelder bugs by everyone. In parts of the Midwest, these insects are known as Democrats. An unusual name compared to other common names of insects. I was once told that the name Democrat reflected the habits of these insects — because they always hang around in little groups and raise a stink. Of course, the fellow who mentioned that fact was a Republican!

Even insects like the boxelder bug aren't immune to politics. ■

Chapter 2

The Year of the Cicada

The cicadas are coming! The cicadas are coming!

Indeed, many folks who live in northern Illinois, southern Wisconsin or in Lake, Porter and LaPorte counties in Indiana will probably see and will certainly hear cicadas this June. You see, Brood XIII of the 17-year race of the periodical cicada will emerge in 1990, announcing its presence with an incessant cadence of high-pitched sound.

The cicadas that emerge this year are termed Brood XIII to distinguish them from other broods of this insect that emerge in different years and localities. For instance, next year Brood XIV will appear in many counties in southwestern Indiana.

Years ago when much of the eastern United States was covered with hardwood forests, a brood of periodical cicadas probably emerged each year. Today, some broods have been lost entirely, and most are confined to localized areas.

Periodical cicadas should not be confused with annual cicadas, which emerge during July and August. Annual cicadas are sometimes called 'harvestmen' or 'dog-day cicadas' because of their emergence time, which is associated with the dog days of summer.

The periodical cicada has the longest developmental period of any insect. As the name suggests, it takes 17 years for the insect to complete its life cycle.

This year's brood of the periodical cicada began its life in 1973. That was before Watergate, so Richard Nixon was still president, and that fall the Oakland A's beat the New York Mets in the World Series. Students graduating from high school this spring may not have been born in 1973 or, at least, were still in diapers.

Periodical cicadas begin their life as an egg laid under the bark of woody plants. The eggs hatch and the nymphs drop to the ground, where they dig into the soil and feed by sucking sap from the roots of trees. Seventeen years later, the nymphs emerge from the soil, where they shed their last shell to become winged adults.

Emergence normally occurs during nighttime hours. The cover of darkness helps protect the insect because the newly emerged adult is soft-bodied and unable to fly. At this time, it is easy prey to cicada eaters, of which there are many.

The new adults begin their appointed role in life, that of mating and laying eggs. Male cicadas attract mates by singing. The noise — or, rather, singing — is produced by two, drumlike membranes on the first segment of the abdomen.

Is it really necessary for the cicadas to make such a racket? No one knows for sure. But wouldn't most folks feel like singing at the top of their lungs after spending 17 years in underground darkness? ■

BUGS

1. What was the original meaning of the Celtic word "bwg"?
2. What insect is responsible for the idea of "debugging a computer?"
3. In what form do boxelder bugs overwinter?
4. What is the scientific name of the only insect order that can correctly be called bug?

Chapter 2

Other Insect Orders

Insect Dragons

Skimmers, Biddies, and Darners. No, these aren't the latest rock bands. They are dragonflies.

Dragonflies are among the oldest of insects. Some call them living fossils. Today's dragonflies look about like their ancestors that lived nearly 300 million years ago. Dragonflies roamed the skies during the 100-million-year reign of the dinosaurs. One such ancient dragonfly was itself dinosaur-sized. This insect had a wing span of nearly 27 inches.

Immature dragonflies, called nymphs, live in the water. Adults do fly far from water on their aerial forays, but they are most commonly found near water habitats.

Both adults and nymphs are predators. They feed primarily on other insects, although large dragonfly nymphs have been known to capture and devour small fish.

Adult dragonflies capture prey while on the wing. Although the dragonfly has a fearsome-looking set of jaws, it procures its meals by an unusual method. The dragonfly shapes its six legs into a basket. Then, in an insect version of an aerial dogfight, overtakes prey from behind, snaring the potential meal in its legs.

The dragonfly sometimes eats on the wing — sort of a "meal to go" in the insect world. For a more leisurely dining experience, the dragonfly will perch on vegetation before devouring the hapless victim.

Because dragonflies destroy a number of insects, including mosquitoes, gnats and flies, they are beneficial. Even though dragonflies are predators, they are harmless to people. These insects neither sting nor bite. However, dragonflies have not always been considered harmless.

There are a number of superstitions associated with the dragonflies. For instance, in some rural areas of the United States, the common name "snake doctor" was acquired because people assumed that the dragonfly acted as a guard to snakes. This may have originated because both snakes and dragonflies share marshy habitats.

Another superstition held that dragonflies could sew together various parts of the human body, including lips, nostrils, eyelids and ears. This belief gave rise to the common name darning needle or devil's darning needle.

Some of the fear of dragonflies, and some of the superstitions, are probably based on the fearsome look of the insect. However, part of the mystique of the dragonfly is due to its territorial nature. Male dragonflies set up territories just as do certain birds and mammals. The dragonfly then defends its territory against other dragonflies. Such territorial defense leads to spectacular battles among these master aerialists. The dragonflies also check out other intruders in their territory — a surveillance activity that some folks might interpret as hostile behavior.

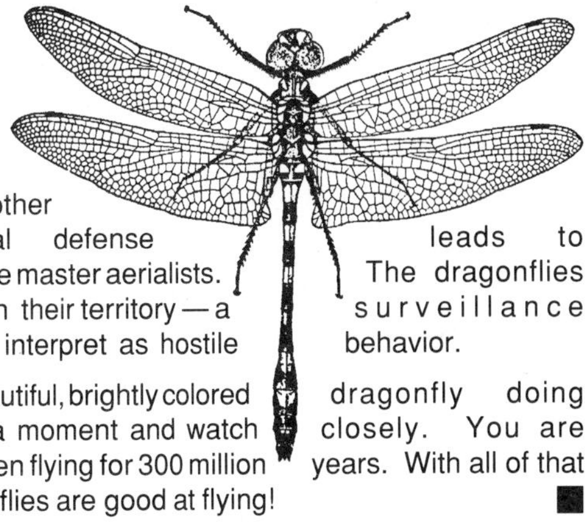

The next time you spy a beautiful, brightly colored dragonfly doing aerial maneuvers, pause for a moment and watch closely. You are watching an animal that has been flying for 300 million years. With all of that practice, it's no wonder dragonflies are good at flying! ■

Fleeting Flies of May

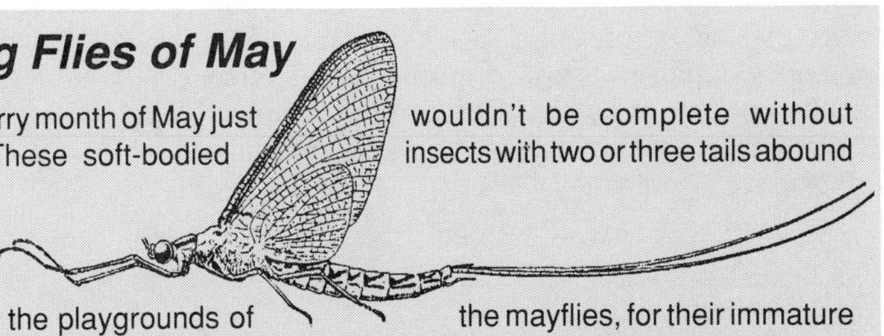

The merry month of May just wouldn't be complete without mayflies. These soft-bodied insects with two or three tails abound this month.

Lakes, ponds and streams are the playgrounds of the mayflies, for their immature stages live in the water and feed upon algae and other aquatic plants.

These insects in both the adult and immature stages are also an important source of food for fish. Consequently, fishermen use artificial lures modeled after the mayfly in their attempts to catch the big ones.

The aquatic stages of mayflies can last a year or more. The adult has one of the shortest life spans of any insect. In fact, these insects are classified in the order Ephemeroptera which is based on the Greek word "ephemero," meaning for a day. This refers to the adults which will live for as little as 24 hours. The adults have reduced mouthparts and do not feed.

The short time the adults have on the wing is devoted to their single biological function, reproduction. Mayflies often emerge in enormous numbers and form swarms. These swarms are normally composed of males which fly up and down in unison in the mayfly version of a mating dance. When a female flies into the swarm, she is claimed by a male and spirited away on a mating flight. The eggs are laid on the surface of the water. Once the biological function of the adults has been completed they die. The dead and dying mayflies don't go to waste, they provide an all-you-can-eat smorgasbord for the fish.

Houses and towns in areas where large emergences of mayflies occur are frequently inundated with these insects. They are attracted to lights where many die leaving piles of dead mayflies several inches deep under store windows or porch lights. In years of high emergence, mayfly bodies may accumulate on river bridges, causing the surface to become slick and hazardous. In some instances, snowplows have been called out to clear the bridges of dead mayflies.

Paul Fleischman in his award-winning book Joyful Noise begins his poem "Mayflies" with these lines:

> Your moment — Mayfly month
> Your hour — Mayfly year
> Your trifling day — Our life

Mayfly adults are indeed ephemeral, that's why entomologists classify them as Ephemeroptera. Such is the fleeting life of the mayfly adult. One last frantic day to ensure the next generation. ■

Chapter 2

Archie: The Famous Cockroach

While archie the cockroach may be famous, most people regard cockroaches as infamous. In fact, cockroaches are despised and with good reason. These pesty insects have invaded our abodes for thousands of years in spite of our best efforts to the contrary.

There is, however, one cockroach that made a name for himself. In fact this cockroach was a writer, and his name was "archie." As the story goes, archie lived in the office of New York Sun Times newspaper writer Don Marquis. Each evening archie would creep on all six legs to the office typewriter and hammer out a column.

Typing was not easy and archie had to use his head, "literally," for the task. He would crawl up on the carriage and do the insect equivalent of a swan dive, striking the selected key head first. This laborious approach to typing produced free verse poetry uncluttered by capitalization or punctuation since archie couldn't depress the shift key while landing on the letter key.

Don Marquis, the writer, began in 1916 to use the literary efforts of archie in a column called "Sun Dial." Even though the style is unorthodox, the wit, wisdom and commentary of archie is timeless.

From the viewpoint of a lowly cockroach, archie has a lot to say about life in general. Consider the following maxims of archie.

don't cuss the climate
it probably doesn't like you
any better
than you like it

live so that you
can stick out your
tongue
at the insurance
doctor

many a man spanks his
children for
things his own
father should have
spanked out of him

insects have
their own point
of view about
civilization a man
thinks he amounts
to a great deal
but to a
flea or a
mosquito a
human being is
merely something
good to eat

Many of us probably hate to admit it, but we can learn a lot from nature, even if the teacher happens to be a cockroach.

La Cucaracha, La Cucaracha

La cucaracha, the cockroach! Probably no insect conjures up more unpleasant thoughts in human minds than the cockroach.

Cockroaches are a very old type of insect. Some scientists estimate that roaches have been on earth for over 300 million years. During most of that time, roaches have devoted their considerable energies to breaking down dead plant material. From an ecological perspective, that is a very noble thing to do.

However, at some point in history, some of these six-legged scavengers took up abode in our dwellings. That, in the humble opinion of humans, was a downright unfriendly thing to do. So we devote a lot of time and energy trying to keep roaches from our homes.

There is nothing inherently bad about sharing our domicile with roaches. To be sure, they have been implicated in disease transmission. And, without question, they are common in unsanitary conditions. But mostly it is just plain socially disgraceful to share quarters with them.

To the modern housekeeper, having roaches is akin to being placed in the public stocks on the town square. For that reason, we have developed ways to overcome the shock of finding roaches in our kitchens. We call some roaches "waterbugs," because somehow it is easier to report to neighbors that the exterminator only found waterbugs. And some pest control companies will make housecalls in unmarked automobiles. That, of course, is so the neighborhood will be unware of the nature of the visit.

Cockroaches are everywhere in the world. Many have expanded their range to include foreign soil in addition to their ancestral homelands. But their names still betray their nationalities, for example, the German, Oriental, Madagascar and American roaches.

Some prefer to earn their fame closer to home though. Back in 1916, columnist Don Marquis introduced a column called "Sun Dial" in the New York Sun newspaper. "archy," a lowly cockroach and self-proclaimed poet, invaded Marquis' office every night to write this free-verse column. A dedicated writer, archy accomplished this feat by diving head first one by one onto the typewriter keys, which explains why he never bothered to add punctuation or capital letters to his poetry. Along with his friend, Mehitabel, the cat, archy provided a delightful commentary on life during those times.

In spite of our disdain for cockroaches, the wisdom of archy is worth repeating. Recognizing that cockroaches were not the favorite insects of people, archy once rejoiced:

there is always
something to be thankful
for you would not
think that a cockroach
had much ground
for optimism
but as the fishing season
opens up i grow
more and more
cheerful at the thought
that nobody ever got
the notion of using
cockroaches for bait.

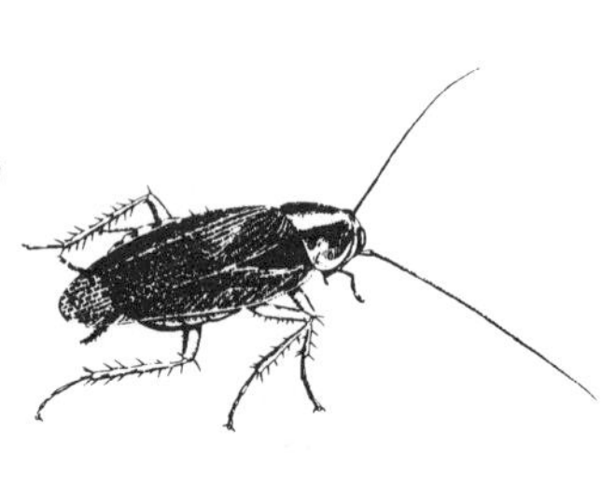

. . . archy

In spite of our disdain for cockroaches, archy and his descendants need not worry. They will be on this earth long after we are gone.

Chapter 2

Chewing Machines

Grasshoppers are among the most recognizable insects on earth. Perhaps it's because of their chewing mouthparts. Grasshoppers have the type that show up in horror movies. Or it might be because of their hind legs. Those legs are used for jumping and, hence, the name—hopper.

But the truth is that grasshoppers are well known for their appetites. The eating habits of grasshoppers make them one of the world's worst insect pests.

Grasshoppers have been known as a pest for thousands of years. The Bible contains several references to grasshoppers—sometimes called locusts — as pests. For example, in Joel 2:3 we read, ". . . the land is as the Garden of Eden before them and behind them a desolate wilderness; yea, and nothing shall escape them." The eighth of the plagues visited upon Egypt preceding the Exodus was a great mass of locusts which, according to biblical account, ate all the vegetation on the land so that nothing was left.

Grasshoppers primarily feed on green foliage, but when food is scarce they will feed on almost anything. Tales have been told of grasshoppers eating straw hats left in the field. In the Dust Bowl days, wooden pitchfork handles were said to have been nearly consumed by hungry grasshoppers.

Grasshopper problems are most pronounced when the weather is dry. Biological control of this insect is reduced under dry conditions. For instance, under wet spring conditions, the egg masses, which are the overwintering state of grasshoppers, are attacked by a fungus disease. This disease eliminates many hoppers before they hatch.

In the arid regions of Africa, the migratory locust is a continual problem. During the drought periods of the 1930s and the 1950s, grasshopper damage to U.S. crops was high. And in unusually dry years, such as 1988, grasshopper problems normally increase.

Many approaches to grasshopper control have been used over the years. During the 1930s in the Midwest, hopperdozers were used. Hopperdozers were grasshopper-catching machines placed on the front end of a truck or tractor. As many as eight bushels of hoppers were collected per acre using one of these devices. Such a grasshopper population has been estimated to consume a ton of alfalfa hay per day in a 40-acre field.

More recently, people in Africa have tried to keep the insects from damaging crops by driving them away. Today, large swarms of grasshoppers are sometimes sprayed during their flights with an insecticide carried by aircraft.

Another way to kill grasshoppers is to include a poison in a bait. An enterprising entomologist during the 1930s even mixed poison with horse manure for use in controlling grasshoppers. Reports are that the bait worked quite well.

As a last resort, some peoples of the world have taken to eating grasshoppers. However, such an approach has not been widely accepted in the United States. It seems that eating up an insect problem—especially grasshoppers—just doesn't appeal to our tastes. ■

Hoppers, Hoppers Everywhere

Ah, July! That time of the year when ol' Sol the sun, almost without human notice, begins a seasonal retreat toward the southern horizon, and the days begin to shorten ever so slightly.

To most folks, July signals the onset of, as Nat King Cole immortalized in song, "Those lazy, hazy, crazy days of summer." However, the declining minutes of daylight stir within plants and many animals a sense of biological urgency. Plants flower; some animals lay in a winter's food supply; others just add on a layer of fat; and many insects rush to lay eggs.

No insect is more closely associated with the dog days of summer than grasshoppers. If baseball players can lay claim to the title of "Boys of Summer," then surely grasshoppers are the "Bugs of Summer!"

Grasshopper egg masses, oviposited the previous fall in the soil, hatch in June and July. As summer days get drowsier, the grasshopper nymphs — typical teenagers that they are — are eating up a storm.

By August, mature grasshoppers begin the process of mate selection. Many grasshoppers attract mates by producing a sound, appropriately named "calling." This sound, called a "song," is most often produced by males in one of two ways. The short-horned grasshoppers — those with short antennae — make sounds by rubbing their hind leg across their wing. The long-horned grasshoppers rub one wing against the other.

It is a bit misleading to term these sounds "songs" though, because the sound has no pitch. It sounds a bit like rubbing two pieces of sandpaper together. For most of us, this sound is relegated to the status of background noise, and it is easy to forget or ignore.

Grasshopper songs are one of the most prominent features of late-summer days. At almost any time of the day, three or four species of grasshoppers can be heard. They, like birds, can even be identified to species by their calls.

It is probably this singing that prompted Aesop to pen his fable of the grasshopper and the ant. To Aesop, it must have seemed that singing away the last days of summer was a foolish thing for a grasshopper to do, especially compared to the ants, who work industriously to store the winter's food supply. But the singing of the grasshopper should probably stand to remind us that its work is done. The grasshoppers late-summer song is really a last laugh. For in the soil are grasshopper egg masses, just settling in for a long winter's nap in preparation for next season's feast.

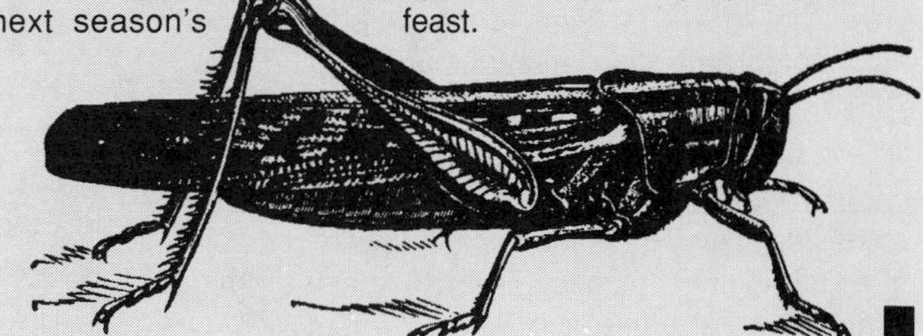

■

Chapter 2

Arsenic and Old Lacewings

Lacewings are the "arsenic and old lace" of the insect world. These insects are small — less than a half-inch in length. To us, they appear quite fragile, soft-bodied with four clear, membranous wings. The many cross-veins in their wings create an image, well, of lace. That is the basis for their name. But to their prey, lacewings are as deadly as arsenic.

Lacewings, which are classified in the insect order Neuroptera, are considered ancient insects. Bearing resemblance to miniature prehistoric monsters, most are greenish or brown with golden-colored eyes. Their long antennae and fearsome chewing mouthparts suggest that lacewings are not part of the gentle, nectar-sipping set of the insect upper crust. Quite the opposite.

Both lacewing adults and larvae are random predators. They roam plants with the fervor of hungry diners scanning a menu as they search for insects. Aphids are a favorite food. Lacewing larvae have a pair of sickle-shaped jaws that are piercing-sucking tubes. When a prowling larva, appropriately called an aphislion, encounters an aphid, the end is swift. The victim is impaled on the lacewing's sharp jaws while fluids are sucked from the victim's body like soda through a straw.

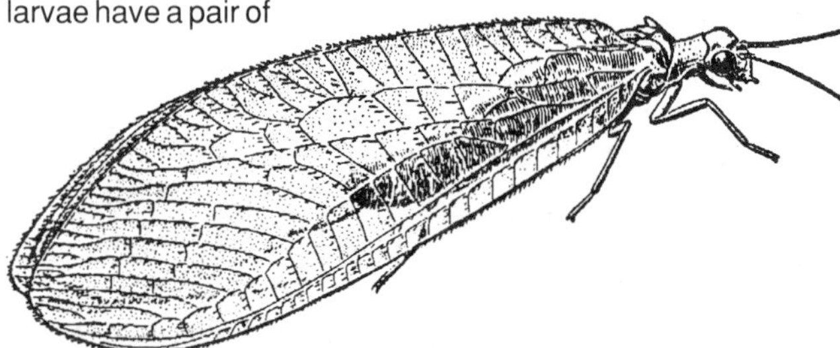

Larval lacewings are such dedicated predators that even their brothers and sisters are potential meals. Among lacewings, the first hatched has an advantage. Newly hatched larvae begin a fervent search for food. Almost anything will do — even an unhatched lacewing egg. No amount of parental cajoling would likely prevent this ultimate expression of sibling rivalry. So lacewing mothers-to-be place their eggs on a stalk, just out of range of hungry little jaws. Of course, when larvae hatch and descend from the safe hatching perch, they're on their own in the dog-eat-dog world of lacewings and aphids.

Many gardeners have gained a great appreciation for the appetite of lacewings. In fact, lacewings have biological control potential and have even gained commercial status. Gardeners can purchase lacewings to help control the undesirable creatures that show up in their gardens — at least undesirable creatures of the insect variety. Lacewings are of no help whatsoever when it comes to hungry neighbors who seem to show up at the garden when the work is done and the harvest begins! ■

Winter Stoneflies

Insects, like snakes, frogs and salamanders are cold-blooded organisms. These animals cannot regulate their body temperature and are generally inactive during the winter.

Some insects, such as the familiar cockroach, cope with cold temperatures by living in our dwellings. But a few hardy insects species are seen during the winter months in the great out-of-doors.

One such insect, the winter stonefly, is appropriately named — at least the season in its name is accurate. Winter stoneflies can be found crawling around during sunny days from January through April.

But stoneflies really aren't flies at all. Some do fly, although their aerial forays are less than spectacular. A few species of stoneflies have given up flying altogether, and for good reason: they lack wings. These wingless individuals depend on their six little feet to get them where they want to go.

Technically, stoneflies are members of the insect order Plecoptera. Insects in this order are rather soft-bodied and have antennae-like appendages, called cerci, protruding from their abdomen.

These rather drab-colored insects are found near streams or rocky, lake shores. The immature stoneflies, called nymphs, live in the water and are often found under stones. That's the basis for their common name, stonefly.

The stoneflies that show up during the winter months are normally active in air pockets that form between the ice and the surface of the water of streams. At a time of year when most insects are out of sight, stoneflies take advantage of the higher temperatures in such miniature greenhouses to be active.

During warm seasons when the ice disappears from streams in midwinter, as it has this year, stoneflies show up in abundance on fence posts, bridges and other structures in the vicinity of the streams where they emerged.

Why are these insects active during the winter? No one knows for sure. One suggestion is that it avoids competition with other insects. The stonefly has discovered a time of year when it doesn't have to compete with the teeming hordes of insects that show up during the warmer months. As far as insects go, it has the whole world to itself.

So what does the winter stonefly do under such circumstances? Like any good adult insect, it does what nature has designed it to do: it mates and lays eggs.

And what does it eat? Nothing at all. You see, the winter stonefly doesn't feed in the adult stage, which is fortunate, since there is probably very little to eat under the ice on a winter's day! ■

Chapter 2

Termites: Nature's Wood Destruction Crew

In nature's grand scheme of things, insects have many jobs, for example, clean-up detail. Being on the clean-up crew may not be your idea of a good time, but it's a job that has to be done. Can you imagine what the world would be like if dead plants and animals remained on the surface of the earth? Combine this with the paper and beverage containers that we humans throw on the roadsides and you've got a real mess. Therefore, be thankful that clean-up is a way of life for some insects!

Termites are one of the insect cleaner-uppers. Their job is to help rid the world of dead trees. Termites destroy wood by eating it. However, eating wood is one thing, digesting it is another. To aid in wood digestion, termites have in their guts protozoa, which are microorganisms, that break down cellulose.

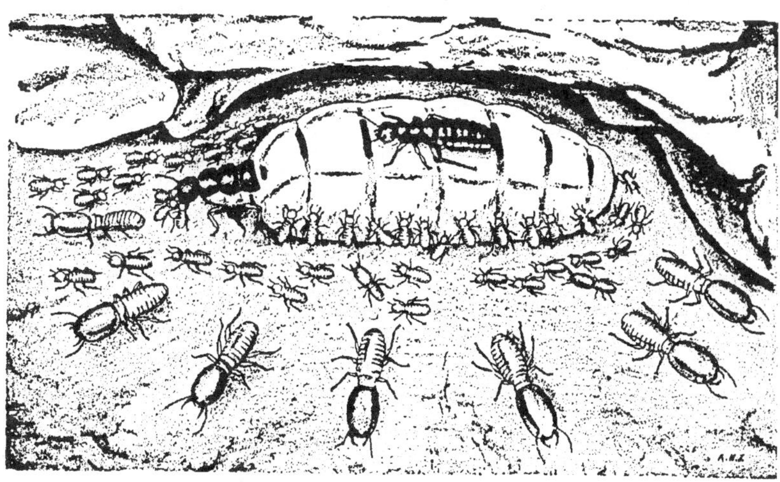

All of this is a nice plan. However, when humans started building structures out of wood, the termites continued to do their ecological task. To a termite, dead wood is dead wood! It matters not that the wood is part of the finest house on the best street in town. Of course, when termites attack houses, people become hostile and call the little creatures pests and try and get rid of them.

Ogden Nash recognized the economic importance of termites as structural pests when he penned the following:

Some primal termites knocked on wood
And tasted it, and found it good,
And that is why your cousin May
Fell through the parlor floor today.

To many homeowners the thought of termites is a sober one indeed. In the springtime, at least in the case of termites, what has been out of sight comes to mind. It is in the spring that termites swarm. Swarming is a process where termites leave the underground nest chambers and disperse. This is one time in the year when the termites can be readily seen. But they can be easily confused with ants, which also swarm.

If termites are detected in a home, the best approach for control is to select a termite control service. However, do not panic! Termites work slowly, so you have time to purchase the service at your convenience. Also, choose a reliable firm; the termite business is one that is attractive to fly-by-night businesses.

Based on fossil records, termites are one of the oldest insects. So when termites eat the wood from which we have fashioned our houses, they are doing what comes naturally, as they have for the last 350 million years or so! ■

Doodlebugs' Charm

James Whitcomb Riley, a Hoosier poet, recognized a doodlebug when he saw one. In his poem *The Doodlebugs' Charm* Riley revealed that it was his Uncle Sidney who introduced him to the unusual six-legged creature. What was the fascination?

Doodlebugs are strange-looking insects with large, flat heads and long, protruding sickle-like jaws. This group of insects is classified in the order of Neuroptera which includes the familiar lacewings. Both lacewings and doodlebugs are predators on other insects.

Doodlebugs live in pits constructed of dry sand or dust. These pits can sometimes measure up to two inches wide at the soil surface. During construction the doodlebugs cleverly set traps by piling sand around the pits. Once inside their homes, the doodlebugs eagerly wait for their meals to "drop in." One by one insects traveling too close to the pits tumble to the doodlebug's dinner tables. Ants are frequently their victims, giving rise to another common name for doodlebugs, "antlions."

Doodlebugs are more common in the south and southwest of the country. Their pits frequently are found in groups and in very dry conditions such as under buildings.

"To call 'em up," Uncle Sidney said, "'Doodle! Doodle! Doodle-Bugs!' An' they'd poke out their head — "'Doodle-Bugs! Doodle-Bugs! Come up an' git some bread!'"

With a little strategy and a whole lot of patience, you may be able to entice the doodlebugs to show themselves. Instead of calling out their name, slowly push grains of sand into one of their pits. The curious and ravenous doodlebugs will be tempted to investigate what they think is their next meal.

If you encounter a group of the hungry larvae, then perhaps like James Whitcomb Riley, you too, will discover the doodlebugs' charm. ■

Prayerful Insects

One of the most recognized insects is the praying mantis. How did the insect get such a pious name?

The word "mantis" is based on the Greek word meaning prophet or soothsayer. While in wait for a victim, the mantis takes a rather pious stance which no doubt suggested its name — praying mantis. The European mantis even has a scientific name descriptive of the posture, Mantis religosa.

The praying mantis is no pacifist. It would probably be more appropriately called the "preying mantis" for it is an effective predator. Most mantises are colored in such a way as to camouflage their presence. They hunt by waiting. They have small heads and are among the few insects with a distinctive neck. The neck allows them to turn their heads so they can better spot their prey, Their large compound eyes give them great vision for detecting movement and judging distance.

All mantises are carnivorous and feed on almost any insect including flies, crickets, moths and even wasps. Mantids are well-equipped to catch their food. Their forelegs are modified into a fearsome insect-catching device that functions like a pocket knife. These raptorial forelegs include spines to aid in holding a victim which is caught in ambush.

Once mantids have procured a meal, they eat with the aplomb of a sophisticated diner at the finest of restaurants. However, their dining manners belie the appetite of a woodchopper. They can consume as many as twenty flies in one day.

It is this appetite and food habit that makes the praying mantis a beneficial insect. The insect is a friend of gardeners everywhere. However, mantis populations are seldom high enough to destroy large populations of pest insects. Therefore, many gardeners give mother nature a little hand by purchasing and placing mantis egg cases in gardens and flower beds.

The purchase of praying mantis egg cases may or may not rid a garden of undesirable insects. However, the act of doing so makes most gardeners feel good. Besides they take great pleasure in seeing a mantis in the garden. Especially if that mantis happens to be chowing down on some other insect! ■

Sticks That Walk

What's the difference between a walking stick and a stick that walks? Six legs!

When we think of a walking stick, we usually think of a staff or cane that aids a person in walking. However, there are walking sticks of the insect variety that walk with six legs.

Walking sticks that are commonly found in the United States resemble twigs. They are wingless, slowmoving insects that feed on trees and shrubs. Their version of a twig look-alike contest is a matter of survival. They blend into their enviornment so that potential predators can't see them easily. Small birds perched upon a walking stick are sitting on a potential meal but often don't know the difference.

Insect walking sticks vary in size. The largest insect found in the United States is a walking stick that reaches a length of 6 to 7 inches. This insect is found in the South and Southwest. Most walking sticks are tropical and those that live in such climates can attain an adult length of about a foot, which is appropriate considering their name.

In some instances, walking sticks have covered trees and consumed all the foliage. Because of their protective coloration most people will not see them. To the untrained eye, they are just another bare twig.

Walking sticks have a single generation per year. Mature female walking sticks drop their eggs wherever they feed, leaving them to endure the winter season on their own. After winter, the little twig imitators hatch in a paradise of fresh, green leaves which they will eagerly devour.

The next time you focus your gaze upon what you think is a twig, and it walks away, don't fret. You've just had an insect encounter of the oddest kind. Walking sticks are one of the many bizarre insects that inhabit earth. ■

Other Insect Orders

1. What kind of an insect was archie?
2. Describe the process of how dragonflies catch food.
3. In what type of habitat would dragonfly immatures be found? What is their food?
4. Where would winter stoneflies be found during the winter months?
5. Under what weather conditions do grasshoppers cause the greatest problems?
6. Why is it appropriate that mayflies are classified in the insect order Ephemeroptera?
7. What is the ecological role of mayflies?

Chapter 3

Insect Biology

Insect Reproduction

Vive La Difference

In the insect world, male and female insects are different in ways other than the obvious physical attributes.

In the insect version of the dating game, insect sounds for attracting a mate are always produced by the male. The songs of crickets, grasshoppers and katydids emanate from an all-male choir. And the not-so-melodious shrill of cicadas results from the vibrations of a drumlike membrane on the abdomen of the males.

In fact, ancient Greeks recognized that male cicadas sang, while females were mute. The old Greek philosopher Zenarchus summarized this fact in his comment, "Happy are the cicadas' lives for they have voiceless wives."

Female insects have their own ways of dealing with the opposite sex. Many females produce mating perfumes called pheromones. Upon release, these chemicals, which are emitted from specialized organs, attract males from considerable distances. Some of the large moths may travel up to 50 miles while following the pheromone trail of a female. Although females dominate the insect perfumery business, a few male insects, such as some of the bark beetles, produce pheromones, too.

Following mating, many male insects go their merry way while the task of laying eggs and caring for the young is left to the females. But some female insects don't let the males off that easy.

For example, the giant water bug female captures a male and attaches her eggs to his back for him to carry until they hatch. Other females — such as the preying mantids, some dance flies and even some fireflies — make a meal of their mate.

In some insect species, the number of males are reduced. The engraver beetle populations are made up of 200 females to each male. And some aphids have eliminated males all together. These females reproduce without benefit of mating through a process called parthenogenesis.

So in the insect world, it may be the males that do the singing, but more often than not, it is the female that has the last laugh! ■

Insects Don't Add; They Multiply

Ever wonder how there can be so many insects in so quickly after the spring thaw? It could be magic, or spontaneous generation. But it isn't either.

It has to do with the birds and the bees — mainly the bees! Bees and other insects are very good at laying eggs in very large numbers. Scientists believe that rapid reproduction is one reason for the phenomenal success of insects on earth.

Consider the honey bee queen. In the warm months of June and July, she can lay between 1,500 and 2,000 eggs each day. Since she must deposit each in a cell of the comb, that production represents a good day's work. You might say she's "busy as a bee" during that time. A honey bee queen will produce around 100,000 eggs during her average 3-year life span. Not a bad record.

But honey bee egg production pales in comparison to that of the large queen termites of Africa. Such queens, real egg-laying machines, may lay as many as 36,000 eggs in 24 hours. That's about 25 eggs a minute and totals over 13,000,000 per year. Such queen termites are believed to live between 50 and 100 years. That figures out to be over a billion eggs produced by one queen.

While the old housefly is no queen termite when it comes to laying eggs, she isn't a slouch either. Average egg production during the life of a housefly is probably around 800 eggs. The record number of eggs measured for one fly is 2,387. But the success of the housefly is not solely due to the rate of egg-laying; it is also due to the speed with which the insect goes through its life cycle.

The same is true for the fruit fly, an insect that almost everyone recognizes. Fruit flies seem to magically appear around overripe vegetables or fruit. The appearance of large numbers of fruit flies in a short time shows how fast this insect develops. Under ideal conditions, fruit flies may produce 25 generations per year. Each female may lay up to 100 eggs, of which about half will hatch into females and half into males.

It has been calculated that by starting with one pair of fruit flies and allowing the original and all succeeding females to reproduce under ideal conditions for one year, the number of flies would be fantastic — about 10^{41} (That's a 10 with 41 zeros behind it.) All those flies would form a ball 96 million miles in diameter, if you assume that 1,000 would fit in a cubic inch. A ball that size would almost reach the sun from the earth!

Of course, all insects that hatch don't survive to reproduce. Many insects die of starvation or exposure to lethal temperatures or are consumed as food by other animals. Among insects, many are hatched so that a few survive. You could say that in the insect world, the battle cry is, "The more, the merrier!" ■

Chapter 3

Insect Eggs

Insect lives are frequently described in terms of a cycle: egg to larva to pupa to adult and back to egg. So the age-old paradox frequently asked of our fine feathered friend, the chicken, might also be relevant to insects. Which came first: the adult or the egg?

Fall Armyworm Egg Mass (left) and Eggs (right) top and side view

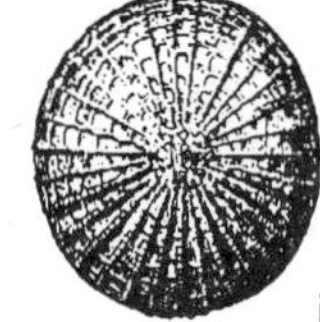

Every insect begins life as an egg. Most insect eggs are laid by the adult before the embryo is fully developed. Therefore, the egg doesn't hatch immediately.

Hatching time is usually short, normally within a few days. Since insects don't incubate their eggs, hatching time is determined by the environmental temperature. For instance, the eggs of the Oriental fruit moth will hatch in three to six days in warm weather, but may take up to 40 days in cooler weather.

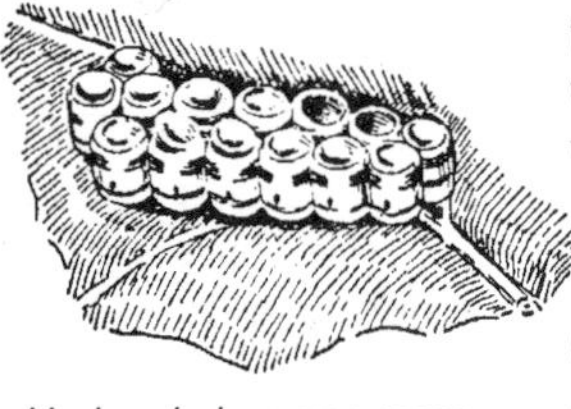

Harlequin bug egg mass

Some insects hibernate in the egg stage. In this case, the egg may not hatch for 6 to 10 months. Grasshoppers and corn rootworms are such insects. And eggs, such as of the walkingstick, may remain unhatched for two years.

Fertilization is generally necessary to produce an insect egg that will hatch. Some insect females have, however, eliminated the middleman in the reproductive process. Insects that lay unfertilized eggs include some bees, ants, social wasps and many aphids. In the social insects, unfertilized eggs develop into males while fertilized eggs become females.

Insects eggs come in various shapes. Some are flat and scalelike. Eggs of the European corn borer look like fish scales, half covering each other on the leaf of the corn. Others look like miniature wine barrels placed neatly on a dock waiting export. Some of the stinkbugs follow this pattern of egg placement.

The shell of the insect egg can be perfectly smooth. However, some insect eggs are sculptured in striking markings that are the envy of human artists. Generally, the thickness of the shell of the insect egg gives a hint of the environmental conditions it must face. Eggs that hatch shortly after they are laid have thin shells. Eggs that must endure the winter tend to have thick shells. An exception is when the egg is laid in some protected place, such as in the soil or under the bark of a tree.

Some insects cover the egg mass with special materials. Many moths cover the egg mass with hair from their bodies. The female bagworm deposits eggs in the bag which served as her home. The praying mantid secretes a brown, frothlike substance in which to enclose her eggs and attaches the mass to a twig or wire fence, where it remains for the winter.

While it is not possible to answer the question of which came first, it is true that the insect egg must survive if there are to be adult insects. Diversity in the shape, size and placement of eggs suggests that insects have opted not to put all their eggs in the same basket!

Say it With Perfume

It's not easy to find someone with whom to share your life. Especially if you are an insect. In fact, most adult insects devote their lives to that most ancient of biological imperatives—finding a mate.

Insects don't have computer dating lists, lonely-hearts clubs, singles bars or even a six-legged version of a matchmaker to help in the mating game. Each insect is on its own when it comes to this business of love and marriage.

Insects employ a variety of activities to attract potential mates. Some, like crickets and katydids, are crooners. Others like the fireflies are specialists in aerial fireworks. Still others "say it with perfume." Yes, for many insects a good scent is worth a thousand sweet words.

Insects that use perfume to announce their availability include butterflies and moths. Technically, these velvet-winged suitors use chemicals called pheromones, which are produced in the insect's body. When released into the environment, these odors are irresistible to the opposite sex. Most pheromones are produced by female insects, but in some species the male is the one in the perfumery business.

How does this all work? The female produces the pheromone and releases it into the environment. To make sure that the chemical gets carried toward potential suitors she flaps her wings about. This creates a plume of air that wafts downwind carrying the sweet scent with it. This process is appropriately named "calling"—sort of the insect equivalent of "Hey, good lookin'"! Males who happen to be downwind at the time will detect the pheromone—that's why male moths have fuzzy antennae—and follow the trail upwind to the source. At that point, one is to assume he politely introduces himself and says something like, "Nice pair of legs . . . pair of legs . . . pair of legs."

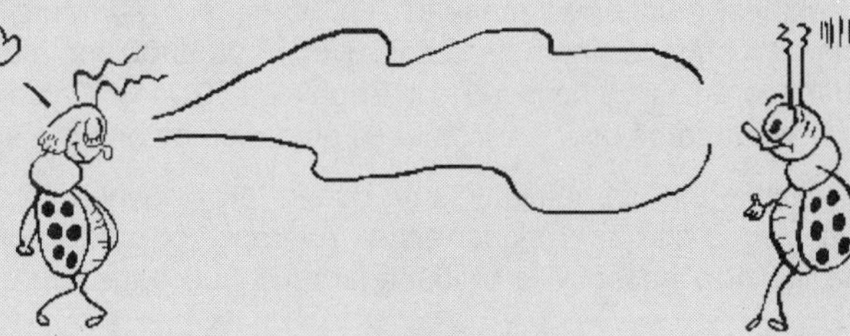

Pheromones are complex chemicals. For

Chapter 3

Insect Songsters

Insects rival birds as the animal world's most note-worthy singers. The rasps, shrills, clicks and chirps of insects aren't as melodious as the tones produced by birds, but, by sheer volume, the insects frequently dominate their avian competition in nature's chorus.

Unlike birds, insects use a variety of mechanisms to harmonize. Some, like mosquitos and bees, produce sound by the vibration of their wings.

Such sound is incidental to the activity of these insects. However, the mosquito's whine has come to be a warning to its human victims. Likewise, the buzzing of bees is widely recognized as a danger sign in the animal world. Some flies even mimic the sound for their own protection. And the sound is so familiar that the composer Rimski-Korsakov used violins to represent it in his popular "Flight of the Bumblebee."

The majority of insect choristers produce sound by stridulation. That is, they rub one body part against another. Some grasshoppers produce sound by rubbing the edges of their wings together. Others "fiddle" by rubbing the back leg across the edge of the wing.

But all insects aren't fiddlers. Some are drummers. The cicadas are the percussionists of the insect world. The drum of the cicada is a membrane located on the abdomen, which is vibrated by the use of a complicated set of muscles to produce the well-known hum of the cicada.

Insect sounds vary throughout the season and over the course of the day. For example, many grasshoppers sing during the day but become silent at nightfall. Many crickets begin to warble when the sun goes down.

Insects sing primarily for the purpose of communicating with others of their species. For instance, some insects court a potential mate by crooning a sweet song, a practice the insects share with birds and, in some instances, humans.

Unlike humans, the male of the species is usually the lead singer. This fact was noted long ago by the Greek philosopher Xenarchus, who wrote, "Happy are the cicadas lives for they have voiceless wives."

Many people over the years have enjoyed the harmonic renditions of insects. Some Oriental cultures keep crickets in cages just for the beauty of their singing. Indeed, a cricket chirping in the house is considered good luck. Such an idea was noted by Charles Dickens in his poem "Cricket on the Hearth."

However, not all people regard the sound of insects as a thing of joy. For instance, an innovative entomology student once proclaimed on a test that cicada killers kill cicadas because, "They can't stand the noise!"

■

instance, the pheromone produced by the European corn borer is technically termed (Z)-9-tetradecen-1-ol formate. But to a corn borer, that chemical probably rivals the world's sweetest perfume.

We humans once had pheromones of our own. Then we became civilized and began taking baths, and the natural pheromones went down the drain. Thinking individuals that we are, we recognized the importance of such odors and adopted a technological solution to the problem. We make our own pheromones and splash them on. We call them perfumes, colognes, aftershaves and such. To add to the mystique, we give our pheromones fancy, and sometimes seductive, names. And pay high prices to buy them.

Do you suppose that we humans should admit that we adopted an approach to selecting our mates that was originally perfected by insects? Why not? It certainly makes good scents!

■

Insect Reproduction

1. What is unusual about the egg laying habits of the giant waterbug?
2. In the social insects unfertilized eggs hatch. What is the sex of the individuals from these eggs?

3. In general how does the covering of insect eggs reflect the environmental conditions the egg will encounter prior to hatch?
4. What are insect "perfumes" called?
5. What is the name of the process when mate attracting chemicals are released into the air by an insect?

Food Habits of Insects

Food is essential to the growth and development of any organism. Insects use a wide range of food sources. Insects can be considered to be saprophagous, phytophagous or zoophagous. Saprophagous insects feed on dead organic matter. Phytophagous feed on living plants and zoophagous insects feed on living animals.

Saprophagous insects could also be called scavengers. Some of the insects that are saprophagous are the cockroaches and houseflies. Both are general feeders on either plant or animal matter. Collembola (sometimes called springtails) feed on soil humus. Termites, however, are restricted to feeding on dead plant tissue (occasionally in semitropical regions they may attack living plants). Carrion feeders such as the flesh flies and the burying beetles are restricted to animal food. Very specialized feeders in this category are the insects that feed on animal dung — the coleoptera and diptera are common in this category. One of the most well known is the dung beetle sometimes called tumblebug that rolls balls of cow manure to bury and feed to its young.

Phytophagous feeders include leaf feeders like grasshoppers. Also in this category are root feeders like grubs, leaf miners, and stem borers (like the European corn borer). The gall makers, the fungus feeders and the sap suckers such as the plant bugs and aphids are common members of plant feeding insects.

Zoophagous insects include parasites of all kinds. Fleas and lice feed on higher animals. Ichneumon wasps and flies are parasites on other insects. Predators — they consume more than one animal during their life — include ladybird beetles, some wasps and some bugs. Included in this category are the blood feeders like mosquitoes and deer and horse flies. ■

It Takes Gall

Almost everyone has, at one time or another, noticed a deformity in plant growth called a gall. These often grotesque plant abnormalities can be caused by insects. Gall-causing insects lay their eggs in plant tissue, and the developing larvae cause the plant to respond with abnormal growth, known as a gall. Some beetles, moths, flies and wasps are among the insect gall-makers.

Galls have been recognized by humankind for centuries, and in fact, galls are better known than the insects that produce them. The galls are numerous and showy; their insect residents, on the other hand, are quite small and difficult to see.

From times of old and even today, galls have been used to produce tannic acid and dyes, including one dye called Turkey Red. The best permanent inks have, for years, been produced from galls. The Aleppo gall, found in Eastern Europe and Western Asia, is used for this purpose. In some places, the law requires that permanent records be made with ink derived from galls. Such an ink is used by the United States Treasury and the Bank of England.

The word "gall" has a double meaning in the English language. The Latin word "galla" meant a gall-nut, the plant growth abnormality. The Anglo-Saxon word "gall" meant bitter, hence the word "gallbladder" to identify the bile-holding sac associated with the liver. Shakespeare, no doubt, had both meanings in mind in "Twelfth Night" when he had Sir Toby Belch tell Sir Andrew to use "gall enough" in the ink to pen a challenge to duel Viola.

Gall insects attack over one-half of all plant families, and almost all parts of the plant are subject to infestation. In general, gall-makers produce the same type of gall on different plants.

Galls are generally named according to the way they look. For instance, we have the hedgehog gall, which must look a bit like a hedgehog. Many galls remind folks of fruits and vegetables, including the apple, potato and pea galls of oak. We also find spindle, hairy and spiney galls on oak. And there are button galls, cup galls and red sea urchin galls. Bullet galls and vase galls have been known to occur on the same plant as the wool-sower galls.

One of the most interesting of the galls is the jumping oak gall. When this gall falls from its oak tree host, the larvae inside cause the gall to jump. The popping activity of the jumping gall is similar to that of Mexican jumping beans, which is also caused by an insect inhabitant.

Even in the insect world, a little gall can sometimes attract attention! ■

Food Habits of Insects

1. What is a purpose of insect sounds other than for attracting a mate?
2. What is the food of saprophagous insects? Name three such insects.
3. Grasshoppers and European cornborers exhibit what general food habit?
4. Name three types of insects that are zoophagous.

Chapter 3

Surviving Winter

Where Have All The Insects Gone?

Each year as fall marches uncontrollably toward winter, nature prepares. Temperatures begin to drop and so do the leaves from trees. Waterfowl wing overhead in their annual southern migration from breeding grounds in the north. Swallows, bluebirds, and redwing blackbirds depart to make way for the birds of winter.

And the insects disappear. Yes, the teeming hoards of insects that occupied every nook and cranny just a few weeks ago are seen no more. The cricket, the cicada and even the mosquito have fallen silent.

To borrow, and slightly modify, a line from an old Peter, Paul and Mary song, "Where have all the insects gone, long time passing?" If the answer is "to graveyards every one," it is a bit misleading. To be sure, many of the insects of last summer have died. But their offspring shall return!

Insects have solved the problem of winter in several ways. Some hibernate. Lady bird beetles, Mexican bean beetles, bald-faced hornets, yellow jackets and cluster flies are among the many that hibernate as adults. These insects seek sheltered places to gain some protection from the winter. They can be found under rocks, in leaf litter, even under the eaves and in the attics of our homes.

Other insects spend the winter as larvae. The larvae of June beetles, known as white grubs, just dig deeper in the soil as the temperature drops. Many caterpillars, such as the wooly bear, crawl into secluded places for their long winter's naps. Most, however, make some provision to keep from freezing. Some reduce the water content of their bodies and replace it with glycerol, the antifreeze of the insect world.

The European corn borer spends the winter as a larvae in corn stalks. A fact of interest to ice fishermen who frequently dig the borers from their hiding places to use as bait.

Some insects avoid the winter by remaining in the egg stage. The mosquito, corn rootworm and praying mantis leave their eggs out in the cold.

Other insects solve the problem of Midwest winters by leaving. Yes, like some of the human species, they go south for the winter. Many of our insect pests repopulate Midwest areas each spring from breeding grounds in the south. Many aphids, cutworms and armyworms use this strategy for dealing with winter. Another insect that migrates back each year is the Monarch butterfly.

Insects have used a variety of tactics to solve the problem of Indiana winters. While insects may be gone, they should not be forgotten. For next spring, when the temperatures begin to warm, the fire of life will be rekindled in tiny insect hearts everywhere. Like the swallows to Capistrano, they shall return! ■

Insect Antifreeze

November is the time to winterize homes, cars, plants and even dog houses. Surviving winter demands preparation. It means caulking, putting up storm windows and doors, covering winter-sensitive plants with mulch, insulating dog houses and possibly getting a flu shot.

What about insects? What do they do when Old Man Winter blows his icy breath across the landscape? Well, they also winterize.

Winterizing for an insect is much like the process we go through to winterize a car. We add antifreeze to the car. Insects add antifreeze to themselves. If the liquid in the cooling system of a motor is allowed to freeze, the expansion during the process will break the radiator and hoses. The same is true of the liquid in insects. If it is allowed to freeze, the crystals that form will destroy the cells and tissues of the insect and cause death.

By adding antifreeze to an automobile's cooling system, the freezing point of the liquid is reduced so that freezing doesn't occur. This protects the system from damage.

As winter approaches, some insects use a similar antifreeze approach. In preparation for freezing temperatures, the water content in the insect is reduced. The water is replaced with glycerol, a compound similar to glycol that's used in antifreeze. Therefore, like the car, the insect is winterized. An insect's biological system is shut down and is protected from freezing during the cold winter months.

When the days become longer and the temperatures creep upward, the insect reverses the process. Glycerol is broken down and replaced with water. The insect is ready to resume normal activities.

In her poem entitled, "About Caterpillars," Aileen Fisher begins with this stanza:

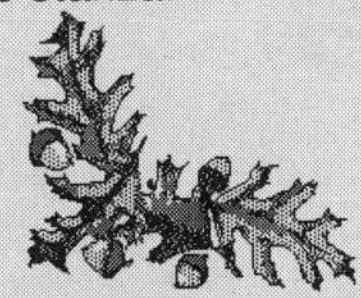

"What about caterpillars?
Where do they crawl
when the stars say, 'Frost,'
and the trees say, 'Fall.'"

Good question. But the important thing about an insect surviving winter is not where they crawl, but what they do when they get there. The successful insects winterize with antifreeze. ■

Southward Bound

The autumnal equinox is the official beginning of fall. 'Tis the season when pumpkins sometimes wear a mantle of frost in early morning. When the fading green of the leaves of summer expose bright but fleeting hues of red and gold.

Fall is a time of harvest and quiet beauty. Mother Nature removes her summer foot from the accelerator and life begins to coast. Slowly at first, then more rapidly, earth's life cascades toward the barrenness of winter.

Fall is a harbinger of death to many of the insect world, but this is not so for the Monarch butterfly. One of the best known of North American insects, it avoids winter by migration. As fall approaches, the adult butterflies begin a truly miraculous journey to their overwintering sites.

Mountainous areas in Mexico and California provide the ideal environment for these travelers to survive the winter. Presently, only two major sites have been identified by entomologists as meeting the Monarch's requirements. In fact, because deforestation endangered one of these butterfly spas, Mexico declared it a protected area.

As these insects travel south, they create major excitement when they stop to spend the night and congregate on a single tree. These trees, sometimes called butterfly trees, are the insect equivalent of a Holiday Inn. Once at the overwintering site, the marvelous Monarch feeds on nectar from flowers to build up energy reserves for a return flight.

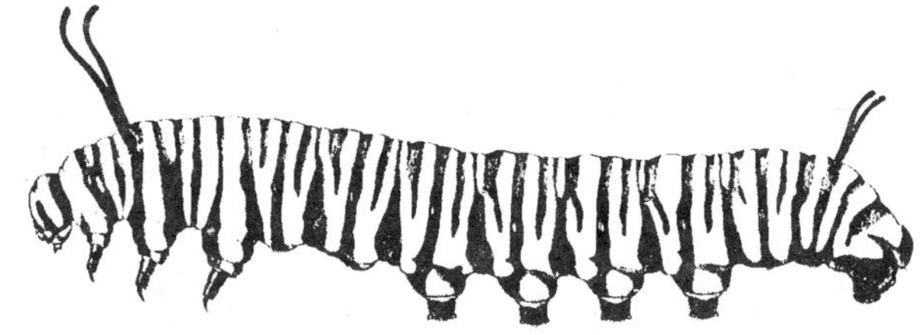

As spring approaches, the overwintered Monarchs begin to wing northward, as their ancestors have done for untold centuries before. During the spring journey, they mate and lay eggs on milkweed plants, a rather inhospitable host.

The milkweed plant contains compounds called cardiac glycosides — chemicals put there by the plant to keep animals from feeding on it. Most animals, that is, but not the Monarch. These insects just store the bitter substances in their bodies. As a result, they acquire a bitter taste, and consequently, insect predators, such as birds, learn quickly to avoid making a meal of the bad-tasting insect.

But bad taste alone is not enough to protect against becoming the main course for some hungry insect eater. So the Monarch wears a bright coat — one that we delight in seeing — that is easily recognized by potential predators. In the insect world, a little catchy advertising pays dividends.

Monarch butterflies fluttering lazily in a southerly direction across an October meadow gives one pause for thought. That rather fragile insect with thin membrane wings covered with soft scales is in the middle of a journey that can cover up to 2,000 miles before it ends. It is on a journey to a location where it has never been, but to which it is unerringly guided by some genetic code.

It is truly a miracle of the biological world. ■

On the Winds of Spring

Ah, the southerly breezes of spring! Those warm and sometimes turbulent air masses signal that Old Man Winter is losing his grip for another year.

Spring breezes seem to spontaneously generate children with kites, enthusiastic and overly optimistic gardeners, April showers, and hordes of insects. But the winds of spring also bring the promise of teeming multitudes of insects. Flying, jumping, crawling, sucking, munching insects.

To some insects, the onset of spring is merely a signal to emerge from their winter hiding places and begin the frenzy of insect activity associated with summer. To other insects, however, the spring weather fronts actually provide transportation to summer feeding grounds.

Many insects cannot overwinter in northern areas, but they survive very well in the more moderate temperatures of the Gulf Coast states. As the spring weather fronts begin to generate, they pick up more than moisture from the Gulf. The fronts also pick up insects that happen to be flying around at the time as well as those insects that are waiting to catch a ride northward.

Many spring weather systems are loaded with insects. In fact, so common are insects in weather fronts that they have become known as the plankton of the air.

Observers have noted that some of the insects fly backwards. These insects, which are actually being carried, flap their wings only enough to keep aloft during the trip. As the weather systems weaken, these passengers, like rain, are dumped rather unceremoniously from the sky.

Some of our common insect pests are weather-front hitchhikers. Many aphids, sometimes known as plant lice, come into the Midwest astride a storm. Leafhoppers, including the potato leafhopper, a pest of alfalfa, also arrive on the wings of a storm.

While aphids and leafhoppers are rather small insects, some larger ones also pick up a ride on the southern zephyr. One major pest of gardens and field crops is the black cutworm, which in the adult stage is a moth nearly an inch in length. This moth isn't at all bashful about spending the winter in the sunny south and then taking the first spring weather front to points further north.

This year, as she has done in the past, Mother Nature will most likely bestow on us one of her famous spring downpours. When she does, some will be tempted to say that it is raining cats and dogs. The truth of the matter is that it's likely raining aphids, leafhoppers and cutworms!

Comforting thought, isn't it? ■

Chapter 3

Plant Chompers

Gardeners know it. So do farmers. It's a little song and dance number that insects do – "the plant chomp."

Eating plants is popular in the insect world. Almost all butterflies and moths eat plants during their caterpillar days. Most crickets, grasshoppers and true bugs are plant feeders as well as many beetles, some flies and a few bees.

This chomping of leaves, chewing of stems and sucking of sap is not good for the plant. So plants have developed defense mechanisms to combat the insect menace. Some plants have physical barriers such as spines and hooks to discourage insects from chomping them. Others contain noxious chemicals that are harmful to insects and animals in search of a plant meal.

These noxious plant chemicals, sometimes called phytotoxins, are effective inhibitors of insect feeding. Some phytotoxins have been discovered to have uses other than keeping insects from feeding.

Long before mankind had available synthetic insecticides, it was discovered that pyrethrin, an extract from chrysanthemums, killed insects. Other such plant-derived insect killers include rotenone and nicotine.

Some of these chemicals have medicinal properties. Quinine from cinchona bark was used to treat malaria. The milkweed plant contains a chemical called cardiac glycoside, because it is useful in treating certain kinds of heart diseases.

Other phytotoxins include mescaline from the peyote cactus and morphine from the poppy. The active compound in marijuana is cannabidiol, the coca plant produces cocaine. Both compounds function to protect the plants from insect attacks. The nice aroma of our morning cup of coffee portends the stimulatory effect of the caffeine. While in the coffee plant, caffeine is a deterrent to insect feeding.

It is interesting that many chemicals that protect plants from insect feeding work as stimulants or hallucinogens when consumed by humans. Could it be that insects that ingest such chemicals are too nervous to eat? Or perhaps the insect just doesn't care enough to worry about food? Or it may be that even a lowly insect is too smart to eat what is bad for it! ■

Surviving Winter

1. What are two methods insects use to survive as a population in an Indiana winter?
2. Where does the Monarch butterfly accquire its bitter taste?
3. Where does the Monarch butterfly overwinter?
4. Name two insects that ride the spring winds into Midwestern states.

Insect Societies

The Swarm

The miniature denizens of the alien society spew forth from the honeycombed labyrinth of their darkened domicile. Armed warriors, in blind obedience to some prehistoric imperative, swarm about their deposed leader. Humans, mere mortals, tremble at the sight and sound of the frightening frenzy.

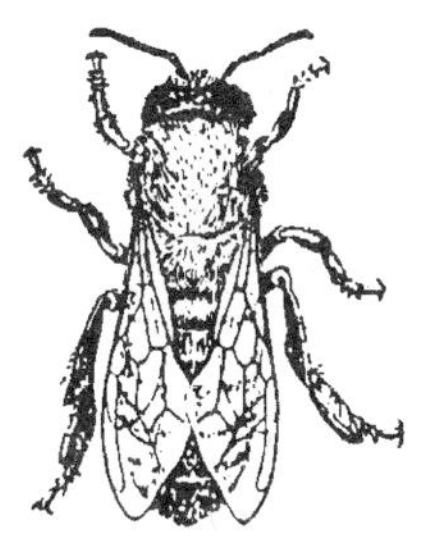
worker

An advertisement for the latest horror movie? No, just one of the rites of spring — the swarming of honey bees. This process, which occurs primarily in the months of May and June, allows honey bees to establish new colonies.

The honey bee swarm is one of the true wonders of nature. First, a new queen is produced in the colony. The presence of the young queen causes the old queen and her loyal workers to leave. Before they leave, the workers fill their crops with honey — the insect equivalent to packing a picnic lunch.

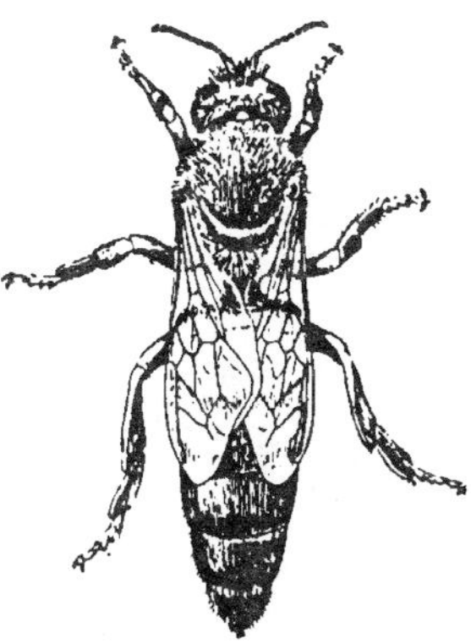
queen

The first flight of the swarm normally takes it to some temporary resting place. The bees cluster around the queen while scout bees search for a permanent abode. The cluster may be on a fence post, a tree limb or a street light. If the swarm happens to land in a populated area, it is sure to create a sensation. The fear of being stung by a swarm of bees is, however, mostly unfounded. Swarming bees are quite docile and seldom sting.

The amount of time the swarm spends at its first landing site is normally limited. Consequently, the best action when confronted with a cluster of bees is to do nothing; they are not dangerous and will soon leave. Once the scout bees have found a permanent site, the cluster of bees takes wing, and the queen is escorted to the new location. At the new site, the bees immediately get down to business and set up housekeeping.

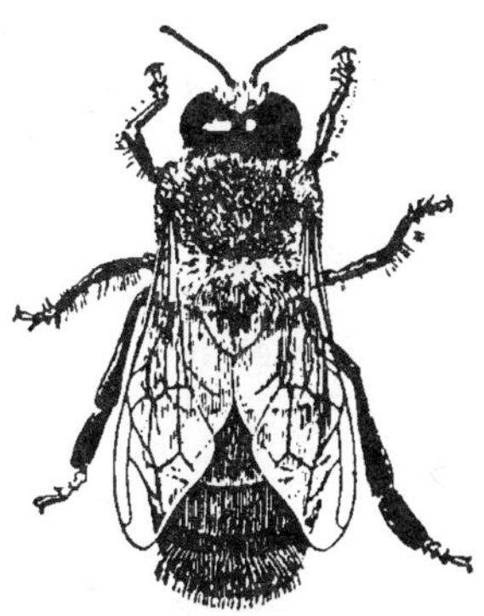
drone

Beekeepers collect swarms and put them in hives as a method of increasing the number of colonies in their apiaries. It's easy to do. Once the queen is in the hive, the dutiful workers follow. However, for a new colony to be successful, it must get established in time to gather enough honey to sustain it over the winter. This idea is incorporated in an old folk saying relative to collecting a swarm of bees. One version is:

A swarm in May is worth a load of hay,
A swarm in June is worth a silver spoon,
A swarm in July, just let them go by!

If in the future you happen to encounter a swarm of bees, don't panic. Just take the opportunity to enjoy one of the natural wonders of the world. Seeing is bee-lieving! ■

Chapter 3

The Yellowjackets are Coming

Fall — the harvest season. That time of the year when pumpkins lie in golden contrast to the fading green vines of their nurturing plants. When sun-ripened apples are turned into sweet mush under the unrelentless crunch of a cider mill. When the quiet serenity of a backwoods picnic or suburban cookout is suddenly broken with a blood-curdling scream — yellowjackets!!

Yes, folks everywhere slightly modify Paul Revere's now-famous warning of Revolutionary War times. "The yellowjackets are coming, the yellowjackets are coming" is an oft-repeated warning of close encounters of the insect kind.

Yellowjackets are common, ground-nesting, social wasps. In the spring, a mated female emerges from her overwintering site and establishes an underground nest in an abandoned rodent burrow. There she begins the task of rearing young wasps. Early growth of the colony is slow, because the queen does all of the work. However, by midsummer other wasps have been produced. These workers take over the duties of food finding, larval care and defense of the nest. By late fall, some yellowjacket nests may contain as many as 3,000 workers.

Immature yellowjackets are fed meat, mostly in the form of arthropods captured by workers. In the fall, when prey species become scarce, the yellowjackets become scavengers. They can be found around garbage cans and are frequent visitors to picnics. That, of course, causes great concern to the humans, who are reluctant to share the feast with six-legged visitors, especially those armed with a stinger.

In general, yellowjackets do not sting except in defense of their nest or when physically abused. Therefore, remaining calm is the best policy when faced with a yellowjacket intent on tearing shreds of meat from your bologna sandwich or skating on the ice cube in your cola. Aggressive behavior normally prompts a like response on the part of the yellow jacket, and in most cases, the insect will be victorious.

If yellowjacket nests in lawns are a continual problem, they can normally be eliminated by finding the hole to the nest and treating with an insecticide during the night. However, such activities can be hazardous to your health, because yellowjackets will not stand idly by while their home is being destroyed.

In most instances, folks are well-advised to leave the nests alone. Yellowjackets are beneficial because of the insects they destroy, and winter will solve the problem for another year. Besides, who wants to be guilty of stirring up a hornet's nest? ■

The Case of the Winter Wasp

Everybody knows that winter is a time when insects are scarce. You see, winter is that season when temperatures turn downward. Cold temperatures and insects don't mix.

Being cold-blooded, the insects can't function when it's cold. We still have our housemates, like cockroaches, fleas and flies, that have come to live in our homes and on our pets. These do quite well during the winter months! But most insects disappear.

Enter the winter wasp. The wasp, that armed warrior of the insect world and flying, poison-loaded hypodermic needle. The wasp, that uninvited purveyor of terror for every man, woman and child within striking distance.

Everybody knows that wasps aren't to be about in winter! Except for a few wasps. Because, for example, there was a wasp in our kitchen the day after Christmas. My daughter vociferously called it to my attention. And what winter churchgoer hasn't been a witness to the quiet hysteria of the congregation that is created by the menacing mid-winter flight of a wasp. Such wasps always seem to gain attention by losing a significant amount of altitude right over the "Amen" pews.

This wasp, out of place, is a quirk of wasp biology brought about by heated buildings, churches, houses and the like. In the fall, with the approach of winter, many female wasps mate and head to sheltered locations to hibernate for the winter. A typical natural location for hibernation would be in the leaf litter of the forest floor, where a wasp would settle down for a long winter's nap.

With the coming of spring, the rays of the sun warm the forest floor. The warmer temperatures signal to the slumbering wasp that it's time to venture from the hibernation location. She heads on her way with the mission of beginning a new nest for the coming season.

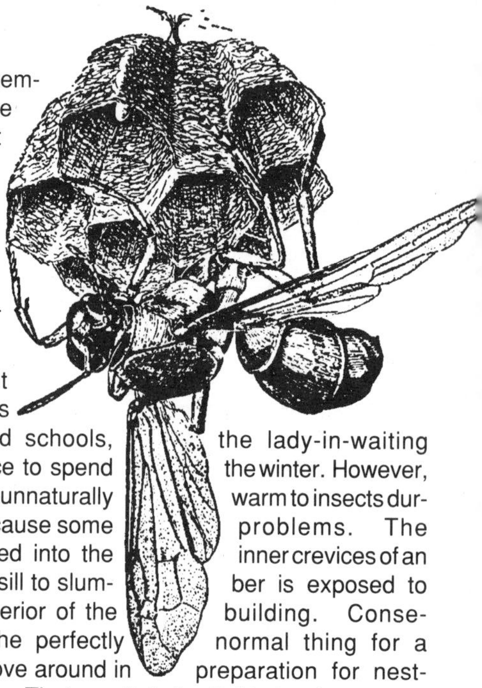

But in permanent buildings, such as houses, churches and schools, the lady-in-waiting wasp has a new place to spend the winter. However, buildings, which are unnaturally warm to insects during the cold months, cause some problems. The wasp that has crawled into the inner crevices of an attic, eave or windowsill to slumber is exposed to the heat from the interior of the building. Consequently, she does the perfectly normal thing for a wasp — begins to move around in preparation for nest-building and egg-laying. That results in the flight of a winter wasp.

The strafing run above the congregation during the sermon on a bright February's Sunday is sure to grab attention. Don't think of that brazen, aerial daredevil as a wasp out of place. Think of her as the first indicator of spring! ■

Chapter 3

Clay Masons

Clay is widely used as a raw material for home construction by insects and people. Adobe and brick houses have sheltered humans for centuries. Insects, however, were using clay for homes long before humans abandoned cave dwellings.

Among the finest of the insect clay masons are the wasps. Two of the most common are the potter wasps and the mud daubers.

Potter wasps, also called mason wasps, are common insects. They construct their nests of mud and attach these jug-like homes to twigs. The homebuilder provisions the nest with caterpillars. From an egg attached to the mud home by a string, the newly-hatched larvae descend to feed on the food that mother supplied.

Mud daubers are aptly named. Their nests are constructed by daubing mud in a somewhat organized fashion in reasonably protected locations. Wasps of this group can frequently be found along the edges of ponds or streams. Here the wasps scoop up the mud in their mouths for transporting to the nesting site. These wasps are frequently blackish-blue in color.

One of the most recognizable of the mud daubers is the pipe-organ mud dauber. The nests of this wasp are laid end to end in tubes. Several tubes are constructed side by side in a pattern similar to the pipes of a fine church organ. Each cell is provisioned with a spider as a food resource for the young wasp. When the wasp has completed development, it chews a hole through the side of the tube.

Some mud daubers use any available facility for constructing a home. In fact, old-fashioned outhouses provide ideal nesting sites! Anyone who has had the occasion to use an outhouse in the summer is well aware of that fact.

The composer of the song "Ode to the Little Brown Shack Out Back" noted the presence of wasps in such a building. However, the wasp was misidentified in the phrase "to the yellowjackets' drone." That non-human singer was certainly a mud dauber. And some people would say you haven't lived unless you have used an outhouse — at least used one while being serenaded by a female mud dauber as she fashions her nest.

Of course, a mud nest under construction requires mud. Mud-laden mud daubers frequently fly from the quarter moon in the door to the nest site. Such a flight pattern is sometimes over the best "seat" in the house. For the human occupant of the outhouse, such flights can be exciting. A little too exciting! Some folks have been known to leave the facility rather abruptly when faced with a low-flying wasp.

That's the way it is with some humans. They just don't appreciate insects like mud daubers — at least when they are sitting in an outhouse reading the Sears and Roebuck catalog. ■

Warrior Ants on the March

It is the stuff horror movies are made of. Hordes of seemingly mindless individuals terrorizing every living thing in their path. Unafraid of humans or any technology that the human mind can conceive, these creatures use fearsome jaws to wreak havoc on all they encounter.

"They" are warrior ants, sometimes called army or driver ants. No wild-eyed scriptwriter has to dream up such a movie tale. It already exists!

Warrior ants live in the semitropical regions of South America and Africa, but unlike most other ants, they do not have a permanent home. Warrior ants form bivouacs from which they raid surrounding areas in search of plunder. Or they go on marches during which it is said they consume all of the animal refuse in their way. During such frenzied marches, they will not hesitate to attack all kinds of vertebrates, including human beings.

Many are the tales of encounters with the warrior ants. Dr. Albert Schweitzer had to conquer the warrior ants, among other things, as he developed his hospital in Africa. Of particular interest to Schweitzer was the chicken house. At the onset of a warrior ant invasion, Schweitzer would jump out of bed and run to open the chicken house door. According to the famous doctor, "Shut in, they would inevitably be the prey of the ants, which would creep into their mouths and nostrils until they are suffocated, and then devour them, so that in a short time nothing is left but their white bones."

Another well-known doctor who devoted his life to Africa also records encounters of the unpleasant kind with warrior ants. This doctor was none other than the one who prompted the journalist Sir Henry Stanley to exclaim upon finding him living on Lake Tanganyika, "Dr. Livingstone, I presume."

Dr. David Livingstone recorded in his diary that the camp "suffered a furious attack at midnight from driver ants." In an attempt to keep the ants away, Livingstone's men lighted grass fires. In his last diary entry for the day, he wrote: "We put hot ashes on the defiant hordes." Apparently to no avail because the good doctor noted that he had suffered bites so numerous that he resembled a person who had smallpox.

In some parts of Africa, criminals were punished a century or more ago by binding their hands and feet and laying them in the path of an ant army. Francois Coillard, a missionary in Africa, reported that under such circumstances, "in a surprisingly short time the writhing victim will have been changed into a skeleton of clean and polished bones that will make the trained anatomist envious."

Over time, such observations of warrior ants have no doubt helped give credence to mother's admonitions to fidgety children: "You're wiggling around like you have ants in your pants!" ■

Chapter 3

Protective Coloration

Insect Societies

1. What is the biological purpose of swarming in honey bee colonies?
2. Swarms of honey bees are normally docile. One reason is an action they take before leaving the old hive. What is the action?
3. Is it the old queen or the young queen that leads a swarm of bees?
4. Warrior ants are found in what kind of climate?
5. What is the larval food of yellow jackets?
6. Why might yellow jackets be considered beneficial insects?
7. What is a common over-wintering form of many social wasps?
8. With what do pipe-organ mud daubers provision their nests?

Insect Eaters

Why are there insects? It's a question as old as the ages. Odgen Nash alluded to it in his poem "The Fly:"

> God in his wisdom made the fly, and then forgot to tell us why.

Nash is not alone. Almost everyone at one time or another has wondered why insects exist.

One important ecological service insects provide is nutrition for other animals. There are a lot of insect eaters out there. Some even have names that reflect their culinary habits.

Most people are aware of anteaters. These animals spend their entire lives dining on ants. And there's a bird called a flycatcher. It's name alone suggests its favorite food — flying insects.

Many different animals use insects as a food source even if their names don't reflect it. Frogs and toads have sticky tongues to capture flying insects. Snakes and salamanders also will dine upon insects.

Many aquatic creatures feed upon insects as well. For that reason fishermen use artificial bait modeled after insects. These models are appropriately called flies. Fishing flies come in many shapes and colors, but you can bet they are designed to entice the fish into thinking it is about to eat a tasty insect.

Mammals also eat insects. Bears eat grubs that they dig out of rotten stumps. Skunks also eat insects. A grub-infested lawn is a great place for a skunk to dig up a meal. This process leaves holes in the lawn, much to the disgust of the homeowner. Even dogs and cats will chow down on an insect or two when given the chance.

Bats, the only flying mammals, depend upon insects for their entire food supply. Bats fly at night and use echlocation to navigate and catch night-flying insects, sort of a meal on the wing.

Many birds consume insects. Woodpeckers peck wood looking for larval insects. Wrens are great insect eaters. Many blackbirds also eat insects. A flock of blackbirds feeding on the lawn in the spring could be a sign of an insect infestation. That domestic fowl, the chicken, also delights in a good insect meal. Years ago, chickens running in the orchard were considered beneficial because they ate the insects that were over wintering in the fallen fruit.

Why are there insects? They keep a lot of animals from going to bed hungry! ■

Turn About is Fair Play

When it's time to dine, insects choose their favorite foods: tasty plant leaves, stems and roots; succulent plant sap, and delectable plant flowers and fruits.

Plants, however, are not eager to be devoured by insects. Many plants have spines and hairs, sticky substances and even bad tastes to thwart hungry mandibles. Yet in spite of their attempts to protect themselves, most plants become the victims of insects.

Still, there are a few plants that have turned the dining tables on insects. These plants, called insectivorous plants, trap insects and make a meal of them.

The best known of the insect-eating plants is the pitcher plant, a native of North America. Its leaves and petioles are modified to form hollow "pitchers." Glands on the inside of the pitchers secrete a substance that attracts insects. Insects trying to reach this substance fall into a liquid at the bottom of the pitcher and are digested by the plant.

The sundew plant has leaves with numerous sticky hairs. Insects that get trapped in the hairs are digested in a fluid secreted by the leaves.

Another insect-eating plant is aptly named, the Venus's-flytrap. This plant has leaves that end in two lobes. The lobes are bordered by a series of spines. The plant just sits around with the lobes expanded waiting for a meal to come by. When some unsuspecting fly wanders into the center of the expanded lobes, the lobes will spring shut like the jaws of a steel trap. The fly cannot escape this plant. It is doomed to be digested by a secretion poured from glands on the surface of the leaf.

For these plants, eating insects is more than a sinister method of getting even. Insect meals provide insectivorous plants with nitrogen. Most plants that eat insects live in wet areas where nitrogen is limited in the soil, so they need to supplement their nutrient uptake.

It's ironic that for a few plants a tasty insect not only provides a fine meal, but also gives them gas – nitrogen gas. ■

Beautiful But Bitter

It's yellow, black and white striped in its youth, has 14 leg-like appendages, fearsome mandibles and a hard-shell head. It feeds on a plant that contains chemicals used as a medicine. Later, as an adult, it's brown with black stripes, and spends the winter in a remote mountainous region of Mexico. Could it be an invader from outer space or a creature from the black lagoon?

Well, actually, it's the Monarch butterfly! One of our best known insects. The bright, striped colors of the larva warns potential predators that it's distasteful.

The bitter taste of the larva comes from the juice of the milkweed plant that it uses for food. The milkweed plant contains bitter substances called **cardiac glycosides**, which are named for their use as a human heart medicine. These compounds benefit the milkweed plant by acting as antifeeding compounds for most animals including insects.

The Monarch, however, has developed the ability to utilize the plant in spite of the presence of the bitter chemicals. The larva stores the toxic compounds in its body. This makes the larva bad-tasting, an attribute that is transferred to the adult following pupation.

Many birds are predators of insects, but they can't tolerate the bitter taste of the Monarch. To advertise their bad taste, the Monarch, in both the adult and larval stages, wears bright colors. So effective is the scheme that the Viceroy butterfly, a good-tasting insect which resembles the Monarch in color and pattern, also is protected.

The Monarch, actually a tropical butterfly, has adapted to more northern climates by leaving the winter behind. Each fall Monarchs leisurely flutter toward overwintering areas in the mountains of Mexico.

Along the way, great flocks of these insects sometimes gather on trees to rest overnight. These resting sites, called butterfly trees, are one of natures truly memorable sights.

The Monarch butterfly is indeed a biological miracle. These fragile insects wing over 1,000 miles to a place they've never been. Come spring they head north to lay eggs on plants too toxic for most animals to eat.

Once egg laying is complete the butterflies die, leaving the younger generation to carry on. Each succeeding generation moves northward to lay eggs until their genetic code unerringly indicates that it's time to turn around.

The butterflies begin the long and treacherous southern journey. They make the trip not so much for themselves, but to ensure survival of future generations of the "beautiful but bitter" Monarch.

■

Deceitful Buzzers

Buzzing is universally regarded as a warning sound. For example, buzzers remind us to fasten our seat belts. Buzzers in smoke detectors alert us that our houses are on fire or that the roast in the oven is slightly overdone. Elevators, airplane guidance systems and even computers buzz when things are amiss.

Buzzing as a warning signal was perfected by insects, especially the bees. The sound is produced by wing vibration as the insect flies. Most animals respond negatively to the buzzing of bees, and for good reason. Bees are equipped with a stinger they can use for defensive purposes. However, in most encounters with other animals, bees do not need to unsheath their stinger. Their buzz alone wards off most sources of potential danger.

So effective is the buzz of bees as a protective device that other insects have adopted it for their own use. Many flies, because their wing-beat frequencies are similar to that of the bees, sound like bees. The sound alone usually provides some protection for these imitators. However, when their color pattern matches that of bees, only an entomologist can tell the difference at first glance.

Some flies even mimic the aggressive behavior of disturbed bees. One group of flies that sounds, looks and acts like bees even claim their mentor's name — bee flies.

Not only flies have benefited from sounding like buzzing bees. One beetle, the green June beetle, is especially adept at convincing folks it is a dangerous insect. This is a large, somewhat flattened, green beetle with yellow body margins. As an adult, the green June beetle feeds on the foliage of fruit trees and on the ripening fruit. When these beetles appear in large numbers and swarm around during their feeding activities, many people have been convinced that they have encountered a swarm of killer bees. The beetle is perfectly harmless, but most folks and other animals don't stay around long enough to find out.

Some might suggest insects that mimic the sound of bees are guilty of fraud or false advertising. But think of it this way, a little benevolent deceit can go a long way toward preventing encounters of the worst kind. At least from the insect's point of view!

■

Stingers and Nettlers

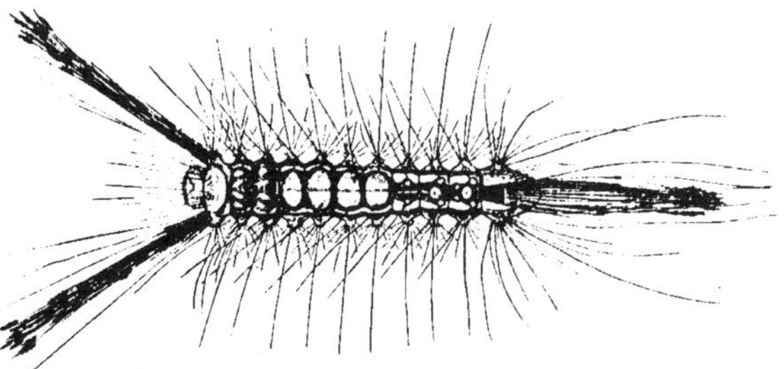

This world is full of stingers and nettlers. Stingers like scorpions, bees, hornets and wasps actively inject poison into their targets. They deliberately and aggressively pursue their victims. The insect stingers even sound dangerous, buzzing menacingly before they sting.

Nettlers are the mild-mannered poison peddlers of the world. Nettlers are passive stingers. They include stinging plants, some are appropriately called nettles, jellyfish and some caterpillars. Nettlers never look for trouble, they simply wait for the victim to contact them. So if you get too close, you are likely to regret it.

Stinging and nettling are methods of protection for these creatures. Stinging allows insects to defend their homes as well as their lives. Both stingers and nettlers use their poison-peddling prowess to avoid becoming a meal for some hungry insect or plant eater.

Even some fuzzy caterpillars are poison warfare experts. These insects possess poisonous hairs which are typically shorter than other caterpillar hairs. The hairs are barbed and connect to a poison gland at their base. When the poisonous hair is contacted, the poison is released, and the victim experiences a stinging sensation.

Some of the nettling caterpillars are brightly marked. One such is the saddle-back, a pale green insect with a brown and white design across its back that resembles a saddle. Other nettling caterpillars include some of the tussock moths, the pus moth and the buck moth.

Years ago, witch doctors of primitive tribes recognized that some caterpillars had natural stinging arrows on their bodies. These witch doctors frequently employed the irritating power of the poisonous hairs of these insects in their witchcraft.

Anyone who has had an encounter with a nettling caterpillar can tell you that they, like fire, are beautiful to behold but dangerous to touch. And that is the way the insect would like to keep it.

■

Protective Coloration

1. How do some flies use the sound of their wings for protection?
2. What type of butterfly gathers to rest on "butterfly trees?"
3. What are cardiac glycosides?

Population Dynamics

A single insect, unless it happens to be a mosquito buzzing in your ear or a bee about to sting, is generally of little consequence to humans. It is populations of insects that really get our attention. Consequently most studies of insects are based on populations, not individuals.

Insects have a tremendous biological potential based on their rates of reproduction and short generation time. This potential is generally characterized as a **logrithmic rate of growth,** a J-shaped curve on a graph that relates population to time (as in the following graph). This rate of growth doesn't continue unbridled in nature, otherwise we would be up to certain portions of our anatomy in insects. Nature applies brakes to logrithmic growth. Those brakes come into play as the population approaches the **carrying capacity** of the environment (depicted as "K" on many graphs).

Some factors that limit a population as it approaches carrying capacity for the environment are lack of food or water, build up of toxic wastes, weather, and predators and parasites. One aspect of insect control is to use the factors that limit populations to our advantage in reducing the number of insects we consider pests. For instance removal of crumbs from behind the sink (limit food) will help keep cockroach populations down. We can also place insect infested dried-flower

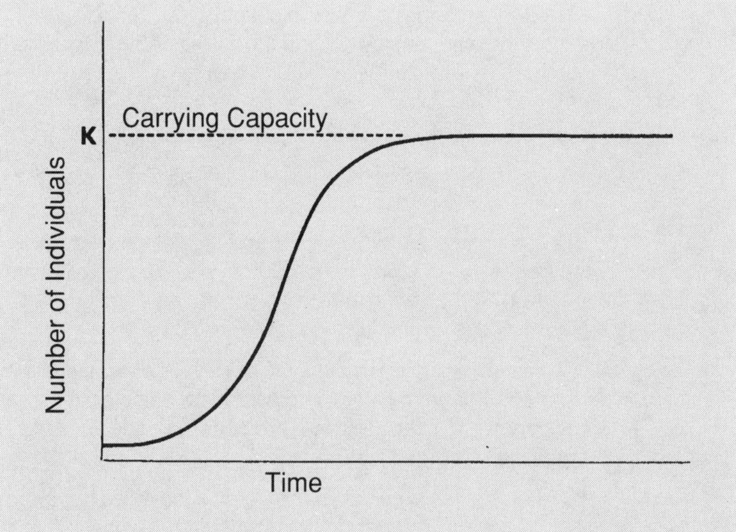

Theoretical Growth Curve of Animal Populations Approaching the Environmental Limit

➔

arrangements in the freezer for a day to remove the undesirable creatures.

Since populations are the key to most insect situations, entomologists frequently try to monitor population build-up. This can be done by either counting the number of insects involved or sampling. Counting all the insects in an area is nearly impossible unless the area is very small (like a jar) so most entomologists estimate populations. Population estimates are done by sampling.

Insect sampling involves several techniques. One is to capture the insects and count them. This can be done with an insect net. Sometimes the traps depend on the insect to come to it. Such is the case with a light trap, a pheromone trap, or a sticky trap (something like fly paper). Of course any such method must be related to the number of insects that are really there. One method of calibrating a sampling method is called **capture-mark-release-recapture.** In this mark and release procedure a given number of insects are captured, marked and released. When a sample is taken the number of marked insects relative to the total captured can be used to estimate the total number of insects available in the area.

Another method of insect sampling is to count symptoms such as holes in leaves or signs such as frass or cast skins. Such methods are especially important in agricultural entomology where the damage and not the insect is the important issue.

It is sometimes important to predict the buildup of an insect population. The build up can be influenced by a number of factors including the population limiting factors mentioned above. In addition, individual insects can leave (emigration) or come into the area (immigration) both of which would change the numbers. In fact with many pest insects it is movement into a house, a field or even a country that is the beginning of the problem.

Since insects are cold blooded their rate of population growth is tied to temperature. Consequently understanding temperature relationships can be useful in predicting a potential problem with insects. One method used to predict insect development has been with heat units. A **heat unit** is based on a threshold temperature (the lowest temperature where development will occur) for a specific insect. As temperatures exceed the specific threshold then heat units accrue and can be used to predict when the insect will reach various stages in development. Such a prediction can be used to schedule scouting or control activities.

■

Population Dynamics

1. Unchecked insect populations have what theoretical growth rate?
2. What is the carrying capacity of the environment?
3. What are the factors that limit population growth of an organism as it approaches "K"?
4. Why are insects marked and released relative to sampling?
5. What is a heat unit and how might it be used in insect control?

Most people have heard of Drosophila, the pomace flies that have been studied so much by geneticists. These flies develop rapidly and, under ideal conditions, may produce 25 generations a year. Each female will lay up to 100 eggs, of which half will hatch into males and half into females. Now, suppose we started with a pair of these flies and allowed them to reproduce under ideal conditions for a year — with the original and each succeeding female laying 100 eggs before she dies, and each egg hatching and the young growing to maturity and reproducing again. The number of flies that would be produced in the twenty-fifth generation is fantastic (about 10 to the 41st power); if the flies of this generation were packed tightly together, 1,000 to a cubic inch, they would form a ball of flies 96 million miles in diameter, or a ball extending nearly from the earth to the sun!

D. J. Borrer and D. M. DeLong

Chapter 4

Interaction With Humans

Insect Products

How Sweet It Is!

Honey has been called the food of gods and kings. Of course, folks of more earthly and less noble birth have also been known to partake of the "fruit of the hive."

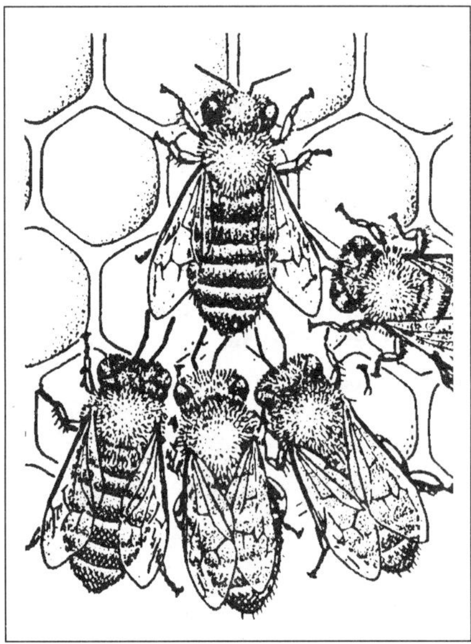

Bees have been depicted in Egyptian hieroglyphics dating back to 3500 B.C. Indeed, for thousands of years, honey was the primary sweetener used by mankind.

Honey is wonderful. It does not spoil. Its acidity and sugar content keep harmful microorganisms from growing in it. It does not freeze. And, as people found out in times before refrigeration, when used on salt-cured foods it covered up some of the taste of the salt.

Honey bees were unknown in North America until the immigration of Europeans. The introduction of the honey bee prompted the Native Americans to dub these insects "the white man's flies." Nonetheless, the Native Americans quickly acquired a liking for honey.

Honey truly results, as an old proverb teaches, from the industry of the bee. It takes 2,000 to 3,000 bees working an entire day to collect enough nectar to make a pound of honey. During the day, each worker bee makes six to eight trips to the field to visit the flowers. She will suck the nectar from the flowers and store it in her crop, a specialized portion of her digestive tract, for the trip to the hive.

Once in the hive, she regurgitates the nectar, which has undergone a chemical transformation while in her crop. The honey is then placed in the cell of the honeycomb, where it is fanned until the water content reaches a proper level for storage.

Honey varies widely in color and flavor, reflecting the type of flowers that provide the nectar. In general, clover plants provide a very sweet and light-colored honey. Honey from the roadside weed goldenrod is very dark in color and not as sweet. Some liken goldenrod honey to sorghum.

Each honey, like a fine wine, has its own bouquet. From orange honey can be detected the odor of, well, orange blossoms. Not surprising because it's the nectar that gives the characteristic aroma to blossoms of all types.

Honey has also been used to make wine, called mead, which was a favorite drink of the Knights of Merry Olde England. In the days of the Middle Ages, it was also customary to provide a newly married couple with enough mead, or honey wine, to last for the first month of their married life. Since a month was roughly equivalent to a cycle of the moon, this time became known as the honeymoon.

So it is entirely appropriate that the most famous line from the long-running TV show "The Honeymooners" should be Jackie Gleason's "How Sweet it Is!" ■

Insect Pests and Their Control

Ecologically speaking there is no such thing as a pest, only consumers. However, when some organism begins to consume something that mankind wants, that organism is branded a pest. From the beginning of agriculture, pests have created problems for farmers. Early farmers learned to live with pests and, through trial and error, how to deal with the more troublesome ones. Ancient Chinese citrus growers maintained colonies of a predatory ant to place in orange trees to reduce the numbers of leaf-feeding insects. Around 1,000 BC, Homer mentioned "pest averting sulfur" as a method of insect control. Long before the discovery of America, Indians in Central America hilled corn to prevent lodging due to the feeding of corn rootworm larvae. Many of the ancient control practices used techniques such as crop destruction, tillage and crop rotation.

In the latter part of the 1800s Paris Green and rotenone were discovered to have insecticidal properties. In 1939, Paul Muller established the insecticidal value of DDT and, in 1948, won a Nobel Prize for his efforts. The use of DDT as an insecticide and the development of dinitro compounds such as DNOC and dimoseb as herbicides signaled the beginning of the chemical age of pest control. From 1950 until 1975, total production of synthetic organic pesticides in the U.S. increased at a steady rate. Pest control literature during this time deals mainly with chemicals. This period was truly the "golden age" of chemical pest control.

In 1962, Rachel Carson published *Silent Spring* a book that dramatized, some say a bit too dramatically, the perils of excessive pesticide use. *Silent Spring* served as a focal point for the general public to push for a change in philosophy regarding the nature of pest control. In 1963, the President's Science Advisory Committee issued a special report that criticized a number of plant protection chemicals, primarily insecticides. Problems regarding chemicals began to surface. Target pests were becoming resistant. New pest organisms that had not existed previously appeared. Chemicals were found to be polluting streams and lakes and were detected in food. The golden age of pesticides began to appear less golden.

In 1972, the President of the United States directed agricultural, public health, and environmental protection agencies of the federal government to take immediate action to develop pest management programs. The goals of the programs were to protect the nation's food supply against the ravages of pests, to protect the health of the population, and to protect the environment.

This federal action signaled the beginning of the pest management era of pest control. This era has been accompanied by intensive regulation of pesticide manufacture and use by various federal agencies including FDA and EPA. Federal money was made available to fund pest management research. The Cooperative Extension Service provided money to establish pest management action programs in all states. The action programs were designed to demonstrate the value of pest management philosophy and associated control tactics for pests of all types. In addition, the Federal program which required certification of applicators of certain "restricted-use" pesticides was an attempt to train users about the hazards of pesticide use. ■

Our Immigrant Insects

Have you ever wondered why many pest insects have foreign names?

It sometimes appears that even insects contribute to the U.S. trade deficit. However, foreign insects began invading our shores long before Washington bureaucrats fretted about the balance of trade. Unfortunately, many of these uninvited insects have stayed here.

German and Oriental cockroaches have infested our homes for many years. Now, in some parts of the United States, the Asian roach has moved in. Many gardeners find Japanese beetles munching on their roses during the summer. Wheat farmers have to deal with Hessian flies and Russian aphids. Corn is attacked by the European corn borer, and soybeans, by the Mexican bean beetle. Apple producers battle the European red mite and the Oriental fruit moth.

American elm trees are now rare because of a disease organism carried by the European bark beetle. All of us have read about the Oriental and Mediterranean fruit flies. Now the African bee is headed our way from Central America.

All of these insects are named for their native areas. When mankind began to travel worldwide, insects hitched a ride. The Hessian fly probably came to the United States in straw bedding used by the Hessian troops during the Revolutionary War. Japanese beetles willingly ride airplanes — many new infestations begin near airports. The Mediterranean fruit fly sneaks into the country concealed in fruit, which is sometimes concealed by travelers.

Some insects that cause problems were actually "imported." For instance, the African bee was introduced to Brazil in an attempt to increase honey production. Gypsy moths, pests of trees, were introduced into the United States by a scientist working on silk production.

All introduced insects are not bad. Some beneficial insects have been successfully introduced into the United States. One such insect is the Vedalia ladybird beetle — a predator of a citrus insect pest.

A few insects native to the United States have managed to find their way to other lands. The American bollworm and the Colorado potato beetle are now worrying farmers outside the U.S. When it comes to pest insects moving around the world, some might say, "share and share alike!" ■

The *Bug Scout* Cartoon - A Teaching Approach

In the late 1960s and early 1970s the concept of controlling insects with a minimum use of insecticides was an ongoing debate among insect control specialists, agriculturalists and environmentalists. The concept now known as pest management was being talked about by administrators at all levels but not really being used at the producer level.

Agricultural educators faced a difficult problem, how to get growers to think about the concept of pest management. The problem was difficult because insecticide use was supported by a powerful pesticide industry that used modern marketing and advertising techniques. Pest management on the other hand was supported primarily by the public sector that did not have access to the mass media in the same way that the pesticide industry did.

Out of this dilemma grew new ways to reach the growers with the idea of pest management. One such idea was the development of the cartoon character now known as "Bug Scout." Bug Scout was based on the stereotypical image of an entomologist on a field trip - short pants, pith helmet and insect net. Scouting was the idea that it was necessary to "scout" crops, go through the field looking for insects and their damage. The character was combined with a short Pest Management Tip column and introduced into a farm magazine "Indiana Prairie Farmer" on a regular basis.

The rationale for the cartoon and short text format was that most readers of magazines will look at cartoons and will only read a short article unless the material is of a great deal of interest to them. It has also been suggested that the same is true of college students!

The experience with Bug Scout and Pest Management Tip proved it to be a good teaching tool. For instance in the first readership survey of the magazine that included the feature it was one of the highest readership items. About 62% of the readers read "Bug Scout" compared to an average of 49% for other cartoons. The pest management tip was read by 46%. This compared to an average readership of 30% for special and regular features of the magazine. Advertisements also attracted about a 30% readership. In general Bug Scout and the Pest Management Tip were a good way to reach growers with pest management information. Furthermore they were quite cost effective - the magazine actually paid for the cartoon and published the information free. ■

Chapter 4

Insects and Germs

A Lousy Subject

Few humans could love a louse, especially one of the insect variety.

Most of us find these little creatures quite distasteful. So much so that when we feel a bit under the weather we are apt to describe the condition as "lousy." Many of us have really "loused something up" at some time or another, and all of us have heard a person described as "a real louse."

What are these insects that have come to symbolize the despicable aspects in our lives? Lice can be described as wingless parasites of warm-blooded animals. Hosts include humans and that is where the rub comes in! To have lice is something to be avoided, or at least not mentioned publicly.

It has not always been so. You see humans have harbored lice for as long as, well, as long as we have been humans. The oldest literature makes reference to lice, including several references in the Bible. Mummies of Native Americans, estimated to be several thousand years old, show evidence of lice infestations.

During the Middle Ages, an infestation of lice was considered a sign of good health, an odd notion since lice were responsible for transmitting the disease typhus. Folks probably developed this idea because lice and fleas leave a body very quickly at death — sort of the insect equivalent of rats off a sinking ship.

So prevalent was the association of lice with health that servants, as a sign of hospitality, would capture and toss lice on guests as they passed through the gates of the castle to attend a royal gala. Ladies of fashion of such times used long hair pins to keep their tresses in place. A practical use of these fashion items, it is said, was to dislodge particularly troublesome lice should the creatures manage to create discomfort near the scalp.

Lice also played a political role in the olden days. In Hurdenburg, Sweden, during the Middle Ages, a louse was used to determine the next mayor. Each year the eligible notable men of the town would sit at a round table with their beards touching it. A louse dropped in the center would determine the next mayor by selecting a beard for a home. Sort of the ancient Electoral College, one is to presume.

Lice are still with us. Each year outbreaks of head lice are experienced in schools around the country. These outbreaks, which are most common during winter months, are frequently found among school children in the lower grades. The reason for this is probably the tendency of young children to share winter clothing, especially stocking caps. This allows lice to travel from person to person. Additionally, these youngsters are at an age when parents encourage children to groom themselves, a task which is accomplished a bit haphazardly at times.

Indeed, the great apes and ancient humans engaged in mutual grooming, the primary purpose of which was to remove lice eggs from the hair. These eggs are called "nits," and the practice of hunting them is called "nit-picking."

So remember the next time you accuse someone of being a "nit-picker," it's probably because they have a lousy job!

■

Flea-Bitten

Have you heard the old saying, "Dogs have fleas to keep them from worrying about being dogs?" Well, it's true that dogs spend a lot of time scratching, and for good reason, flea bites itch. Fleas can cause their host animals to be unthrifty. Thus, another saying, "The fatter the fleas, the leaner the dog."

Fleas are among the most modern of insects. Some scientists believe that fleas are just flies that have lost their wings. Fleas live on mammals. So they can move easily through the hairs on their hosts, fleas are flattened from side to side.

Adult fleas are known for their jumping ability. A flea can leap up to 13 inches. If a human could do as well, the world long-jump record would be nearly 800 feet. Such a comparison is not fair. Fleas have rubber-like pads at the base of their back legs. These pads are compressed when the flea is preparing to leap. Thus, flea jumps are spring aided!

Immature fleas live in the nest of the host and feed on feces and other organic materials. Before changing into adults, young fleas enter a resting stage that can last for months. The fleas emerge from the resting stage when a host animals enters the nest. Either the motion or the heat from the hosts body triggers the emergence. Such behavior ensures that a food source is available to the newly-emerged and hungry flea.

Some fleas are named after specific animals such as the cat flea and the dog flea. However, most fleas will feed on any warm-blooded animal. In fact, the most common flea found on dogs is the cat flea, not the dog flea.

It is hard to be positive about fleas, but they have been trained to pull carts and perform in flea circuses. The training is the easy part, but finding a harness to fit a flea is another matter.

Humans have long been bothered by fleas. In the Middle Ages, ladies even wore "flea furs." This piece of fur was worn around the neck as an attraction for fleas. The collar with its collection of fleas could then be removed and the fleas destroyed.

Ogden Nash recognized the long association of humans and fleas in his poem entitled "Fleas." The entire poem is "Adam Had'em."

■

Chapter 4

The Parable of the Beans and the Bean Eaters

Once upon a time in some ancient land the first farmer, no doubt a woman, planted some beans. The farmer watched the beans grow and discovered that a whole host of bean eaters came to eat the beans. Indeed, the bean eaters, (insects, rodents and diseases) were so good at eating beans that they got most of the beans before the farmer was able to harvest.

The farmer was unwilling to share her beans, so she began to do what she could to discourage the bean eaters, but alas the bean eaters persisted and always shared in the harvest. To this very day, whenever a farmer plants beans, the bean eaters come to the bean fields and the farmers do what they can to discourage the bean eaters, but the bean eaters always get their share, more or less.

Insect Products
Insect Pests and Their Control
Insects and Germs

1. Why do harmful organisms not grow in honey?
2. What alcoholic beverage is made from honey?
3. Where did the term honeymoon originate?
4. What does the foreign name of an insect generally indicate?
5. Why were gypsy moths introduced into the United States?
6. For what general purpose are insects deliberately introduced into other countries?
7. Typhus is transmitted by what insect?
8. What are lice eggs called?

Insecticides

Chemical Safety Starts with Mice and Men

"How was I to know that this rodent was the only survivor of your insecticide toxicity test?"

Don't underestimate the value of rats and mice! As farm pests they are quite undesirable. As laboratory animals they can be used to estimate the toxicity of agricultural chemicals to humans. This information is necessary to determine safety precautions needed when handling toxic chemicals.

The benchmark for measuring the toxicity of a compound is LD50. An LD50 is the dosage required to kill 50% of the test animals. Lethal doses can be based on oral or dermal exposure, depending on how the chemical was administered to the animals.

Lethal dose information is used to determine the signal words required on pesticide labels. These signal words - caution, warning, or danger - indicate the toxicity of the pesticide.

The next time you look at the toxicity of a pesticide, remember that mice and men might have more in common than you thought! ■

Pesticides are Poisons

BUG SCOUT

"The skull and crossbones? Oh, it's used to signal danger. What I mean is...Well, we're taking about insects!"

All pesticides are poisons. However, pesticides are not equally hazardous to humans. Thus, federal law requires that all pesticide labels include a signal word. The signal word indicates the poison category for the product.

The most hazardous compounds have the signal word "Danger" and a skull and crossbones on the label. Moderately hazardous pesticides have the signal word "Warning." The least hazardous of the pesticides have the signal word "Caution".

These signal words are meant as a guide to the user. However, regardless of the signal word, all pesticides should be handled carefully. People who handle pesticides should know the location of the nearest poison control center. That knowledge might be valuable in case of pesticide poisoning.

Remember, you can never be too careful when handling pesticides. Treat pesticides as it if they are poison. They are! ■

Chapter 4

Pesticide Cover-up Good for Health

"Safety with pesticides is important, but don't you think the suit of armor is going a bit far?"

Farmers handle more pesticides during the spring and summer months than any other time during the year. More handling of pesticides means more exposure and more potential for accidents.

You can minimize pesticide accidents by following these suggestions.

- Do not smoke or eat while applying pesticides.
- Mix pesticides carefully to avoid splashing.
- Avoid breaks in pesticide containers.
- Wash with soap and water after using pesticides and launder clothes before wearing again.
- Wear protective equipment as prescribed on the label.

Remember that the use of common sense around pesticides is good advice. Many government officials will tell you that suggesting a "cover up" is bad advice. However, when handling pesticides the smart farmer will "cover up" every chance he gets! ■

Store Pesticides Safely

Storage of pesticides in unlabeled containers is a dangerous practice. Pesticides stored in feed bags frequently end up in livestock rations, often with disastrous results. A significant number of human poisonings each year also result from pesticides being stored in other than original containers.

Be safe! When cleaning pesticide application equipment, put any unused product back in original bags. In addition, always store pesticides away from your livestock feed. Insist that your feed dealer do the same with his pesticides.

A pesticide out of place is an accident just waiting to happen! ■

BUG SCOUT

"Let's see, I put the rootworm insecticide in the cattle feed bag . . . or was it the potato sack? Now the herbicide . . ."

Insecticides

1. What is an LD50?
2. Name the signal words that can be used on a pesticide label.
3. What are some suggestions useful to minimize pesticide accidents?
4. In what kind of container should pesticides be stored?
5. In addition to wind speed what are two other factors that will contribute to spray drift from a field application of pesticides?

Control Spray Drifts

Spray drift to non-target areas can be a problem when applying pesticides. Drift can be due either to vapors moving from the target area or due to movement of spray during application. Spray movement, however, is the primary cause of drift problems.

The amount of spray drift is due to droplet size, wind speed, and spray height above the ground or crop.

Drift can be minimized by eliminating the fine spray particles. This can be done be decreasing pressure or increasing water volume. However, more spray drift is due to wind problems than to any other factor. You can't do anything about the wind, but spraying in high wind is sure to create problems.

Remember, good fences and lack of spray drift makes good neighbors. ■

BUG SCOUT

"Oh, he's not spraying here . . . he's spraying way over there!"

Alternatives to Chemical Control

BUG SCOUT

"Either they're attracted to the pheromone in the vial or your deordorant has failed!"

Pheromones Aid Insect Control

Pheromones are complex chemicals produced by insects. These chemicals are used by insects to communicate with other members of the same species. For instance, some female insects produce a pheromone that attracts males at mating time. Some pheromones are known to attract males over long distances - 10 miles or more in some cases.

Scientists have been able to identify the chemical structures of many insect pheromones Synthetic pheromones are now available for European cornborers and black cutworm moths.

Entomologists use synthetic pheromones to attract insects to traps. Insect counts from these traps are used to determine peak periods of insect activity. This information is helpful in timing scouting and control procedures.

Some entomologists thinks it's a dirty trick to use a sex pheromone to attract a moth to a trap. But some farmers think it's an even dirtier trick for cutworms or cornborers to attack a corn crop. ■

BUG SCOUT

"I don't care if your contract is for corn and soybeans, you're going to help me control cabbage worms!"

Consider Biological Control

Cabbage worms can cause severe damage to cabbage, cauliflower, or broccoli in the home garden.

Many chemical insecticides can be used for control of cabbage worms. Control can also be achieved with Bacillus thuringiensis, a species of bacteria that attacks and kills larvae of moths or butterflies.

Bacillus thuringiensis is available under the trade names Bistrol, Dipel, and Thuricide. The use of a bio-control agent like Bacillus thuringiensis has advantages for the home gardener. There is no harvest restriction for the treated plants. It is not toxic to honeybees and is safe to handle.

If the prospect of a few uninvited cabbage worms on the dinner plate isn't appetizing to you, Bacillus thuringiensis may be helpful. ■

"It's one way to get rid of grubs!"

Crop Rotation Aids Insect Control

An old adage recommended planting three seeds in every hill of corn. The reason – "one for the grub, one for the crow, one for to grow."

Today grub damage to row crops is very low. Grubs are the immature forms of May beetles. The beetles lay their eggs in the soil of sod pastures or grassy areas in other crops. Newly hatched grubs feed on plant roots for one to three years before emerging as adults.

Grubs become a problem when corn follows sod in the crop rotation. Grubs then feed on corn plants and reduce the stand. Because very little corn is planted following sod today, grub problems are very minor.

When it comes to grubs in corn, it's just not like it was in the good ol' days. Thank goodness! ■

Clean Grain Bins

Clean and inspect grain bins before harvest. Don't forget combines, trucks, wagons, and other grain handling equipment. Stored grain insect infestations seldom originate in the field. Most insect infestations begin in old grain in and around the grain bins.

When cleaning reveals insect infestations, use a residual spray in grain bins and grain handling equipment. If an infestation is detected in old grain, fumigate with a recommended insecticide before adding new grain.

Don't forget to inspect grain monthly during storage. Remember when dealing with Indian meal moths, grain weevils, and other stored grain pests: "An ounce of prevention is worth a pound of insecticide."

BUG SCOUT

"Having Bug Scout inspect grain bins sure keeps the rats exercised!"

Good Sanitation Cuts Fly Problem

Sanitation is an important aspect of fly control. Flies found around farm buildings develop in moist manure or other wet decaying organic matter. Some flies can complete a generation, from egg to adult, in as little as 10 days during August. So, it is easy to see why fly populations appear almost overnight.

Insecticides can effectively kill flies. However, without proper sanitation, use of insecticides is a losing battle. Manure removal at least twice a week is needed to break the breeding cycle. Let wet manure dry and dispose of old damp straw or hay away from buildings.

You can probably control more flies with a pitchfork or manure shovel than with any insecticide on the market. And you really can't control flies without a spreader!

"Hey, Bug Scout, from here it's hard to tell whether the flies are attracted to you or the manure pile!"

Reduce Overwintering Pests

Some pests survive unfavorable environmental periods in crop residue. For instance, the apple maggot and plum curculio cause infested fruit to drop from trees. The dropped fruit then serves as an overwintering site for these insect pests. Removing and destroying fruit is a good way to reduce populations of these pests.

The anthracnose fungus and the European cornborer both overwinter in cornstalks. Fall plowing reduces winter survival of these pests. Reduced tillage tends to increase infestations of pests that remain in crop stubble.

When it comes to managing pests, a good "house cleaning" can work wonders.

"It could be caused by apple maggot or plum curculio or even gravity!"

Prune Fruit Trees Now

"But you said to prune apple trees close!"

Fruit production may be affected by many pest problems. These pests include diseases, insects, mites, mice, and weeds. Proper pest identification is necessary to select an effective control program.

Pruning is an important aspect of most control programs. Removing and destroying dead or dying branches eliminates some sources of disease. Pruning also allows proper penetration of pesticides applied to the tree for disease, insect, or mite control.

This is the time to prune fruit trees to aid pest control next summer. Remember a fruit tree is like a lot of organizations: a good pruning to cut out dead wood works wonders. ■

Alternatives to Chemical Control

1. For what insect management purpose are synthetic pheromones used?
2. Name a species of bacteria that is widely used for insect control.
3. Name three beneficial insects that are either predators or parasites on insect pests.
4. What is the most likely source of insects that start infestations in stored grain?
5. Other than insecticides what is an important aspect of housefly control?
6. Why does removing and destroying fallen fruit in an orchard enhance insect control?
7. How does pruning trees affect the control achieved with pesticides?

Control in Home and Garden

Insect Devices Give Partial Control

There are a lot of gadgets on the market purported to provide insect control. These devices are sold to reduce insect problems in and around homes, barns, yards, or gardens. Most are designed to attract insects for purposes of extermination.

Other machines repel the undesirable insects. All such devices will provide satisfactory relief from insects only when used with other control measures.

No collection device will provide satisfactory fly control unless breeding sites are eliminated. The same is true for mosquitoes in the back yard. Thus, sanitation remains the number-one control measure for flies, even with the miracles of modern technology.

Remember, unless used with other controls, the only benefit of insect gadgets might be the pleasure of seeing and hearing flies commit suicide on the electric grid. ■

"Not only is it approved by EPA, but it serves as a burglar alarm, starts your coffee maker, and ...."

Chapter 4

Bug Lights

All across America the signs of summer are evident. Wrens have returned to backyards to belt out two-ton songs from two-gram bodies. Neighborhoods drone with the weekend sounds of lawnmowers, hedge trimmers and sprinkler systems.

Many homeowners also are engaged in another suburban ritual known as "hanging the bug light." Illuminating the bug light heralds the onset of summer as surely as lighting the tree signals the Christmas season.

In the good old summertime the age old battle between humans and insects reaches its peak. Bug lights (not to be confused with that popular beverage Bud Lite!) are another weapon in the war.

Although they vary in size and shape, all bug lights have a singular purpose . . . insect incineration! The device functions by using ultraviolet light to attract insects. Many night-flying insects are lured to light, but ultraviolet is the most attractive of all wavelengths. Modern technology has combined this light with open electric wires to form bug-killing devices known generally as bug zappers or bug killers.

Humans have flocked to these devices as surely as moths circle a flame because bug lights kill lots of insects. However, research has shown that the insects most homeowners are trying to avoid are not affected by these electrifying devices.

Most female mosquitoes – the ones that bite and the ones we want to get rid of – are not attracted to the light.

In the case of Junebugs, many are killed but many more miss the trap. Subsequently, they land on vegetation in the area and lay eggs in the soil. These hatch into grubs that will feed in the lawn.

Generally, most of the insects that end up being killed in the light traps would not have been there if the light had not been hung in the first place. By using light traps we end up attracting insects, just the opposite of what homeowners had hoped would happen.

So why do we pay good money for these devices? It's because we like to kill insects. There just is something pleasurable about the snap, crackle and pop of an insect being fried on the wires that gives us pleasure.

Nothing compares to sitting in a porch swing on a summer evening and listening to insects commit suicide in a bug light. But, hopefully, it is your neighbor's bug light. That way you know your insects are being attracted to the neighbor's place and not bugging you! ■

Control in Home and Garden

1. Why will insect control gadgets such as light traps not provide satisfactory control?
2. Why is sunning considered a method of control for clothes moths or carpet beetles?
3. What are three physical characteristics that will distinguish ants from termites?
4. What is the only ant that will cause structural damage to houses?
5. What is the absolute best (the big number one) way to prevent ants from invading a house?
6. Name six species of cockroaches likely to be found in homes in Indiana.
7. The chances of successful roach control are greatly increased if what preceeds the application?
8. Wiggle-tails are the larvae of what insects?
9. What is the most effective control procedure for mosquitoes around the home?
10. Name five groups of insects that are considered pests of home-stored foods.
11. List five procedures useful in preventing infestations of stored foods.
12. What are symptoms of grub infestations in lawns?
13. What are the common names of three insects with larvae known as white grubs.

Sir Knight Bug Scout and his trusty steed, Threshold

'Twas a sleepy June day for Farmer Krupperstrap. Corn was growing lickety-split, the first alfalfa cutting was in the barn and the old white-faced cow had just dropped twin heifers . . . .

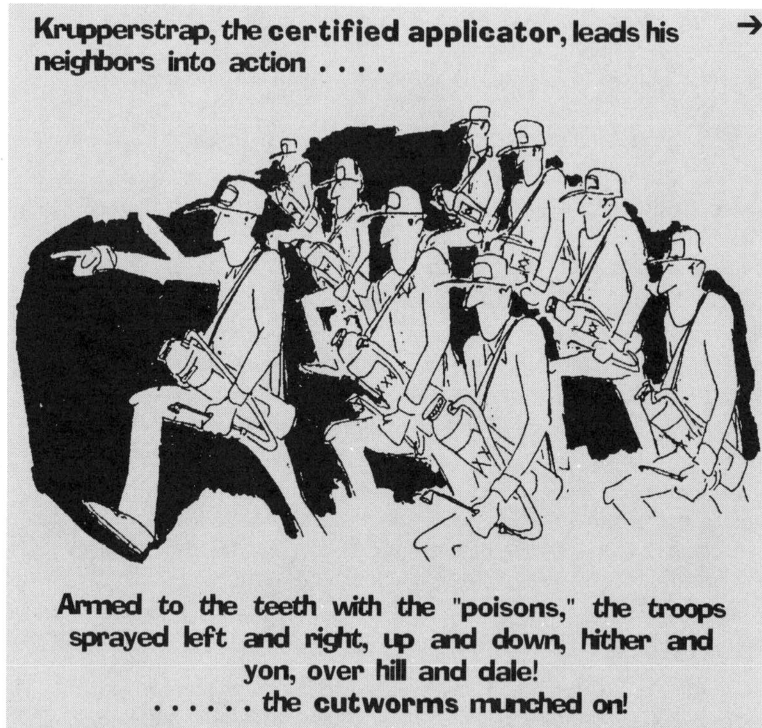

Meanwhile, back at the ranch that gallant Sir Knight Bug Scout, astride his faithful steed, Threshold, had just departed for a foray in the field. Gliding smoothly over rough terrain, equine and rider were as one.

Suddenly . . . .

Threshold senses danger . . .

he balks,

But Bug Scout's humiliating introduction deters him not.

Look here, Meteorus leviventris, the cutworm's natural enemy!
Waste not chemicals here!

and so Sir Knight Bug Scout rides off into the sunset. Krupperstrap, his hard working wife and wholesome semi-beautiful daughter wave a fond farewell as a voice trails from the horizon,

Hi ho Threshold, *Away!*

Chapter 4

Pest Management

Introduction

Pest management is the current philosophy of agricultural pest control. As terminology, pest management, is relatively new, having only during the past decade risen to a place of prominence in the vocabulary of most agriculturists. Because it is a philosophy, pest management is difficult to define. Pest management is a concept of crop production incorporating effective and economical crop protection components that minimize the undesirable side effects of pest control actions. It is important to understand the following fundamental aspects of pest management.

1. Pest management is a part of total crop production.
2. Crop protection must be economical.
3. Pest control actions can result in undesirable effects.
4. In its broadest sense pest management refers to all pests including weeds, plant pathogens, nematodes, vertebrates and insects.

Ecologically the term "pest" has no meaning. Mankind has classified certain organisms as pests because they compete for available food, destroy structures or carry disease. In agriculture, organisms were probably first recognized as "pests" when mankind began to cultivate crops. Under these conditions it was readily apparent that other organisms fed on crops and shared the harvest. As mankind progressed in agriculture and introduced monocultures the impact of pests, under such unstable ecological systems, could be disastrous. In fact, many practices of modern agriculture may have evolved because of pest problems. Pests have probably influenced the course of civilization. The ancient Greeks and Romans knew of and used pesticides in the Mediterranean Basin. Crop losses due to pests during those times might have spelled the difference between adequate food supplies and famine.

During the last century agriculture in industrial countries has changed from small, labor-intensive to large, highly mechanized operations. As modern agricultural practices were widely adopted, pest problems frequently became more severe. In addition, the new mobility of the human population allowed pests to move around the world and proliferate in areas free of natural controls.

➔

Pest Management Isn't Poured Out of Cans

"He said one - half pound in the row, with light incorporation, provides excellent control!"

Almost everyone has a philosophy of pest control. Some people promote pesticides as the only approach to pest control. They have been described as being of the "kill'em and count 'em" philosophy. Some people would never use a pesticide. Their philosophy has been termed that of an "eco-freak" or "bug and bunny lover."

A true pest management philosophy of pest control is somewhere between these extremes. The use of pesticides is an important tactic in pest management. Resistant plants and crop rotation as well as use of parasites and predators are also control options. Concern for the environment is important, as is economic benefit from control.

Remember, pest management is a philosophy. You can't go down to the local agri-chemical dealer and buy a can of pest management. When it comes to pest management, it's the philosophy that counts. ■

As a result of the increasing need for pest control methods, several crop protection techniques have evolved. These include pest resistant plants, cultural controls, biological controls and pesticides.

The success of the synthetic organic insecticides such as DDT following the conclusion of World War II began the pesticide era of pest control. The new chemicals were effective, easy to use, and cost effective. As a result most insect control programs quickly abandoned the technology that was currently being used in favor of pesticide spray programs. These spray programs led to the development of problems. Target insects began to develop strains which were genetically resistant to insecticides. Insecticides were destroying target insects and non-target organisms alike, and in cases where the non-target organisms were biological control agents, the pest population continued to increase in density. Pesticide residues began to build-up in eco-systems around the world, often ending up in the human food chain.

These and other events created an atmosphere of concern regarding the magnitude of use and dependence on chemical pesticides in pest control. These developments have led to a general recognition of the need for improved crop protection systems. The pest management concept and associated philosophy developed in response to this need.

The Economics of Pest Management

Economic Injury Level

A basic concept underlying all pest management decisions is the economic injury level. Stern *et al.* (1959) defined the economic injury level as . . .

"the lowest pest population density that will cause economic damage." Other definitions include a pest density where . . .

"the loss caused by the pest equals in value the cost of available control measures" (National Academy Science 1969);

"the pest population that produces incremental damage equal to the cost of preventing the damage" (Headley 1972). Regardless of how the economic injury level is defined it boils down to whether or not treatment makes money for the producer, thus the term ECONOMIC injury level. For example, if the value of crop damage prevented by a pesticide application is $12 per acre and the cost associated with treatment (pesticide materials, application equipment costs and labor) is greater than $12, the pesticide application is not economical. We say that in this instance the pest population has not exceeded the economic injury level.

➔

Find Economic Threshold

Pesticides don't increase crop yields. Pesticides can prevent yield losses when used against pest populations that reach damaging levels.

Pest managers refer to pest population levels where treatment is required as "economic thresholds." An economic threshold is the point at which the yield loss prevented will pay for the cost of treatment. Pesticide application to pest populations below the economic threshold means money wasted - straight out of the profit column.

Find out the economic thresholds for your crops. Thresholds vary according to the stage of plant growth, stage of the pest, and according to the type of growing season.

Some crop producers like to kill bugs or weeds every chance they get. Killing pests at populations below the economic threshold doesn't make "cents." ■

*"Aha! One of the *!#!* little rascals is still kicking!"*

Economic Threshold

When the density of a pest population reaches the economic injury level the crop has already sustained damage and loss in yield. In many cases this is a "tolerable loss" in that control would be un-economical. However, when pest populations increase in density through time it becomes desirable to implement control procedures at a level below the economic injury level in those instances when pest populations will ultimately exceed the economic injury level.

The pest population level at which controls are employed to prevent the population from exceeding the economic injury level is the ECONOMIC THRESHOLD (Stern *et al.* 1959). In pest management the economic threshold is often referred to as the ACTION THRESHOLD.

Equilibrium Position

The economic injury level is always tied, in some way, to the pest population. Pest population density, like the population density of all organisms on earth, fluctuates over time. *The average population level of an organism over a period of time is termed the* EQUILIBRIUM POSITION. Changes in population numbers away from the equilibrium position can be caused by environmental factors (i.e. rainfall, adverse temperatures), biological control agents (i.e. parasites, disease) or competition between members of the population for food or space. Those populations that remain close to their equilibrium position are termed STABLE POPULATIONS, while those that fluctuate widely are termed UNSTABLE. Pest populations are frequently divided into groups according to the relationship of the equilibrium position and the economic injury level.

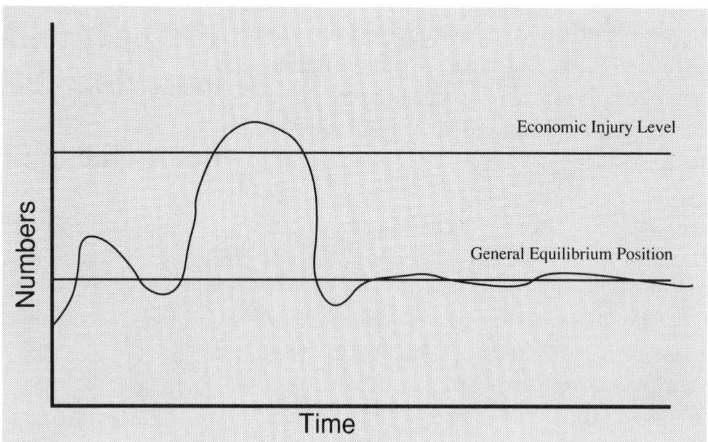

Theoretical Concept of the Economic Injury Level Relative to Pest Numbers Over Time

Economic Classes of Insects

Many insect species feed on crops but never reach densities high enough to cause economic injury. These insects are NON-PESTS and treatment is never required. Metcalf and Luckman (1975) include the cow-pea aphid, *Aphis craccivora* Koch, on alfalfa; the yellow wooley bear, *Diacrisia virginica* (Fab.) on corn;

Base Control on Economic Injury Level

Pest management decisions are based on economic injury levels. The economic injury level is the number of pests needed to cause a loss in yield equal in value to the cost of control. Pest management specialists recommend control action when the economic injury level is reached.

The economic injury level is not constant. For instance, fewer pests are required to create an economic loss as the value of the crop increases. On the other hand, more pests would be required to reach the economic injury level as the cost of control increases. In addition, the number of pests required to cause economic damage changes as the plant grows and matures.

The economic injury level is just a way to indicate whether or not a pest control treatment will make money. Making money is the primary objective of crop producers and pest management tactics. ■

and the painted lady, Vanessa cardui (L.), on soybeans as examples of non-pest insects.

Some insect species have very unstable populations and under conditions of favorable environment their numbers grow rapidly and exceed the economic injury level. These insects are termed OCCASIONAL PESTS. Many insects fit into this category of pests and include corn rootworm beetles, *Diabrotica* spp., feeding on corn silks; the green cloverworm, *Plathypena scabra* (Fab.) on soybeans or the fall webworm, *Hyphantria cunea* (Drury), on trees.

A number of insects have populations that nearly always exceed the economic injury level and are termed PERENNIAL PESTS. The cotton boll weevil, *Anthonomus grandis* Boheman; and the Colorado potato beetle, *Leptinotarsa decemlineata* (Say) are frequently used examples of perennial insect pests.

The final group of insects are termed SEVERE PESTS. Severe pests have an equilibrium position above the economic injury level and always require control intervention to prevent economic loss. The corn earworm, *Heliothis zea* (Boddie), on sweet corn; the codling moth, *Laspeyresia pomonella* (L.), on apples; and the house fly, *Musca domestica* (L.) in dairy barns are common examples.

Check Before You Spray

'Tis the good old summertime. That means bright sunshine, hot days and nights, and insects. Insects in our homes, our gardens, and our crops. The presence of insects does not automatically mean that control is necessary.

"That masked hombre? The fastest spray can in the West, that's who!"

Some insects are beneficial. Lady beetles and lacewings destroy many aphids each day. Pest insect populations don't always reach damaging levels even though they feed on the crop. Control is not profitable under these conditions. Corn rootworm beetles feeding on silks of corn frequently do not require control.

Sometimes the damage is done before the insects are noticed. For instance, aphids on the tassels of corn have already damaged the plant. Aphid control at this stage is not cost effective.

When insects appear on your crops, decide whether control will be economical before spraying. Being quick on the spray can is important when control is needed, but don't be stampeded into spraying when its unnecessary. ■

Basis of the Economic Injury Level

The economic injury level is frequently based on a direct measure of the pest population, for example, insects per stem, or "grubs" per cow. However, many economic injury levels are based on indirect measures which are often easier to obtain than actual pest population counts. These indirect measures fall into two general categories:

1. The damage that is of interest is measured and includes a sampling for the percentage leaf defoliation, or the number of fruit with oviposition scars etc.

2. The measure of a factor that is not in itself damaging to the plant, but which indicates the presence of a pest population that will create damage later. Leaf feeding by early instar European corn borer, *Ostrinia nubilalis* (Hubner), larvae on corn leaves is such an indicator.

It is important that a damage index, such as exists for the corn borer, be used in association with an estimate of the insect population. It is possible that unfavorable environmental conditions might reduce the pest population below damage thresholds. This would eliminate a control action, even though early leaf feeding exceeded the economic threshold indicated by the damage index. Indirect indices of pest damage can be fairly useful for determination of economic injury levels; however, their limitations should be considered when making control decisions.

Factors Influencing the Economic Injury Level

Economic injury levels are dynamic values. The value for any pest is influenced by a number of factors including value of commodity, cost of control, host plant tolerance, interaction of pest species and environmental stress on the crop. In general as the cost of control measures and the tolerance of the crop to the pest increase the economic injury level also increases. This means that as the cost of an insecticide treatment increases from $10 to $15 ➔

Count Rootworm Beetles

"Did ya count that one, Bug Scout?"

Count beetles now to help determine the need for rootworm control on next year's corn crop. Beetles present during August lay eggs that hatch into rootworm larvae next spring. An average of one beetle per plant is needed before the use of a soil insecticide is profitable.

Count the beetles on a minimum of 25 plants, five plants at each of five locations per field. Be sure to look behind leaf sheaths and in silks. For the best results, select plants that are typical of the crop and avoid sampling only in the border areas of your field.

Fields that do not have beetle populations and are in brown silk normally do not need further scouting. However, fields in green silk will attract beetles from neighboring fields and might require additional field visits.

A visit to a cornfield in August may not be a pleasure trip. But many corn farmers have found that it's a management tool that pays dividends. ■

per acre a producer would need a more damaging pest population before the yield savings would pay for the additional pesticide cost. Also, if tolerant varieties were used, larger pest populations would be required to justify treatment. Thus, the economic injury level goes up.

As the value of the commodity increases, the economic injury level goes down. Fewer soybean pests are needed to pay for the cost of treatment when soybeans sell for $8 per bushel than when they sell for $6 per bushel. In general, seed producers of any crop have lower economic injury levels than commercial growers. This is due primarily to the greater value of a unit of the crop. In addition, the plants used to produce seed might also be less tolerant than commercial varieties, thus reducing the economic injury level.

It is difficult to say that environmental stress and interaction of pests always affect the economic injury level in the same direction. As a general rule increased stress on the plant, whether from the environment or other pests tends to decrease the economic injury level. Treatment may be economically justified at lower pest levels when the plant is under moisture stress than when adequate moisture is available. The important point is that many factors influence the economic injury level and it may change from area to area, year to year, and even from field to field.

Zero-Damage Concept

A concept that is essential to a discussion of the economic injury level is what has been called the ZERO-DAMAGE LEVEL. *For every pest there exists a population level that will not have an impact on the yield or quality potential of the plant.* When the pest population is at or below this level, it no longer has pest status. Thus, considerations regarding changes in the economic injury level are no longer relevant. Unfortunately, many farmers have unnecessary production costs because they have become accustomed to killing pests, regardless of demonstrated need.

Furthermore, there is increasing evidence that populations at or below the zero-damage level may produce a positive yield response as shown with alfalfa and the alfalfa weevil by Hintz and Wilson in Indiana. →

Windshield May Be Clue

Bugs on the windshield! To most people that means poor driving vision and the need for strong windshield cleaner fluid. The pest management specialist may view the situation differently.

The presence of large numbers of insects on the windshield might signal an approaching pest problem. For instance, large numbers of moths on the windshild on a quiet night may mean that it's time to scout corn for cornborer eggs and larvae. The same might be true for moths of fall armyworms or sod webworms.

Entomologists also use light traps or pheromone traps to collect adult insects to determine the time for scouting operations. Philosophers still debate whether the chichen on the egg came first. Entomologists, on the other hand, know that after you see the moth the larvae can't be far behind. ■

"Thanks for the specimen, but your collection technique leaves something to be desired!"

The Sporadic Nature of Certain Pests

The economic injury level is normally defined in terms of a plant or animal unit of production. However, it is equally important to consider the economic injury level in terms of the field or throughout years. Many pests are not only sporadic in time, but also occur sporadically throughout a field. The desirable approach would be to spot treat those areas where the pest infestation exceeds the economic injury level. However, when spot treatment is not feasible the pest manager must decide whether the potential losses from areas of the field economically infested would pay for the cost of treating the entire field. Generally, in these situations a farmer must learn to tolerate some damage in small areas in order to make money.

In the same way, the sporadic nature of certain pests over years must also be considered. It doesn't make economic sense to treat in "insurance fashion" a field that faces a low level loss in 1 year of 6 when the cost of the treatment over the years exceeds the value of the crop saved. An alternative would be to attempt to control the pest in those years when it appears. However, in some situations a small probability of high crop damage from pests exists. Such damage could seriously impair the financial stability of a farm operation. In this instance the application of insecticides, even though the added cost is higher than the potential gain, is the safe approach in terms of the total farm operation. It is important to consider the relevance of the nature of the pest population over years in making a pest control decision.

The economic injury level is the basis of most pest management decisions. Farmers are in business to make money and the use of unneeded pest control chemicals is a production cost that comes straight out of the profit column on the balance ledger.

Pest Management does indeed make "CENTS!" ■

Utilizing Heat Units

"That will teach you not to run around outdoors in the winter wearing those silly short pants!"

Insects are cold-blooded organisms! This means that the body temperature of an insect is close to the temperature in the environment. For this reason, biological functions of insects depend on temperature. Up to a point, insects move more quickly, eat more, and grow faster as temperature increases.

Pest Management specialists use this basic fact to predict activity of insects. Heat units are calculated by summing temperatures above temperature thresholds for a specific time period. The threshold is the temperature where activity begins and is often referred to as the base. For example, it may take 670 heat units at base 50 for an insect to develop from egg to adult. Such information is helpful in timing scouting for insect damage.

Heat units are another tool utilized by pest management specialists to help farmers economically control insect pests. ■

Pest Management

1. What is pest management?
2. Define economic injury level.
3. How would an occasional pest be different than a severe pest according to pest management concepts?
4. What are the two most important considerations that influence the economic injury level?
5. Why might it be said that pesticides, unlike fertilizers, don't increase crop yields?
6. How might heat units be used in insect management programs?
7. How might monitoring corn borer moth flights contribute to management of this insect?
8. What biological agent can be used for European corn borer control?
9. In addition to corn what other crops might have European corn borer problems?

Chapter 4

Entomophobia

Who's Afraid of the Big, Bad Bugs?

The ancient Greeks used the word "entomo" to mean insects and almost anything creepy or crawly, which likely included snakes, lizards, frogs, toads and worms of all sorts. Today, we use entomo as a combining form to mean anything dealing with insects. For example, entomology is the study of insects. And a person who studies insects is known as an entomologist.

Not everyone finds insects as interesting as entomologists do. In fact, some people react quite differently — that is, with an extreme fear of insects. These folks have a disease known as entomophobia.

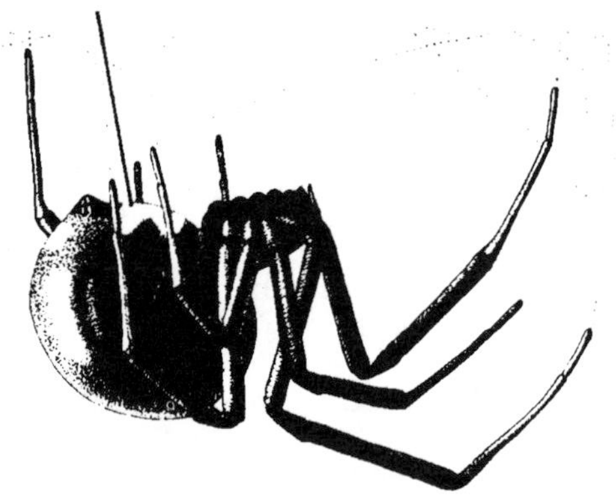

A phobia is an unfounded fear of something, and entomophobia is an unfounded fear of insects. Estimates indicate that nearly 10 percent of the U.S. population suffers from this disease.

Phobias are interesting diseases in that medical science cannot explain what causes them. Certainly, entomophobia is not a contagious disease — it is not caused by some disease organism that can be transferred from person to person. Nor is it likely that the disease is hereditary, passed from parents to offspring through their genes.

Most entomologists agree that entomophobia is learned. We learn to fear the little six-legged creatures because of the behavior and advice of those around us.

Most insects pose little danger to humans. Some, however, can be hazardous to human health. It makes sense to be somewhat wary of bees and wasps. And avoiding biting flies and mosquitoes might prevent the discomfort these insects can inflict.

If there is a real basis for entomophobia, it might be related to the role that insects play in disease transmission. Insect-borne diseases, including malaria, sleeping sickness and typhus, have caused untold human suffering and death. Consequently, in ancient times it might have been logical to fear the insects that were purveyors of death. Since many insects are difficult to tell apart, except maybe to entomologists, it could have been a matter of survival to fear them all.

This attitude is, no doubt, supported today by the reality that some insects, such as some flies and cockroaches, prosper under less-than-sanitary conditions. No one wants to be associated with such filth-loving organisms.

Never mind that the vast majority of insects are not harmful to humans and don't even live in filth. Most insects are pronounced guilty because of their "cousins."

Entomophobia may prevent some people from making friends with insects. But insects probably won't shy away from people. After all, many insects don't suffer from anthrophobia — the fear of humans. ■

Scratch When It Itches

The thought of insects crawling on humans make some people itch. Thanks to modern technology, having insects on our persons is not as common as decades ago. But we still worry about the prospects of such intimate intruders. Thoughts of lice, fleas and mites still crawl through our heads as their ancestors did on our ancestors in years gone by.

So creative is the human mind, and so real is the sensation of sharing our persons with guests of the insect kind that some people actually conjure up a personal infestation of little "beasties." Imagining that insects are crawling on our persons is a disease known as delusory parasitosis.

"Delusory" means something really doesn't exist. "Parasitosis" is the medical term for having parasites on the skin. Delusory parasitosis differs from other hallucinations in that it is a tactile sensation. Other hallucinations cannot be felt.

People suffering from delusory parasitosis frequently suffer in silence. Society today, unlike in ancient times when it was considered fashionable to harbor a personal crop of insects, frowns on such infestations. To admit to being infested is certain to elicit raised eyebrows if not downright scorn.

Such folks frequently take drastic measures to deal with the problem. They have been known to spray their homes daily with insecticides. This normally does not work since insecticides cannot kill imaginary insects.

The solution to overcoming this phobia involves working with a trained therapist who is aware of this disease. In this case, an entomologist isn't prepared to deal with what "bugs" people suffering from delusory parasitosis. ■

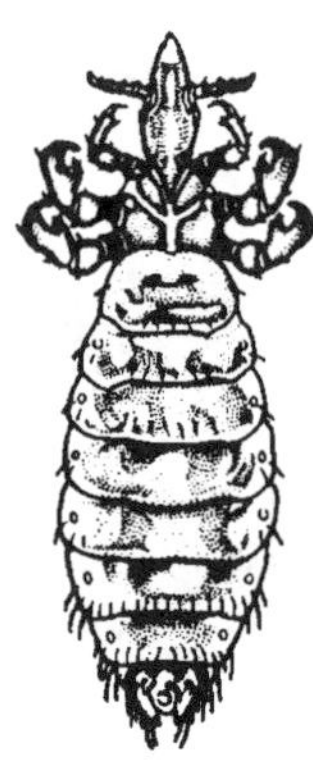

Chapter 4

A 'Bug' Phobia

Panic sets in as a large dot, which you thought was part of the wallpaper design, begins to noticeably move toward you. Your heart pounds loudly in your chest as you realize that the dot is at least an inch long, and has six, ugly legs. How dare this nasty insect invade your home. You then swat it with a newspaper and declare victory over the invader.

Why is it that we humans fear these little creatures? The vast majority of insects are harmless to people although some can sting and bite. Therefore, most insects need not be feared. However, a high percentage of the human population approaches interactions with the insect world on the premise that they never met an insect they didn't hate. It has been estimated that nearly 10 percent of us big, brave humans show an irrational fear of insects, a condition known as "entomophobia."

Scientist have long debated the basis for entomophobia in the human population. It has been suggested that there is a biological tendency for this phobia based on the potential harm some insects can cause such as stinging or even transmission of diseases. Entomophobia may be an extension of generalized animal phobias, where children are said to first enjoy and then develop a phobia for animals in their environments.

In the book *Dragons of Eden*, Carl Sagan has suggested that a fear of insects might be a modern remnant of early human conflict with large reptiles. Regardless of the basis for this irrational fear of insects, it is clear that this is a learned behavior and our experiences modify our attitudes toward insects. There is no question that the onset of entomophobia occurs in childhood. In general, fear of insects is more common among children than adults and greater among women that men, although this may be that men are unwilling to admit that they are afraid of a little "bug."

Even the syndicated columnist Ann Landers responds to letters from entomophobics. Ann's advice in a Sept. 3, 1980 column was "to read up on bugs and become informed. They are fascinating creatures." Indeed education is the key to overcoming most fears, including entomophobia.

Whether or not education would have worked for a entomophobic young lady by the name of Muffet is unclear.

Little Miss Muffet
Sat on a Tuffet,
Eating of curds and whey;
There came a big spider,
And sat down beside her,
And frightened Miss Muffet away.
— Mother Goose, 1916

Even though a spider is not technically an insect (it has too many legs) Miss Muffet's response is a common one when coming face to face with an insect. ■

Entomophobia

1. What is a phobia?
2. What percentage of the U.S. Population suffers from entomophobia?
3. What is delusory parasitosis?
4. How does delusory parasitosis differ from other hallucinations?
5. What is said to be the key to overcoming most phobias including entomophobia?

Chapter 4

Forensic Entomology

An entomological who done it!

We all know that insects can cause problems. They eat our plants, animals, possessions and even feed directly upon us. Sometimes when we are bitten, or our animals, plants or possessions have been damaged, it is not clear what kind of a creature caused the problem. If the perpetrator of the crime remains at the scene long enough to be caught - for example when we swat a mosquito or dig up a grub in our lawn - it is easy to determine the culprit. However in many situations by the time we notice damage the insect is long gone. The question is a common one, "Who done it?"

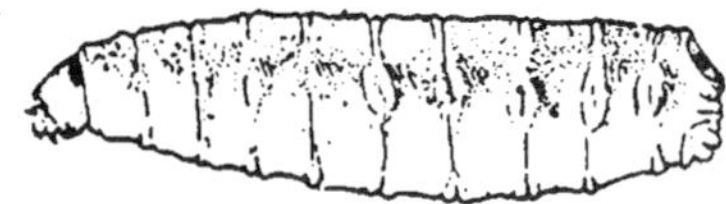

Solving mysteries has always played a prominent role in law enforcement. Most criminals are long gone when a crime is discovered. So crime scene investigations involve the collection of evidence that will aid in determining who committed the crime.

Society in general is fascinated with mysteries and criminal investigations. Our bookstores are filled with mysteries including Sherlock Holmes, Agatha Christie, Nancy Drew and the Hardy Boys. By the millions we have watched on TV — Magnum PI, Hawaii 5-0, Jake and the Fat Man, Mike Hammer, Cagney & Lacey, Simon & Simon, Kojac, Columbo, Hart to Hart, Knight Rider, Matlock, Get Smart, and Murder She Wrote to name a few.

Another of the famous TV crime solvers was Quincy. Quincy was officially billed as a **forensic** pathologist. Quincy gathered all kinds of evidence from murder scenes and through his laboratory tried to determine the facts relative to the case. The word forensic comes from the L. *forensis* from forum or public place. By definition forensic means "belonging to courts of judicature or to public discussion and debate." Thus debate and speech teams are sometimes known as forensic clubs. Relative to crime investigations forensic means that the evidence will be presented in public, as in a court of law.

In recent years the concept of forensic entomology has gained prominence. Forensic entomologists use insect evidence to determine facts surrounding a crime scene. While using insects to help solve a murder is an appealing one to the press, the idea of using facts to pinpoint the cause of a problem that might have been due to insects has long been an important aspect of entomology.

In entomological "who-done its" as in police work all the evidence collected must stand up in a court of law, since that is always the potential final outcome of a case. This in general means collecting and logging samples and taking photos. An important aspect of evidence photos is that they must be able to be identified as to location. This means landmarks in the background that can be used to place the photo. It is also good planning to include involved parties (land owners, farmers, chemical dealers) in some photos.

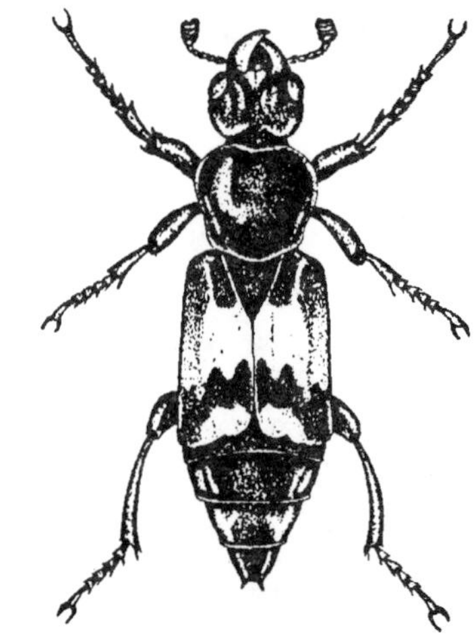

For police and entomologists the easiest way to solve a crime is to catch the criminal (insect pest or human) at the scene. However investigators must make sure that the suspect is the actual criminal. This is especially true of insects in a field that has been damaged by something - almost any insect that happens to be there is an immediate suspect!

➔

Chapter 4

If you can't catch the criminal the next best way is to be able to place the suspect at the scene. This can be done by personal belongings. For insects personal belongings could be things like pupal cases or frass. Indeed insect frass is sometimes a good indicator of just what insect, if any, has been at the scene. Another good indicator used to detect human criminals would be fingerprints or blood. For the insect a similar indicator would be a feeding pattern, the type of chewing marks or whether the feeding was on leaves or stems.

Good investigators of insect damage also like to consider the pattern of damage in fields being considered. For instance insect damage can sometimes be confused with equipment malfunction, such as planting problems, or soil type or water drainage patterns. One thing to remember in such situations is that insects seldom follow down single rows, something that can be related to equipment functioning.

A far more visible aspect of forensic entomology is the use of insects to help solve crimes related to humans. This is most commonly used to solve murders. Most frequently insects are used to determine the time of death. In general time of death in forensic investigations is determined through one of four general methods.

1. Histological methods - based on structure changes of tissue.

2. Chemical methods - based on chemical changes in the body.

3. Bacteriological methods - based on microbial changes.

4. Zoological methods - based plants and animals including insects.

Research using pigs as the model animal has shown that there is a succession of insects that invade an animal carcass following death. These come in what is known as waves. The waves occur over a period of years. The first wave includes the blow flies. These flies show up almost as soon as death occurs. It has been said that a blow fly is the first creature to show up at a crime scene other than the perpetrator. In the middle waves, once the fluids are gone from a body, the sexton beetles show up. In the last waves when the only things that remain are hair and bones the insects that occur are the dermestid beetles and the mealworms (Tenebrio). This may take as long as 3 years to reach that stage.

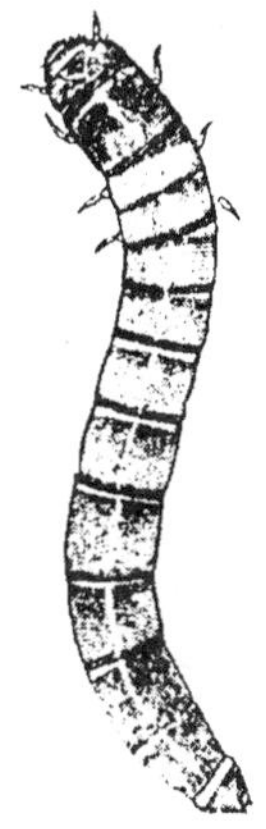

Using such information entomologists can place the time of death by determining the development of blow fly maggots. By knowing the species of blow fly and the temperature it is possible to calculate precisely how long the insect has been developing. Thus the time of death can be determined. Consequently police investigators are being trained to take notice of insects around a crime scene - they may have an interesting story to tell! ■

Forensic Entomology

1. What are the first insects to arrive on a carcass?

2. What animal is used as a model for human decomposition and insect infestation?

3. What is forensic entomology?

4. What meteorological factor must be considered in addition to insect development in estimating postmortem interval?

Chapter 5

Insects and Human Culture

Insects and Music

1. Jim Crack Corn (The Blue Tail Fly)

When I was young I used to wait
On master and hand him the plate:
Pass down the bottle when he got dry,
And brush away the blue-tail fly.

Chorus:
Jim crack corn, I don't care,
Jim crack corn, I don't care,
Jim crack corn, I don't care,
Ol' Master's gone away.

Then after dinner master sleep,
He bid this fellow vigil keep;
And as he's 'bout to shut his eye,
He tells me watch the blue-tail fly.

An when he rides in the afternoon,
I follow with a hickory broom;
The pony being very shy
When bitten by the blue-tail fly.

One day he rode around the farm.
The flies so numerous they did swarm;
One chanced to bite him on the thigh,
The devil take the blue-tail fly!

The pony ran, he jump and pitch,
And tumbled master in the ditch'
He died and the jury wondered why,
The verdict was: the blue-tailed fly.

They laid him under a 'simmon tree,
His epitaph is there to see;
"Beneath this stone I'm forced to lie,
All because of the blue-tail fly."

Old master's gone, now let him rest,
They say all things are for the best;
I'll never forget, till the day I die,
Old master and the blue-tail fly.

2. Shoo, Fly, Don't Bother Me

Chorus:
Shoo, fly, don't bother me!
Shoo, fly, don't bother me!
Shoo, fly, don't bother me!
I belong to Company G.

Verse:
I feel, I feel, I feel,
I feel like a morning star.
I feel, I feel, I feel,
I feel like a morning star.

3. Charlie Caterpillar

Look at all the bees and ants
standing all around,
Making fun of Charlie crawling on
the ground.
"But wait!" cried Charlie.
"Wait and see,
For next week a butterfly I'll be!"

(spoken) Uh-huh!

4. La Cucaracha

La cucaracha, la cucaracha,
ya no quiere caminar.
Porque no tiene, porque le
falta marijuana que fumar.

Ya se van los Carranzistas,
Ya se van para Laredo.
Ya no son Convencionistas,
Porque tienen mucho miedo.

5. The Blackfly Song

'Twas early in the spring when I decide to go,
For to work up in the woods in North Ontario;
And the unemployment office said they'd send me through
To the little Abitibi with the survey crew.

Chorus:
And the black flies, the little black flies,
Always the black fly no matter where you go;
I'll die with the black fly a pickin' my bones
In North Ontari-o-i-o, in North Ontario.

Now the man Black Toby was the captain of the crew.
And he said: "I'm gonna tell you boys what we're gonna do.
They want to build a power dam and we must find a way
for to make the Little Ab flow around the other way."

Chorus: With the black flies . . .

So we survey to the east and we survey to the west,
And we couldn't make our minds up how to do it best.
Little Ab, Little Ab, what shall I do?
For I'm all but goin' crazy on the survey crew.

Chorus: Oh, the blackflies . . .

It was blackfly, blackfly, blackfly everywhere,
A-crawlin' in your whiskers, a-crawlin in your hair;
A-swimmin' in the soup and a-swimmin' in the tea;
Oh the devil take the blackfly and let me be.

Chorus: And the blackflies . . .

Black Toby fell to swearin' cuz the work went slow,
And the state of our morale was a-getting pretty low,
And the flies swarmed heavy; it was hard to catch a breath
As you staggered up and down the trail talkin' to yourself.

Chorus: And the blackflies . . .

Now the bull cook's name was Blind River Joe;
If it hadn't been for him we'd've never pulled through.
For he bound up our bruises and he kidded us for fun,
And he lathered us with bacon grease and balsam gum.

Chorus: For the blackflies . . .

At last the job was over; Black Toby said, "We're through
With the Little Abitibi and the survey crew."
"Twas a wonderful experience and this I know –
I'll never go again to North Ontario.

Chorus: And the blackflies . . .

---

6. The Boll Weevil

The first time I seen the Boll Weevil
He was a sitting on the square.
The next time I seen the Boll Weevil
He had this whole darn family there,
Just looking for a home; just looking for a home.

The Boll Weevil said to his loving wife,
"Honey, stand up on your feet;
Look over yonder in Arkansaw
At all the cotton we've got to eat.
We'll have a home; we'll have a home."

The Boll Weevil said to the lightning bug,
"Can I get up a deal with you?
If I was a lightning bug,
I'd be working the whole night through,
I'd have a home; I'd have a home."

The Boll Weevil ate half the cotton,
And the banker got the rest;
Didn't leave that farmer's wife
But one old cotton dress,
And it's full of holes, and it's full of holes.

7. *Excerpts from* **Praying Mantis**

Chorus:
"I feel like a praying mantis, her scent's around me
I feel like a praying mantis, I sense your antics
but I can't help it, I've been too frantic too long.

"She had insect eyes, but I could still see
That the look she gave him, you gave to me"

She bit off his head so he would not feel the pain
She wanted his body so much she ate his brain
Yeah, but I'll survive. No you won't catch me.
I'll resist the urge that is tempting me
I'll avert my eyes, keep you off my knee
But it feel so good when you talk to me."

8. *Excerpts from* **Glowworm**

"Glow little glowworm, fly of fire,
Glow like an incandescent wire.
Glow for the female of the species,
Turn on the AC and the DC."

"This life could use a little brightin'
Light up you little ol' bug of lightnin'.
When you gotta glow, you gotta
glow!"

"Not every nautical boll weevil,
Illuminates yon woods primeval."

"Glow little glowworm, turn the key
on,
You are equipped with a taillight
neon.
You've got a cute vest, sparkin'
master,
Which you can make both slow and
faster."

9. *Excerpts from* **Black Light Trap**

"In the ballet of black light
And the agony of the fly"

IN THE BLACK LIGHT TRAP
We make all our mistakes
IN THE BLACK LIGHT TRAP
Go in and out like tiny snakes
IN THE BLACK LIGHT TRAP
We fool around but that's okay
IN THE BLACK LIGHT TRAP
In the black light trap"

10. *Excerpts from* **Moths**

(Jethro Tull, Heavy Horses)

The leaded window opened
to move the dancing candle
flame
And the first Moths of summer
suicidal came
And a new breeze chattered
in its May-bud tenderness

"Creatures of the candle
on a night-light-ride
Dipping and weaving – flutter
through the golden needle's eye
in our haystack madness.
Butterfly-stroking
on a Spring-tide high."

"Life's too long (as the lemming said)
as the candle burned and the
Moths were wed.
And we'll all burn together as the
wick grows higher
before the candle's dead."

Chapter 5

Insects in Poetry and Literature

To Err Is Poetic

Insects are everywhere—even in poetry! It's probably not too surprising that animals as common as insects might have attracted the attention of a poet or two down through the ages.

Poets use insects in a variety of ways. In a line from "Haunted House," poet Thomas Hood created a sense of the supernatural: "And on the wall, as chilly as a tomb, The death's-head moth was clinging."

Frequently insects are used to make a philosophical commment or to teach a moral lesson. Such an approach was used by Solomon in his admonition: "Go to the ant, thou sluggard; consider her ways, and be wise." Shelly, in "Adonais," pens these worm-eaten verses:

We decay
Like corpses in a charnel; fear and grief
Convulse us and consume us day by day,
And cold hopes swarm like worms within our living clay.

But in spite of their assumed wisdom, poets frequently make mistakes about the insects that are the target of their vaulted pens. For instance, many poets ascribe the wrong sex to the insects in their writings. This is especially true of bees. Ingelow, in "Parnell," refers to the industry of the honey bee: "From sun to sun, from bank to bank he flies, With honey loads his bag, with wax his thighs." Of course, we all recognize that it is the female honey bee that does the work!

Even the Bard himself, William Shakespeare, made an entomological error when he assumed the head of the honey bee colony was a male. In "Henry V," we read: "They have a king, and officers of sort." And:

To the tent-royal of their emperor:
Who, busied, in his majesty, surveys
The singing masons building roofs of gold;

In this case, the head man turns out to be a woman. On the other hand, some poets made female insects out of males. Oliver Wendell Holmes wrote:

Thou art a female, Katydid!
I know it by the trill
That quivers through thy piercing note
So petulant and shrill.

Holmes failed to recognize—or at least admit—that it is only the male katydid that sings!

Thirty years before scientists confirmed it, Longfellow aluded to the relationship between mosquitos and malaria. In "Hiawatha," Nakomis urges Hiawatha to:

Slay this merciless magician,
Save the people from the fever
That he breathes across the fen-lands
And avenge my father's murder!

Longfellow was partially correct. The merciless magician was the mosquito; however, in true poetic fashion, Longfellow blames the male mosquito for transmitting the disease. It is the female that bites and, thus, carries malaria.

We, of course, are obliged to excuse the entomological errors of poets—just call it poetic license! ■

Biblical Curses

Of all the curses in the Bible, none were more enduring than the "Battle of the Bugs." Most of the 120 references in the Bible are of pest insects — those who brought plagues and curses to the people of that time.

The locusts were the leaders of the insect antagonists. These insects are a type of migratory grasshopper and are mentioned 24 times in the Bible. Plagues of locusts, even today, can be devastating in parts of Africa. In Exodus 10:15 read: "For they (the locust) covered the face of the whole earth, so that the land was darkened; and they did eat every herb of the land, and all the fruit of the trees. . ."

Locust devastation was predicted in Deuteronomy 28:38, "Thou shalt carry much seed out into the field, and shalt gather but little in; for the locust shall consume it." And "All thy trees and fruit of thy land shall the locust consume" (v. 42).

Flies also pestered mankind during biblical times. Flies are mentioned nine times in the Bible. Of the ten plagues of Egypt, six were insects and two were flies. Not just flies but "there came a grievous swarm of flies into the house of Pharaoh, and into his servants' houses," (Exodus 8:24).

And then there were lice. "And the Lord said unto Moses, Say unto Aaron, Stretch out thy rod, and smite the dust of the land, that it may become lice throughout all the land of Egypt" (Exodus 8:16).

Moths' damage was frequently used as an analogy. In Isaiah 51:8, we read the following: "For the moth shall eat them up like a garment, and the worm shall eat them like wool; . . ." ". . . lo, they all shall wax old as a garment; the moth shall eat them up" (Isaiah 50:9).

Of course nothing could be more loathsome than to be devoured by worms. Thus in Job 21:26 "They shall lie down alike in the dust, and the worms shall cover them."

By modern standards, living in the biblical times would not have been much fun, especially if locusts, moths and worms bug you. ■

Chapter 5

Biblical Insects

References to insects, like insects themselves, creep into the most unlikely places — even into the hallowed pages of the Bible. The all-time best-seller contains not two, not three, but 120 references to insects and their invertebrate relatives.

Most biblical references chronicle the negative side of insects — damage to crops, possessions and people. But in a few instances, the Bible speaks of insects in positive ways.

King Solomon used examples from the insect world to enhance his teaching. To the lazy idlers among us, Solomon recommends in Proverbs 6:6, "Go to the ant, thou sluggard; consider her ways, and be wise:" And what does wise, old Solomon expect us to learn from the ant's ways? In verses 7 and 8, Solomon points out that even though she has "no guide, overseer, or ruler, provideth her meat in the summer, and gathereth her food in the harvest."

In Proverbs, Solomon states that there are four things which are little upon the earth, but they are exceedingly wise. These small, but wise things included: "The ants are a people not strong, yet they prepare their meat in the summer;" (30:25) and "The locusts have no king, yet go they forth all of them by bands" (30:27).

Some insects were used as food in biblical times. In Leviticus 11:22, we learn that approved food included, "Even these of them ye may eat; the locust after his kind, the bald locust after his kind, and the beetle after his kind, and the grasshopper after his kind." John the Baptist dined upon locusts and wild honey when he was wandering in the wilderness. Both Matthew (3:4) and Mark (1:6) recorded John's culinary habits in their Gospels.

It has even been suggested by some entomologists that manna — the Heaven sent food of biblical times — was actually produced by scale insects that grow abundantly in the region of the world in which biblical history was recorded. With or without "Manna from Heaven," people in biblical times did occasionally find insects to be useful. But to these ancient folks, insects were mostly troublesome, but that's another story. ■

Poems

References to insects are introduced into poetry for a variety of purposes, some of which are as follows:

As a figure of speech.

1. *"Here in her hairs*
The painter plays the spider; and hath woven
A golden mesh to entrap the hearts of men,
Faster than gnats in cobwebs."

Shakespeare – *The Merchant of Venice*

In pastoral scenes as a part of rural life.

2. *"Now fades the glimmering landscape on the sight,*
And all the air a solemn stillness holds,
Save where the beetle wheels his droning flight,
And drowsy tinklings lull the distant folds."

Gray – *Elegy*

To impress with a sense of the supernatural or weird.

3. *"The air was thick, and in the upper room*
The bat - or something in its shape – was winging;
And on the wall, as chilly as a tomb
The death's-head moth was clinging."

Hood – *Haunted House*

To use insect behavior as a subject for philosophic comment.

4. *"Dreams, empty dreams. The millions flit as gay*
As if created only like a fly,
That spreads it motley wings in th' edge of noon,
To sport their season and be seen no more."

Cowper – *The Task*

To accentuate the jest.

5. *"Your mouth, it was then quite a bait for the bees,*
Such nectar there hung on each lip;
Though now it has taken the lemon-like squeeze,
Not a blue-bottle comes for a sip!"

Hood – *Hymeneal Retrospections*

6. *"That pest of the gardens, the little Turk,*
Who signs with the crescent his wicked work
And causes the half-grown fruit to fall."

Bryant

7. *"Or as a swarm of flies in vintage time,*
About the wine press where sweet must is poured,
Beat off, returns with humming sound."

Milton – *Paradise Regained (Book IV)*

8. *"The housefly, stealing from his narrow grave,*
Drugged with the opiate that November gave,
Beats with faint wing against the sunny pane,
Or crawls, tenacious, o'er its lucid plain."

Holmes – *Spring*

9. *"He, the mightiest of magicians,*
Sends the fever from the marshes,
Sends disease and death among us!"

"Slay this merciless magician,
Save the people from the fever
That he breathes across the fen-lands
And avenge my father's murder!"

"All the air was white with moonlight,
All the water black with shadow,
All around him the Suggerma
The mosquito, sang his war song."

Longfellow – *Hiawatha*

10. *"Of the black-wasp's cunning way,*
Mason of his walls of clay,
And the architectural plans
Of gray hornet artisans."

Whittier – *Barefoot Boy*

11. *"Let earth withold her goodly root,*
Let mildew blight the rye,
Give to the worm the orchard's fruit,
The wheatfield to the fly."

Whittier – *The Corn Song*

12. *"The armyworm and the Hessian fly*
And the dreaded canker-worm shall die,
And the thrip and the slug and the fruit-moth seek
In vain to escape that busy beak,
And fairer harvests shall crown the year,
For the Old-World sparrow at last is here."

Bryant

13. *"Alas for the sparrow's vaulted "pep";*
He has fallen down and lost his "rep";
And the armyworm and the Hessian fly
Ne'er cease to gnaw as he flutters by;
And tho' fair harvest garnered be
This is not due to such as he;
But science with her helping hand
Has put to flight this robber band."

George Ade

14. *"In her suit of green arrayed,*
Hear her singing in the shade –
Caty-did, Caty-did, Caty-did!"

Philip Freneau

15. *"This lady-fly I take from off the grass,*
Whose spotted back might scarlet red surpass,
'Fly, lady-bird, north, south, east or west,
Fly where the man is found that I love best."

John Gay – *The Shepherd's Week*

16. *"Little inmate, full of mirth,*
Chirping on my kitchen hearth,
Whereso'er be thine abode,
Always harbinger of good,
Pay me for thy warm retreat
With a song more soft and sweet;
In return thou shalt receive
Such as strain as I can give."

Bourne – *The Cricket*

17. *"How comes he to dis colda clime*
To seeng so far from homa?
I catch him manny, manny time
W'en I am boy in Roma.
I catch heem een da fields an' tak'
Heem back eento da ceety,
Where reecha people try to mak'
Deir gardens fine an' pritty.
Dey are so glad for hear heem seeng
Dey no can gat too manny
An' so for evra wan I breeng
Dey geeva me a penny.
Dough here hees song ces justa same,
Hees name I no can speak eet —
Eh? w'at you call hees Anglaice name?
Ah! 'creecket,' yes, 'da creecket.'
Sh! nevva mind da snow,
An' how da weend ees blow:
Hoo-woo! Hoo-woo! Hoo-wee!
For here eet's warm, an 'O!
Il grillo seenga so:
Cher-ree! cher-ree! cher-ree!"

Thomas Daly – *"Il Grillo"*

18. *". . . Therefore doth heaven divide*
The state of man in divers functions,
Setting endeavour in continual motion;
To which is fixed, as an aim or butt,
Obedience: for so work the honey bees;
Creatures that, by a rule in nature, teach
The act of order to a peopled kingdom.
They have a king, and officers of sort:
Where some, like magistrates, correct at home;
Others, like merchants, venture trade abroad;
Others, like soldiers, armed in their stings,
Make boot upon the summer's velvet buds;
Which pillage they with merry march bring home
To the tent-royal of their emperor:
Who, busied, in his majesty, surveys
The singing masons building roofs of gold;
The civil citizens kneading up the honey;
The poor mechanic porters crowding in
Their heavy burdens at his narrow gate;
The sad-ey'd justice, with his surly hum,
Delivering o'er to executors pale
The lazy yawning drone."

Shakespeare – *Henry V*

19. *"The shrilling locust slowly sheathes*
His dagger voice, and creeps away
Beneath the brooding leaves where breathes
The zephyr of the dying day:
One naked star has waded through
The purple shallows of the night,
And faltering as falls the dew
It drips its misty light.
O'er garden blooms,
On tides of musk,
The beetle booms adown the glooms
And bumps along the dusk.

The katydid is rasping at
The silence from the tangled broom:
On drunken wings the flitting bat
Goes staggering athwart the gloom:
The toadstool bulges through the weeds;
And lavishly to left and right
The fireflies, like golden seeds,
Are sown about the night.
O'er slumb'rous blooms,
On floods of musk,
The beetle blooms adown the glooms
And bumps along the dusk."

James Whitcomb Riley

20. **The Dragon-flies and Damsel-flies**

"Blue dragon-flies knitting
To and fro in the sun,
With sidelong jerk flitting
Sink down on the rushes,
And, motionless sitting,

With level wings swinging
On green tasseled rushes,
To dream in the sun."

Lowell

21. *"Little brook, sing to me:*
Sing about a bumblebee
That tumbled from a lily-bell, and grumbled mumblingly
Because he wet the film
Of his wings, and had to swim
While the water-bugs raced round and laughed at him!

Little brook, sing a song
Of a leaf that sailed along
Down the golden-braided center of our current swift and strong,
And a dragon-fly that lit
On the tilting rim of it,
And rode away and wasn't scared a bit."

James Whitcomb Riley

22. *"Under the high-top sweeting,*
Many a playmate came to share
The sports of our merry meeting:
Zigzag butterflies, many a pair,
Doubled and danced in the sunny air;
The yellow wasp was a visitor there;
The cricket chirped from his grassy lair;
Even the squirrel would sometimes dare
Look down upon us, with curious stare;
The bees plied fearless their honeyed care
Almost beside us, nor seemed aware
Of human presence; and when the glare
Of day was done, and the eye was fair,
The fireflies glimmered everywhere,
Like diamond-sparkles in beauty's hair,
In the boughs of the high-top sweeting.
The humming-bird, with his gem-bright eye,
Paused there to sip the clover,
Or whizzed like a rifle bullet by;
The katydid, with its rasping cry,
Made forever the same reply,
Which laughing voices would still deny;
And the beautiful four-winged dragon-fly
Darted amoung us, now low, now high,
And we sprang aside with a startled cry,
Fearing the fancied savagery
Of the harmless and playful rover.
The flying grasshopper clacked his wings,
Like castanets gayly beating;
The toad hopped by us, with jolting springs;
The yellow spider that spins and swings
Swayed on its ladder of silken strings;
The shy cicada, whose noon-voice rings
So piercing shrill that it almost stings
The sense of hearing, and all the things
Which the fervid northern summer brings –
The world that buzzes and crawls and sings –
Were friends of the high-top sweeting."

Elizabeth Akers

23. *"'Tis a woodland enchanted!*
The great August moonlight,
Through myriad rifts slanted,
Leaf and bole thickly sprinkles
With flickering gold;
There, in warm August gloaming,
With quick, silent brightenings,
From meadow-lands roaming,
The firefly twinkles
His fitful heat-lightnings."

Lowell

24. *"The shrill Cicadas, people of the pine*
Making their summer lives one ceaseless song."

Byron

25. **In a Garrett**

"Here, in the summer, at a broken pane,
The yellow wasps come in, and buzz and build
Among the rafters; wind and snow and rain
All enter, as the seasons are fulfilled.

Here where the gray incessant spiders spin,
Shrouding from view the sunny world outside,
A golden bumblebee has blundered in
And lost the way to liberty, and died."

Elizabeth Akers

26. **The Grasshopper and the Cricket**

"The poetry of earth is never dead:
When all the birds are faint with the hot sun,
And hide in cooling trees, a voice will run
From hedge to hedge about the new-mown mead:
That is the grasshopper's he take the lead
In summer luxury – she has never done
With his delights; for, when tired out with fun,
He rests at ease beneath some pleasant weed.
The poetry of earth is ceasing never:
On a lone winter evening, when the frost
Has wrought a silence, from the stove there shrills
The cricket's song, in warmth increasing ever,
And seems to one in drowsiness half lost,
The grasshopper's among some grassy hills."

John Keats

27. **Moths**

"Ghosts of departed winged things,
What memories are those
That tempt you with your damask wings
Here where my candle glows?

Vainly you hover, circling oft
The tongue of yellow flame:
A tiger by caresses soft
You vainly seek to tame.

Here is no hope for you: nay, here
Death lurks within the light
To leap upon you flying near
And sweep you from the night.

Moon-butterflies, back to your blooms
Born of the dew and stars!
Hence, ghosts, and find again your glooms
Hidden by shadow-bars.

Quick – speed across the dusky blue,
Lest, in a sudden breath,
This tawny tiger wake, and you
Endure a second death!"

Frank Dempster Sherman

28. *"O the South Wind and the Sun!*
How each loved the other one –
Full of fancy – full of folly –
Full of jollity and fun!
How they romped and ran about,
Like two boys when school is out,
With glowing face, and lisping lip,
Low laugh, and lifted shout!

Over meadow-lands they tripped,
Where the dandelions dipped
In crimson foam of clover-bloom,
And dripped and dripped and dripped;
And they clinched the bumble-stings,
Gauming honey on their wings,
And bundling them in lily-bells,
With maudlin murmurings.

And the humming-bird, that hung
Like a jewel up among
The tilted honeysuckle-horns,
They mesmerized, and swung
In the palpitating air,
Drowsed with odors strange and rare,
And, with whispered laughter, slipped away
And left him hanging there.

And the golden-banded bees,
Drowning o'er the flowery leas,
They bridled, reigned, and rode away
Across the fragrant breeze,
Till in hollow oak and elm
They had groomed and stabled them
In waxen stalls that oozed with dews
Of rose and lily-stem.

Where the dusty highway leads,
High above the wayside weeds
They sowed the air with butterflies
Like blooming flower-seeds,
Till the dull grasshopper sprung
Half a man's height up, and hung
Tranced in the heat, with whirring wings,
And sung and sung and sung!

And they loitered, hand in hand,
Where they snipe along the sand
Of the river ran to meet them
As the ripple meets the land,
Till the dragon-fly, in light
Gauzy armor, burnished bright,
Came tiling down the waters
In a wild, bewildering flight."

James Whitcomb Riley

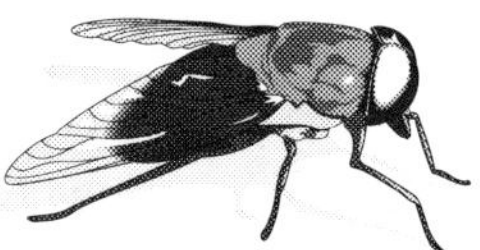

29. *Excerpts from*
I Heard a Fly Buzz When I Died

"I heard a fly buzz when I died;
The stillness round my form
Was like the stillness in the air
Between the heaves of storm.

With blue, uncertain, stumbling buzz,
Between the light and me;
And then the windows failed, and then
I could not see to see."

Emily Dickinson

30. *As the moths around a taper,*
As the bees around a rose,
As the gnats around a vapor,
So the spirits group and close
Round about a holy childhood,
As if drinking its repose.

E. B. Browning, *A Child Asleep*

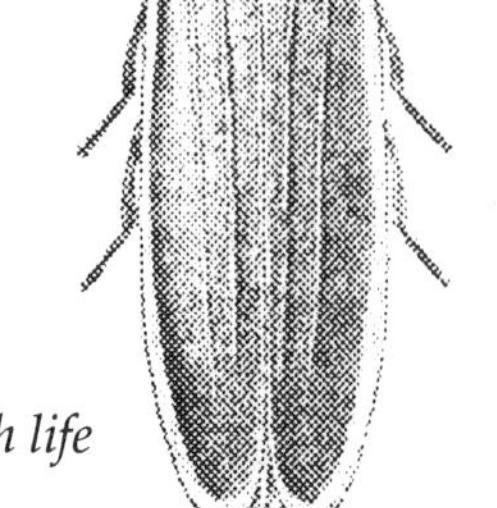

31. *The firefly is a funny bug,*
He hasn't any mind.
He blunders all the way through life
With his headlight on behind.

from the ***Poems of A. Nonny Mouse***
(Jack Prelutsky)

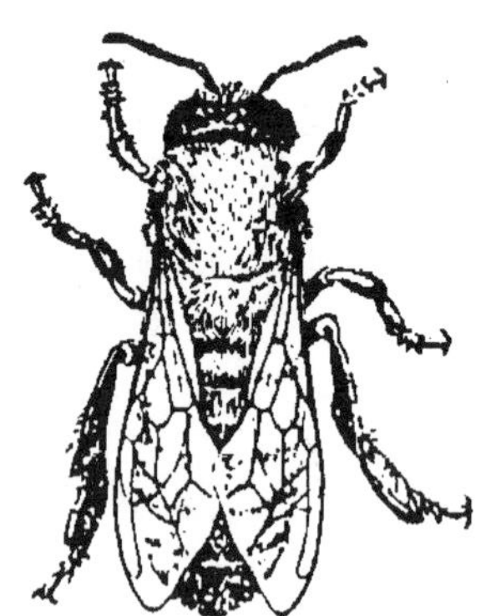

32. *Excerpts from*
Buzzy Old Bees

"There wouldn't be apples
on apple trees,
or daisies or clover
or such as these,
if it weren't for fuzzy old
buzzy old bees."

Aileen Fisher

33. *Excerpts from*
About Caterpillars

"What about caterpillars?
Where do they crawl
when the stars say, "Frost,"
and the trees say , "Fall?"

Some go to sleep
in a white silk case
when the winds say, "Blow!"
and the clouds say, "Race!"

Aileen Fisher

Chapter 5

Insect Folklore

1. **Zuni Indian Saying:** *"When the white butterfly comes, comes also the summer."*
2. **Proverb:** *"He who would gather honey must bear the sting of the bees."*
3. **Old American Saying:** *"If you kill a glowworm you will put the light out in your house."*
4. **Proverb:** *"The bee from his industry in the summer eats honey all the winter."*
5. **American Saying:** *"When the gnats swarm, rain and warmer weather are believed to be coming."*
6. **Proverb:** *"None preaches better than the ant and she says nothing."*
7. **Zuni Indian Saying:** *"When the white butterfly flies from the Southwest, expect rain."*
8. **Proverb:** *"What is good for the swarm is not good for the bee."*
9. **Trinidad Proverb:** *"Ants take over all de grease."*
10. **Blackfoot Indian Belief:** *"Dreams are brought to us in sleep by the butterfly (ap-u-nni)."*
11. **American Folk Belief:** *"It is a folk belief of long standing that local winter weather may be predicted by observing the width of the reddish-brown band of woolly bear caterpillars. The theory is that the narrower the reddish-brown band, the colder and longer will be the winter; the wider the band the milder the winter."*
12. **Ancient Proverb:** *"Patience and the mulberry leaf become a silk gown."*
13. **Proverb:** *"Stirring up a hornets' nest."*
14. **American Slang Expression:** *"A buggy person."*
15. **Proverb:** *"The fatter the flea the leaner the dog."*
16. **Proverb:** *"Take not a musket to kill a fly."*
17. **Descriptive Language:** *"Nit Picking!"*
18. **Proverb:** *"Busy as a bee."*
19. **American Ditty:** *"A swarm of bees in May is worth a load of hay. A swarm of bees in June is worth a silver spoon. A swarm of bees in July is not worth a fly (or just let them go by)."*
20. **Cherokee Indian Saying:** *"Katydid has brought the roasting ear-bread."*
21. **Proverb:** *"The diligence of the hive produces the wealth of honey."*
22. **Ancient Proverb:** *"A worm is in the bud of youth and at the root of old age."*
23. **Irish Saying:** *"Butterflies are souls of the dead waiting to pass through Purgatory."*
24. **Ancient Proverb:** *"Cockroaches never get justice when the chicken is the judge."*
25. **Ancient Proverb:** *"Make yourself honey and the flies will devour."*
26. **American Superstition:** *"If one hive of bees is sold the contents of two hives will die."*
27. **American Saying:** *"Ants in your pants."*
28. **Midwest Saying:** *"When flies collect on the screen door it is going to rain."*
29. **Indiana Saying:** *"When the workers toss the drones out of the hive expect a long dry spell."*
30. **Midwest Saying:** *"Seeing caterpillars late in the fall predicts a mild winter."*
31. **Ancient Proverb:** *"The butterfly that brushes against thorns will tear its wings."*
32. **American Saying:** *"When swallows fly low, rain is on the way."*
33. **Ancient Saying:** *"A fly in the ointment."*
34. **American Folk Saying:** *"When hornets build nests near the ground a harsh winter is expected."*

The Kite and the Butterfly

Ivan Andreyevich Krilov

A Paper Kite, which some boys were flying until it soared above the clouds, called down from on high to a Butterfly far below in the valley.

"Really and truly, friend Butterfly, I hardly recognized you from way up here. Confess, now, that you envy me when you see me flying."

"Envy you? No, indeed!" replied the Butterfly, "you have no reason for feeling so proud of yourself! You fly high, to be sure. But you are always tied by a string. Such a life my friend, is far from a happy one. As for me, humble though I am, I still can fly where I choose. I should not want to spend all my life as the tool of someone else's foolish amusement!" ■

Chapter 5

The Lion and the Mosquitoes (Chinese Folk Tale)

Once in the summer time the lion was very thirsty. But the sun had taken all the water near the lion's home, and he went to many places seeking for it. In time he found an old well, but the water was not fresh. As the lion was very thirsty he said, "I must drink, even though the water is stale."

But when he reached down into the old well, he found that it was the home of all the mosquitoes of the wilderness.

The mosquitoes said to the lion, "Go away, we do not want you. This is our home and we are happy. We do not wish the lion, the fox, or the bear to come here. You are not our friend. Why do you come?"

The lion roared and said, "Weak and foolish things! I am the lion. It is you that should go away, for I have come to drink. This is my wilderness, and I am king. Do you know, weak things, that when I come out from my place and send forth my voice, all the creatures of the wilderness shake like leaves and bow their heads to me? What are you that you should have a place you call your home and tell me that I may or I may not?"

Then the mosquitoes answered, "You are only one. You speak as if you were many. Our people had this old well for a home before your roar was heard in the wilderness. And many generations of us have been born here. This home is ours, and we are they that say who shall come or go. And yet you come and tell us to go out of our own door. If you do not leave us, we will call our people, and you shall know trouble."

But the lion held his head high with pride and anger and said, "What are, oh, small of the small? I will kill everyone of your useless people. When I drink, I will open my mouth only a little wider, and you shall be swallowed like the water. And tomorrow, I shall forget that I drank today."

"Boastful one," said the mosquitoes, "we do not believe that you have the power to destroy all our people. If you wish battle, we shall see. We know your name is great and that all animals bow their heads before you; but our people can kill you."

The lion jumped high in his rage and said, "No other creature in the wilderness has dared to say these things to me-the king. Have I come to the vile well of the silly mosquitoes for wisdom?" And he held his head high, and gave the mighty roar of battle, and made ready to kill all the mosquitoes.

Then the mosquitoes, big and little, flew around him. Many went into his ears, and the smallest ones went into the nose, and the big old ones went into his mouth to sting. A thousand and a thousand hung in the air, just over his head, and made a great noise, and the lion soon knew that he could not conquer.

He roared and jumped, and two of his front feet went down into the well. The well was narrow and deep and he could not get out, for his two hind feet were in the air and his head hung downward. And as he died, he said to himself:

"My pride and anger have brought me this fate. Had I used gentle words, the mosquitoes might have given me water for my thirst. I was wise and strong in the wilderness, and even the greatest of the animals feared my power. But I fought with the mosquitoes and I die-not because I have not strength to overcome, but because of the foolishness of anger."

Ee-Sze (meaning): The wise can conquer the foolish. Power is nothing, strength is nothing. The wise, gentle, and careful can always win. ■

Insect Weather Predictors

Everybody is interested in the weather. If we aren't talking about it, we are trying to predict it.

Today, weather forecasters use a variety of scientific tools and equipment, but that hasn't always been the case. There was a time when nature provided the primary information used in weather predictions. For instance, insects and insect behavior.

Flies, it is said, bite sore just prior to a rain. When rain is on the way, gnats swarm and flies collect on the screen door. Swallows also fly low just before a rain or a change in the weather. This is because the swallows are feeding on flying insects that also fly low just before a rain. Butterflies flying from the southwest also indicate the approach of rain.

Folklore holds that stepping on an ant will bring rain. Maybe that ancient belief gave rise to the Indian rain dance when some overzealous individual got into an ant nest!

Insects have been used to predict the onset of the seasons. It is said that a yellow butterfly flying in one's face indicates a frost within the next 10 days that is sufficient enough to turn the leaves the color of the butterfly. The first song of the dog day cicada means six weeks to frost. A Zuni Indian saying indicates, "When the white butterfly comes, comes also the summer."

Where a butterfly chrysalid is suspended is said to indicate weather trends. If the chrysalid is on a heavy branch, expect rain. If it is found on the underside of slender branches, then we are in for a spell of fair weather.

Foraging behavior of bees gives a hint of weather to come. Someone put these ideas in a poem:

When bees to distance wing their flight,
Days are warm and skies are bright.
But when the flight ends near their home,
Stormy weather is sure to come.

THE EAGLE AND THE WORM

(Russian) Anonymous

Upon the summit of a lofty rock,
An Eagle chanced to espy
A Worm; whom thus he gave in taunting tone to mock:
"Reptile! What raised thee thus high?
How haps it I so vile a creature see
Arched on the same imminence with me, Here daring to abide?"
"By my own strength," the Worm replied,
"I hither made my way; and small in
My opinion, the difference of the mode
In which to the same point we took our road,
What you by soaring did, I did by crawling." ■

(Hopefully the writer's observation of nature was better than his poetry.)

The insect really comes into its own in predicting the severity of winters. A harsh winter is sure to follow when bees lay up an unusually large store of honey. Hornets, it is said, build nests near the ground when a severe winter is expected.

The champion of the insects used to predict winter has to be the wooly-bear caterpillar. This fuzzy black caterpillar, with a reddish-brown band around its midsection, wanders around in the fall looking for a place to spend the winter. According to legend, the narrower the band, the longer the winter. However, don't sell the snowplow based on wide bands on wooly-bears; scientists say the width of the band has to do with what the caterpillar ate! ■

Insects in Cartoons and Children's Literature

Bugfolk

We human beings sometimes impart our characteristics to other animals, a habit called anthropomorphism. Through the ages, we have conjured up creatures like the Centaur, which was half man and half horse, and the Mermaid, a combination of woman and fish. We have even humanized insects, producing a creature that Charles L. Hogue of the Natural History Museum of Los Angeles County calls "Bugfolk."

There aren't, however, many bugfolk, because it's hard for humans to imagine themselves in something as lowly as an insect. Some of the early bugfolk in human history were merely humans with insect wings. One of the earliest was the Greek Goddess Psyche who represented the soul. She was depicted as possessing butterfly wings. Aesop's fables included insects with the ability to use human language. In Shakespeare's "A Midsummer Night's Dream" elves were depicted with butterfly wings.

Yet Jiminy Cricket is the most recognizable of the bugfolk. Jiminy, that loveable little creature with top hat and umbrella, played a starring role in Disney Studio's film "Pinocchio." Except for his small size and his ability to sing, Jiminy exhibits few insect characteristics. However, viewers of the film have little doubt that Jiminy is indeed . . . cricket.

Modern cartoonists have made good use of bugfolk. Hart uses ants frequently in his B.C. comic strip. Hart's ants live in anthills, are sometimes zapped by anteaters and have insect-like antennae protruding from their heads. Instead of six legs, the insect compliment, these creatures have two arms and legs. That's probably the way it should be since the ants in Hart's comic strip are beset with all kinds of human problems that they address with the full range of human emotions.

Gary Larson is the king of modern cartoonists when it comes to use of bugfolk. Such creatures are commonplace in his Farside cartoon. Larson's insect characters cover a wide range of types and are anatomically correct with antennae, six legs, two or four wings, mandibles and distinct body segments. However, Larson's insects are folk, because they walk upright and talk. His bugfolk frequently address issues pertinent to insect life such as shedding of the exoskeleton or food habits, but always with the moral issues that only we mere mortals can appreciate.

Bugfolk are showing up in increasing numbers today to help us see ourselves and even get us to consider some profound truths. Of course the real question of a truth learned from a bugfolk is whether the truth was from the insect or the human portion of the creature. ■

Chapter 5

The Butterfly's Ball and the Grasshopper's Feast

"Come, take up your hats, and away let us haste to the Butterfly's Ball and the Grasshopper's Feast: The trumpeter, Gadfly, has summon'd the crew, and the revels are now only waiting for you."

So said little Robert, and, pacing along, his merry companions came forth in a throng; and on the smooth grass, by the side of a wood, beneath a broad oak that for ages had stood, saw the children of earth and the tenants of air for an evening's amusement together repair.

And there came the beetle, so blind and so black, who carried the Emmert, his friend, on his back;

And there was the Gnat and the Dragonfly too, with all their relations, green, orange, and blue;

And there came the Moth, with his plumage of down, and the Hornet, in jacket of yellow and brown, who with him the Wasp, his companion, did bring, but they promised that evening to lay by their sting.

And the sly little Dormouse crept out of his hole, and brought to the feast his blind brother, the Mole.

And the Snail, with his horns peeping out of his shell, came from a great distance-the length of an ell.

A mushroom their table, and on it was laid a water dock leaf, which a tablecloth made.

The viands were various to each of their taste, and the Bee brought her honey to crown the repast.

Then close on his haunches, so solemn and wise, the frog from the corner look'd up to the skies; and the squirrel, well pleased such diversions to see, mounted high overhead, and look'd down from a tree.

Then out came the spider, with finger so fine, to show his dexterity on the tight line. From one branch to another his cobwebs he slung, then quick as an arrow he darted along; but just in the middle-oh, shocking to tell!

From his rope in an instant poor harlequin fell; yet he touch'd not the ground, but with talons outspread hung suspended in air at the end of a thread.

Then the grasshopper came with a jerk and a spring, very long his own praises the rest of the night;

He took but three leaps and was soon out of sight, then chirp'd his own praises the rest of the night.

With step to majestic the snail did advance, and promised the gazers a minuet to dance.

But they all laugh'd so loud that he pull'd in his head, and went in his own little chamber to bed.

Then, as evening gave way to the shadows of night, their watchman, the glowworm, came out with a light.

"Then home let us hasten, while yet we can see, for no watchman is waiting for you and for me." So said little Robert, and, pacing along, his merry companions return'd in a throng.

William Roscoe Esq. (1806)
Parliament for Liverpool Gentlemen's Quarterly

Chapter 5

Insects in Arts and Crafts

Artists from ancient to modern times have included images of insects in their work. Insects are nearly as pervasive in art and crafts as they are in nature.

Insects are common in jewelry. One of the most common insects used as a motif in jewelry is the scarab beetle. This sacred insect of the ancient Egyptians is a dung beetle, seemingly not the kind of insect most people would want as jewelry. Because of the religious significance of this insect the ancient Egyptians used them in burial rituals. From there the insect itself and carvings of the insect came to adorn living humans. Dung beetles, — excuse me — scarab beetles are still popular today as jewelry.

The great age of entomological jewelry was the Victorian era. During the reign of Queen Victoria of England (1837 to 1901) folks had a great interest in nature and ornate design in, among other things, architecture, furniture and jewelry.

Buttons also have been adorned with insects. As in most art butterflies are the most common insect depicted in buttons. The next most numerous insects on buttons are beetles, followed by flies, bees, dragonflies and grasshoppers.

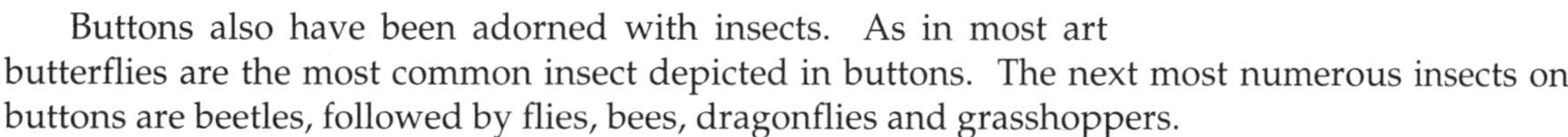

M. C. Escher even let insects creep into his renderings. His "Infinity" shows ants locked in an endless path around the infinity symbol. High atop historical old Faneuil Hall in downtown Boston is a weathervane that was modeled after a grasshopper. That grasshopper weathervane has been there since 1742.

➔

Beetle Brooches and Diamond Dragonflies

Many people have "worn" insects under protest, as the little creatures look for a resting place during their travels. Other people choose to wear insects . . . in the form of jewelry, that is. Our chief ecological competitors are used in almost all societies to create articles of adornment.

Many beetle species, with their brilliant colors, are a popular motif in jewelry, appearing as necklaces, pins, earrings and the like. But while most of these items are a mere facsimile, a few are the genuine article. In fact, the idea of wearing live insects as jewelry probably inspired the insect designs found in the jewelry made of precious metals and gems.

Live jewelry can still be found today. Some beetles are extremely hardy and do not feed in the adult stage. Such insects are commonly collected in Mexico and, with rhinestones and a delicate chain, cemented to a wingcover to become a living brooch. Tourists who purchase such a piece of jewelry seldom get to show it to the relatives back home though. Federal law prohibits importing live insects into this country without a permit. Consequently, live-beetle brooches are confiscated at border inspection stations.

Probably the first insects to be used as jewelry were the scarab beetles of ancient Egypt. These dung beetles were thought to have magical powers and were worn by soldiers into battle for protection. The scarab is still a common motif for jewelry. Indeed, many high-society ladies decked out in the finest of designer clothing have attended a gala affair wearing none other than a jeweled dung beetle.

Another popular beetle, the common lady beetle, has been used as a cover for a fine, Swiss, pendant watch. When the antennae of the insect were compressed, its wings spread to expose the face of the watch.

Of course, beetles are not the only insects to show up in jewelry. Butterflies, bees, and dragonflies are commonly depicted in jewelry. And termites and flies have dangled from human earlobes under the guise of jewelry.

Insect jewelry was common during the Victorian era, when there was a great, popular interest in insects and other products of nature. Some of the finest examples of Victorian insect jewelry were included in the sale of the late Dr. Moser Lyon Stadiem of New Orleans in 1969. Some of his brooches were described in the sale brochure as "bizarre rarities with wings that seemed to fly on their hidden coil springs at the slightest movement." Most items sold for a few thousand dollars, but one item - an 1890 diamond dragonfly brooch - brought $27,500.

The use of insects as jewelry would probably come as no surprise to many children who grew up in areas where cicadas were common. Many kids have attached to their clothing the newly emerged cicadas or their shells. In most people's minds, cicadas make a first class brooch . . . well, at least they would in comparison to dung beetles. ■

Chapter 5

Stamps frequently depict insects. In the U. S. one set of butterfly commemorative stamps was issued at Indianapolis, IN on June 6, 1977. Worldwide there are literally thousands of stamps with an insect motif.

Native Americans also admired, and sometimes worshiped insects. The Hopi of the Southwest are well known for the butterfly dance. This dance was a supplication for good crops. Other dances suggestive of arthropods include the tarantella which is said to be a lively folk dance that resembles a nervous affection caused by the bite of the tarantula. A more modern version of such uncontrolled dancing is known as the jitterbug! ■

Chapter 5

Insects and Holidays

Creepy Crawlies

Allhallows' Eve is approaching and soon the celebration of Halloween will begin. According to tradition, all sorts of ghosts, goblins and ghoulish creatures creep and crawl from their dark, dank domiciles on the night of October 31 to terrorize the earth's human inhabitants.

Of the horrifying creatures that run rampant on Allhallows' Eve, some are grotesque human figures and some are animals including bats, snakes, spiders and even an insect or two.

It's not surprising that insects and spiders are part of the ghastly crew relegated by generations of humanity to a starring role on Halloween. Spiders as a group have earned their spot by being somewhat reclusive and stringing their webs in every nook and cranny. Of course the food habits of spiders and the presence of poison fangs in some adds to the macabre atmosphere. The Black Widow spider may even be considered the queen of Halloween trick or treaters. She has earned her haunting title because of her murderous behavior.

Mating in predatory insects and spiders is a dangerous and somewhat deadly game. In these arthropods, the male sometimes becomes a meal for his mate. In Black Widow spiders, the small male tries to sneak away from his mate but is not often successful. Hence, she becomes the Black Widow.

Moths have been associated with Halloween scenes. These night-flying insects are attracted to lights. No doubt the presence of moths dancing around a candle flame during a spiritual event, such as a funeral wake, has contributed to a mystical view of the insect. In the Middle Ages and earlier, the moth was considered to be a spirit, a human soul.

One moth is appropriately named for a role in Halloween celebrations. It is called the Death's Head Moth (one of the largest moths found in Europe), because it has wing markings in the shape of a skull and crossbones. In the poem "Haunted House," Thomas Hood makes use of this insect in a refrain suitable for any Halloween celebration:

The air was thick, and in the upper room
The bat - or something in its shape - was winging:
And on the wall, as chilly as a tomb
The death's head moth was clinging.

It's not surprising that spiders and insects are used to spice up many Halloween celebrations. After all, some people consider these arthropods the chief of the world's creepy crawlies. ■

Boo Bugs

Even at Halloween, not all skeletons rattle -- thanks to some boo bugs that lend a hand, or a mandible. Never mind that they only produce skeletonized leaves. Among the insect skeleton producers are the larvae of moths, including the oak skeletonizer, the birch skeletonizer, the apple-and-thorn skeletonizer, the western grape leaf skeletonizer and the blackberry skeletonizer.

The hickory horned devil is appropriately named for the Halloween season. It is a fearsome-looking larva with, you guessed it, horns. It turns into a moth in the adult stage. The fiery hunter, a ground beetle that feeds on caterpillars, might just appreciate the heating system employed by Satan.

Pirates are favorites on the trick or treat scene. Two insects have names suggesting they might have been despicable characters that sailed the seven seas -- the warehouse pirate bug and the minute pirate bug. Do you suppose these insects lack an eye or a leg or two?

Of course a mask is appropriate on Halloween. Some insects oblige. The masked chafer, a white grub that damages lawns, probably needs to hide its face -- at least when homeowners are around. The masked hunter, a bug that feeds on bed bugs but will also bite humans, is named because it frequently picks up lint on its head and appears masked as it runs around the house.

Nothing is better fitted to the spirit of the season than assassins. Among the insect assassins is the leafhopper assassin bug. There is also a red assassin bug and a redmargined assassin bug. It may not be quite the same, but the name of this insect suggests it could be part of the gang -- the sunflower headclipping moth!

The smeared dagger moth has a name that suggests it has committed a crime suitable for a Halloween gallery of despicable insects. The truth is that it has wing markings suggestive of its name. Too bad. In this Halloween season, it would be fun to speculate that the smeared dagger moth might have been responsible for the name of a beetle that is black with two red spots. That beneficial insect is known as the twice-stabbed lady beetle. It's beneficial because, like most lady beetles, it feeds on a common plant pest -- aphids.

Now there is a story suitable for Halloween: a black and red beetle consuming every aphid in sight. To aphids it's a nasty trick, but it's a treat to humans. ■

Chapter 5

Halloween Insects

Halloween - a day notorious
For ghosts and goblins so euphorious,
For witches, warlocks and spiders venomous,
For slithering snakes and horsemen headless.
But in this gruesome creature listing,
The insects are completely missing.
Did ancient people superstitious,
By forethought or intent malicious
Exclude insects from this day
That's set aside for ghoulish play?

Such neglect just cannot be
Tolerated by folks who see,
That some insects are vile and evil
Creating anguish and upheaval
In the human populations
Of the world and all the nations.

For as long as time exists,
Pesty insects won't resist,
Halloween - a chance to play,
Tricks on humans in their way.

Mosquitoes seem to thrive
On making miserable our lives,
By stealing blood as vampires do
From arteries, a vein or two.

There are bedbugs, night time thugs,
Sneaking from crevices; crawling from rugs,
On human flesh to leave their mark
Under cover of the dark –
Like a ghost that needs to reason,
To join the spirit of the season.

Bees and wasps shan't be neglected
Amongst insects to be selected
For the list of vengeful creatures
With Halloween's distasteful features.
Six-legged witches through and through,
Concocting an evil, painful brew
Of poison, which they with humming glee,
Through stingers, inject in you and me.

On second thought, it might be right
To ignore all insects on this night.
The nasty things that insects do
Is not one day, but all year through! ■

Christmas Feasting

Christmas comes but once a year. The good cheer of the season often involves lots of food and goodies! Turkey and dressing, sweet potatoes, mashed potatoes, cranberry sauce, yeast rolls and fruit salad for starters. Then come the desserts. Fruit cakes, sugar cookies, cheesecakes and pies. Mincemeat pies, pumpkin pies, cherry pies, cream pies and even lemon meringue pies.

We humans are what ecologists call "omnivores." We eat a variety of food, especially during the holiday season.

Most insects, on the other hand, are food specialists. Even during a special holiday, their meals are of the one course variety.

Some insects, ecologically called "herbivores," prefer salads for breakfast, lunch and dinner. Larval silkworms make a real feast of mulberry leaves. They like mulberry leaves so well that they won't feed on anything else. Monarch butterflies feed on milkweeds during their worm stage. Because of the close association of Monarch butterflies with these plants, the milkweed is sometimes called the butterfly weed.

The names of some insects indicate their favorite food. There is little doubt about the eating habits of corn borers, cabbage worms, alfalfa weevils, potato beetles or cucumber beetles.

Other insects prefer fruits over leaves. Consider the apple and cherry maggots, the corn earworm and the acorn weevil. Some insects aren't real specific about the fruit they eat. The ubiquitous fruit fly will find apples, oranges and our Christmas fruit salad equally attractive.

Like humans some insects prefer animal food to the leafy, green stuff. Examples are cattle grubs, cat fleas and human lice. Mosquitoes prefer their animal food in liquid form, blood. Some insect meat eaters like their entree well done—in this case dead. Scavenger beetles feed on any dead animals they can find. A road kill, an opossum or a skunk, also would make a great holiday feast for a brood of blowfly maggots.

Like humans a few insects are omnivorous. Chief among these creatures is the cockroach. That's probably the reason why so many cockroaches enjoy living in our homes. It's certain that after our Christmas feast this year, cockroaches will be happy to eat the leftovers. That may explain the success of cockroaches—they aren't picky eaters. Was that a piece of fruit cake that fell behind the kitchen cabinet? ■

Chapter 5

The Insects' Wish List

At this time of year, it seems that almost everyone anticipates the holidays by preparing a wish list. And what if that were true of the insects? Perhaps an insect's letter to Old Saint Nick might include the following requests:

The monarch butterfly would like a new crown, while the emperor moth needs a new throne. The royal walnut moth, on the other hand, would like a large kingdom. The queen butterfly wants a pretty carriage.

The bedbug needs a nightcap, and the Mexican bean beetle wants a new sombrero. The earwig and the earworm could both use some earmuffs.

The wooly bear needs a haircut, and a mirror would be put to good use by the handsome fungus beetle. The painted lady butterfly might request some more makeup. How about some deodorant for the stinkbugs, the sweat bees, and the odorous house ants? And maybe some salve for the blister beetle? And the dung beetle? Well, how about some toilet paper?

A brass spittoon would be appropriate for the spittlebug, and a trumpet for the hornworm. The engraver beetle would like a trophy.

The billbug could use some extra cash. The paper wasp would like a subscription to the New York Times, and the praying mantid needs a new Bible. The book louse could use a volume of Shakespeare.

The cutworms can always use new scissors. A few building permits would suit the cranefly just fine. For the carpenter bee, a new saw and hammer, perhaps? And the inchworm sure could benefit from having a metric ruler.

A dinner could make a hungry mealy bug happy. The rice weevil could use a supply of soy sauce. The Japanese beetle could use some chopsticks.

Several yards of canvas would come in quite handy to the tent caterpillar. The lacebugs would appreciate some shuttles for tatting. And the webworm, being a master weaver, could certainly use a loom.

The stag beetle would be most appreciative of a date, and the damselfly has been wishing for a knight. The ladybug would like to be introduced to a gentleman. The toad bug, on the other hand, would settle for a kiss. The dance flies would appreciate a gift certificate to Arthur Murray's.

The robber fly could use a mask. A tungsten light would be welcomed by the leaf miner, and his friend, the digger wasp, needs a shovel.

Skipper butterflies and the red admiral might like boats, while a map would be just the thing for the rove beetle. A gypsy moth might like a new crystal ball, and a new trampoline would be great for the circus beetle.

The sharpshooter leafhopper needs a target, and the armyworm could use some new fatigues. The wool maggot needs a sweater, while the snow flea would like some skis.

The corn borer and the drone fly would like to be more witty, and the crazy ant might want the name of a good psychiatrist.

The questionmark butterfly would like an answer, and the comma butterfly could use a misplaced phrase.

No-see-ums and the obscure scale have one very simple request. They would just like to be seen during this holiday.

But even though these insects' wishes might not come true, one of our wishes certainly does when we wish that the insects leave us alone so we can enjoy our holiday. ■

A Buzzing Christmas

Christmas comes 'round but once a year,
A happy season with friends drawing near,
But a great joy of Christmas, some fogey might say,
Is that the insects of summer have all gone away.
But what if those pests would just happen to stay
And share the good tidings of our Christmas Day?

Would picnic beetles so lively and quick
Fall from the skies in place of St. Nick?
Would the yuletide dinner not seem quite right
In the presence of mosquitoes that buzz and that bite?
And a Christmas hot toddy could provide a REAL sting
If to it a stray yellow jacket would wing.

Of course, tasty egg nog with nutmeg suspended
Would cover up gnats unintentionally upended.
The sweetness of punch, not to mention the candy
Would certainly attract ants and come in quite handy
For these insects to carry as they march underground
To their nest where their larvae can always be found.

A ladybug ornament, a fine decoration,
May just brighten up any yule celebration,
But how disconcerting it certainly would be
To find real, live insects chewing the tree!
Not to mention webworms on wreaths filled with snow,
Or beetles and loopers throughout mistletoe.

So when carols are finished and Christmas is done,
Look back and count all your blessings — each one.
Reflect on the times and the season so great
And holiday magic we all celebrate.
'Tis indeed a season of good will and great cheer,
For not even one bug did dare interfere! ■

Chapter 5

St. Valentine has let his name
To a day where love's the game.
A time when Cupid, armed with is bow,
Shoots darts and arrows to take in tow
All those folks who, if you please,
Are thinking of the birds and bees!

We all know that birds bill and coo.
But what is it that insects do,
Or at least have perfected
To justify being selected
As creatures emblematic of
A natural process known as love?

Males of katydids and crickets
Sing from bushes, trees, and thickets.
By rubbing legs, these insects make
Sounds heard by humans as click and scrape.
Lest we are tempted to malign,
Their females hear a song divine!

Some female moths perfume the air
To attract males who would dare
Fly upwind toward an unknown fate
And select by scent alone – a mate.
This approach let's not criticize;
Remember it pays to advertise!

Insects in their mating antics
Use food and dance as common tactics,
Two-step, four step, or the old soft shoe.
But be specific, any dance won't do.
Some insect dances appear formidable,
But human criticism would be hypercritical!

On Valentine's Day if the one you adore
Is dragged out on the old dance floor,
Or played a favorite romantic song,
Or given some perfume – and goes along –
Then you've done it, if you please,
Practiced an art perfected by bees! ■

Hit Parade of Insects

E-Series

E-17 European Corn Borer in Field Corn, Sweet Corn, Peppers, and Snap Beans

E-18 Clothes Moths and Carpet Beetles

E-22 Ants

E-23 Cockroaches

E-26 Mosquitoes in and Around the Home

E-37 Insect Pests of Home Stored Foods

E-61 Turf Insect Management

Presenting your

"Hit Parade of Insects"

Featuring this year's top 80 insects. Each hit insect is listed according to order with a genus and species or family name to help place it in its proper place in the world of insects. Pest insects are identified with a large **P** - for pest of course!

Order *Ephemeroptera* (from Greek ephemero meaning "for a day")

1. Mayfly

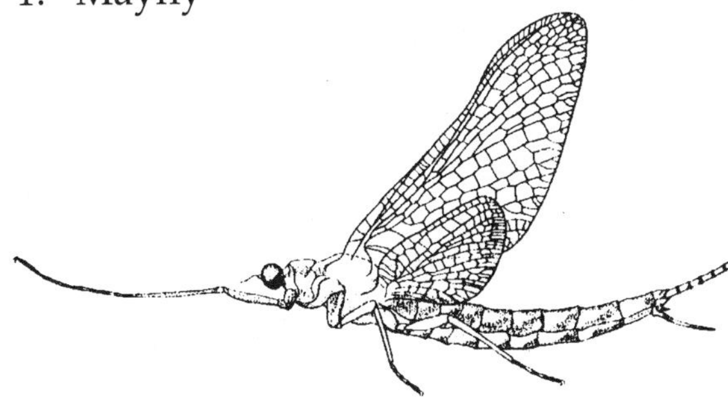

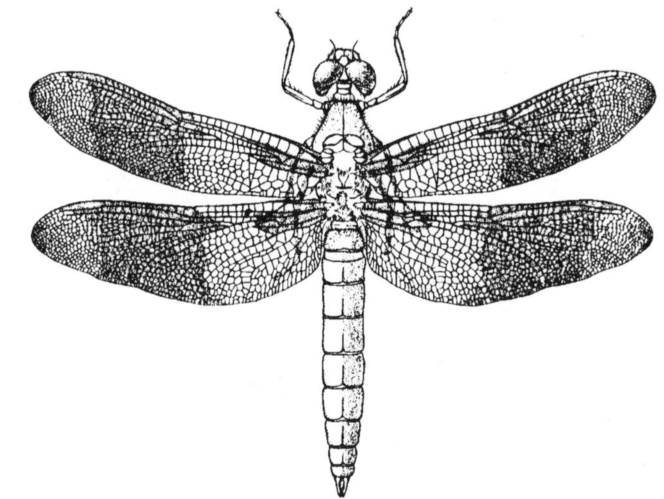

Order *Odonata* (from Greek word meaning tooth - on mandible)

2. Darner Dragonfly - F. Aeschnidae

Order *Dictyoptera*

3. Carolina Mantid - *Stagmomantis carolina*
4. **P** American Cockroach - *Periplaneta americana*
5. Madagascar Hissing Roach
6. Walking Stick - F. Phasmidae

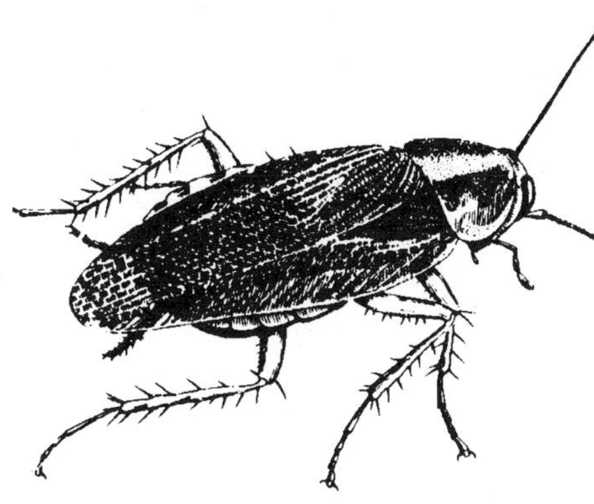

Order ***Orthoptera*** (ortho means straight)

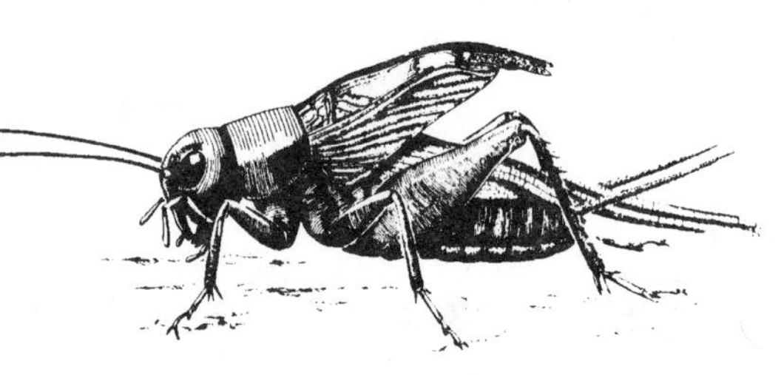

7. **P** House Cricket - *Acheta domestica*
8. Snowy Tree Cricket - *Oecanthus fultani*
9. Katydid - F. Tettigonidae
10. **P** Mole Cricket - *Gryllotalpa hexadactyla*

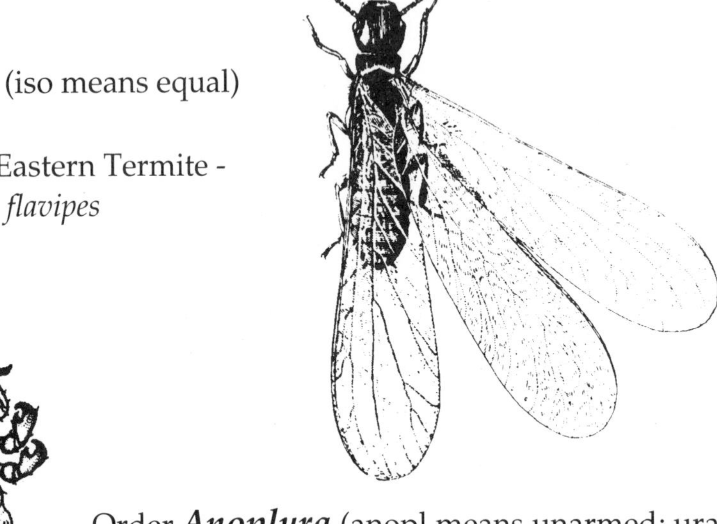

Order ***Isoptera*** (iso means equal)

11. **P** Common Eastern Termite - *Reticulitermes flavipes*

Order ***Anoplura*** (anopl means unarmed; ura means tail)

12. **P** Human Body Louse - *Pediculus humanus*
13. **P** Crab Louse - *Pthirus pubis*

Order ***Hemiptera*** (hemi means half; refers to texture of front wings)

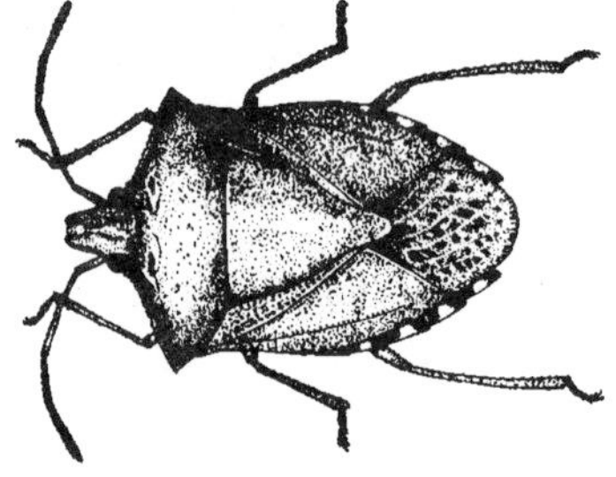

14. Water Boatman - F. Corixidae
15. Giant Water Bugs - F. Belostomatidae
16. **P** Common Bed Bug - *Cimex lectularius*
17. **P** Stink Bug - F. Pentatomidae
18. Water Strider - F. Gerridae

Order ***Homoptera*** (homo means alike; refers to uniform texture of front wings)

19. **P** Periodical Cicada - *Magicicada* sp.
20. **P** Potato Leafhopper - *Empoasca fabae*
21. **P** Rosy Apple Aphid - *Anuraphis rosea*

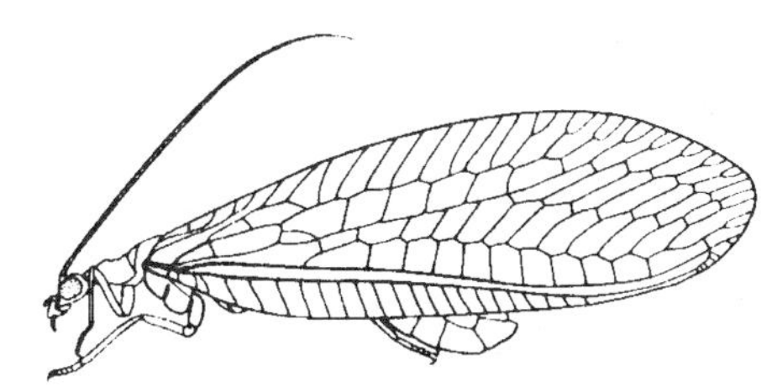

Order ***Neuroptera*** (neuro means nerve, referring to wing veins)

22. Lacewings - F. Chrysopidae

Order ***Coleoptera*** (coleo means sheath, referring to elytra)

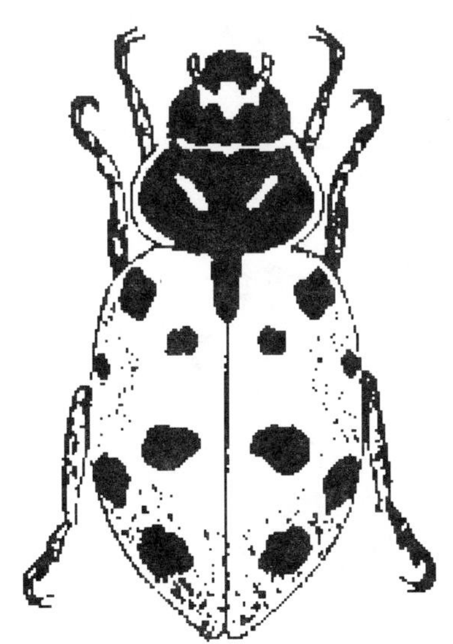

23. Burying Beetles - *Necrophorus* sp.
24. Soldier Beetles - F. Cantharidae
25. Lightning bug - F. Lampyridae
26. P Dermestids - F. Dermestidae
27. Ladybugs - F. Coccinellidae
28. Mealworms - *Tenebrio molitar*
29. **P** Blister Beetles - F. Meloidae
30. Scarab Beetles - F. Scarabaeidae
31. **P** Junebug - *Phyllophaga* sp.
32. **P** Corn Rootworm - *Diabrotica* sp.
33. **P** Alfalfa Weevil - *Hypera postica*
34. **P** Elm Bark Beetle - F. Scolytidae
35. **P** Boll Weevil - *Anthonomis grandis*
36. Tiger Beetle - F. Cicindelidae
37. **P** Click Beetles - F. Elateridae
38. Glowworm - F. Phengodidae

Order ***Lepidoptera*** (lepido means scale)

39. **P** Tomato Hornworm - *Protoparce guinguemaculata*
40. Tiger Moth - F. Arctiidae
41. **P** Black Cutworm - *Agrotis ipsilon*
42. **P** Corn Earworm - *Heliothis zea*
43. Silkworm - *Bombyx mori*
44. **P** Angoumois Grain Moth - *Sitotroga cerealella*
45. **P** Bagworms - F. psychidae
46. **P** Clothes Moths - F. Tineidae
47. Monarch Butterfly - *Danaus plexippus*
48. Black Swallowtail - F. Papilionidae
49. Luna Moth - *Actias luna*
50. Cecropia Moth - F. Saturnidae
51. Mourningcloak - F. Nymphalidae
52. Viceroy - F. Nymphalidae
53. **P** Cabbage Butterfly - *Pieris rapae*
54. **P** Gypsy Moth - *Lymantria dispar*
55. Dead-leaf Butterfly - *Kallima inachus*

Order ***Diptera*** (Di means two)

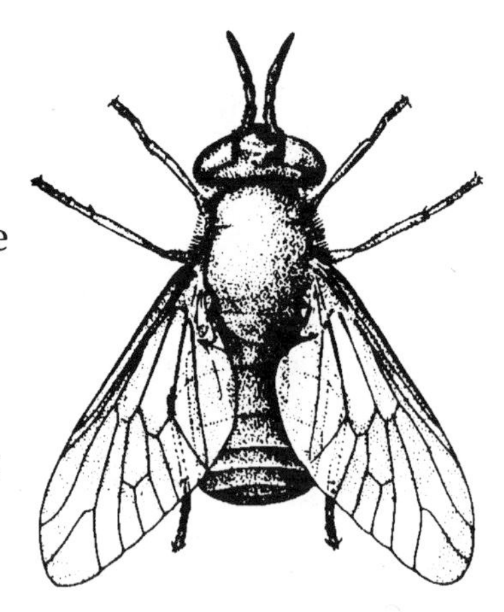

56. **P** Black Fly - *Simulium* sp.
57. **P** *Anopheles* sp. mosquito - F. Culicidae
58. **P** Horse Fly - F. Tabanidae
59. Syrphid Flies - F. Syrphidae
60. **P** Fruit Fly - *Drosophia melanogaster*
61. Screwworm Fly - *Callitroga hominivorax*
62. **P** House Fly - *Musca domestica*
63. **P** Sheep Ked - *Melophagus ovinus*
64. Blow Flies - F. Calliphoridae

Order ***Siphonaptera*** (Siphon means tube, aptera is wingless)

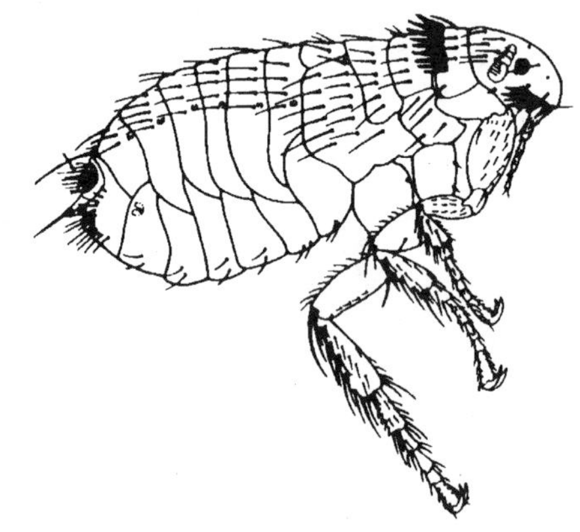

65. **P** Cat Flea - *Tenocephalides felis*

Order ***Hymenoptera*** (hymeno means membrane)

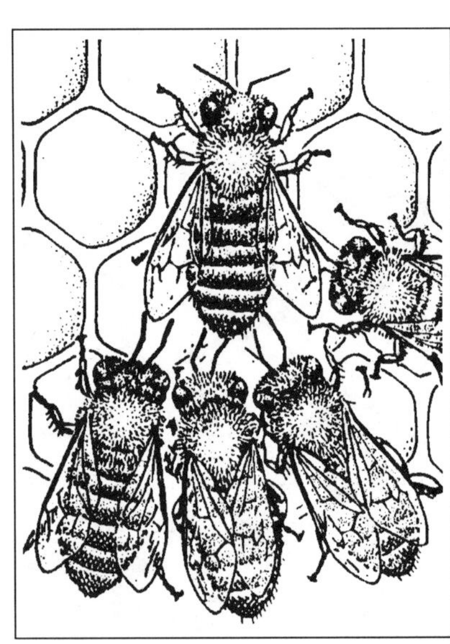

66. Horntails - F. Siricidae
67. Trichogramma - F. Trichogrammatidae
68. Gall Wasp - F. Cynipidae
69. Velvet Ant - F. Mutillidae
70. **P** Imported Fire Ant - *Solenopsis soevissima richteri*
71. **P** Carpenter Ants - *Camponotus* sp.
72. Leaf-cutting Ants - *Alta* sp.
73. Bald-faced Hornet - *Vespula maculata*
74. Spider Wasp - F. Pompilidae
75. Organ-pipe Mud-dauber - F. sphecidae
76. **P** Carpenter Bee - F. Apidae
77. Honey Bee - *Apis mellifera*
78. Bumble Bee - *Bombus* sp.
79. Fig Wasp - *Blastophaga* sp.
80. Cicada Killer - *Sphecius speciosus*

DEPARTMENT OF ENTOMOLOGY

field crop insects

EUROPEAN CORN BORER IN FIELD CORN, SWEET CORN, PEPPERS, AND SNAP BEANS

C. Richard Edwards, Rick E. Foster, and F. Thomas Turpin, Extension Entomologists

Corn borer populations vary greatly from year to year and from field to field. In corn, damage may be caused by the first or second, or sometimes the third, generations of the borer, but seldom by all three in the same planting. Early planted corn is most susceptible to first generation attack and late planted corn to second and third generations. Larvae of the first generation bore into the stalks, whereas the second and third generations also attack the tassels, ears, and ear shanks. Corn borers may also attack peppers and snap beans, as well as many other plants. Monitoring moth activity is crucial for commercial producers to plan management strategies. For the seasonal life history of the European corn borer, see Figure 1.

PREVENTING BORER DAMAGE

Cultural Practices. Corn borer damage can be reduced by avoiding, if possible, extremely early or late planting. However, farmers who are prepared to apply an insecticide for borer control should plant as early as possible. This practice may increase the potential for first generation attack, which is easy to control with insecti-

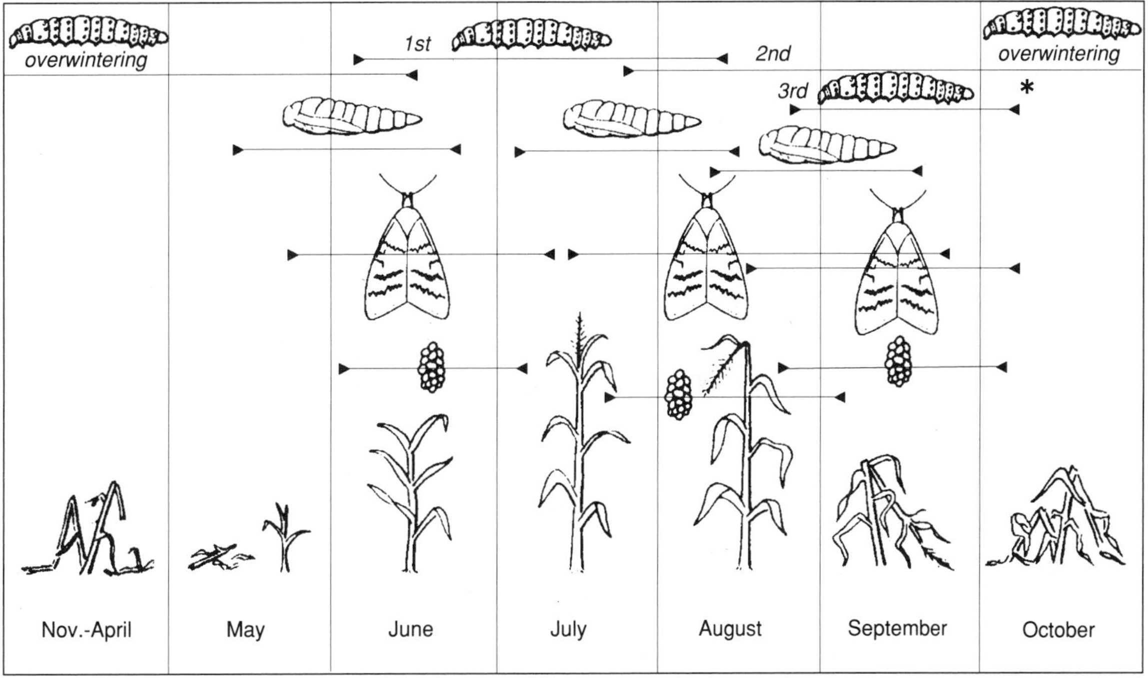

Figure 1. Seasonal life history of European corn borer in Indiana.

* Prior to 1991, third generation larvae had not been observed overwintering in Indiana. However, in the Fall of 1991, some third generation borers did reach the overwintering fifth instar stage before the first killing frost.

PURDUE UNIVERSITY COOPERATIVE EXTENSION SERVICE • WEST LAFAYETTE, IN 47907

cides; but it will reduce second or third generation attacks, which are more difficult to control.

Some hybrids that are adapted to Indiana show some corn borer tolerance and should stand up, hold the ears, and produce high yields in spite of borer attack most years. Some varieties may carry a degree of resistance to first generation larvae (check with your seed dealer). To date, no resistance to second or third generations has been successfully incorporated into commercial varieties. Hybrids which have derivatives of B73 in their parentage are usually more susceptible to damage. In fact, over the past several years, a good share of the increase in damage can be attributed to the use of B73 derivatives.

Although the destruction of corn stalks and other refuse in which the borers overwinter may reduce the overwintering populations in individual fields, there is no evidence that such "clean-up" will eliminate subsequent borer damage. For this reason, practices such as clean plowing, stalk shredding, low cutting, and ensiling are recommended only to the extent that they are good cultural practices.

Insecticide Treatments. Economic corn borer populations can usually be controlled if insecticides are correctly applied at the proper time. As a rule, one application will control first generation borers on field corn; but two or more applications may be needed for subsequent generations, because egg laying occurs over a longer period of time and the borers are harder to reach with an insecticide. Treatment with an insecticide usually is practical on market sweet corn, canning corn, and hybrid seed corn fields. On field corn, treatment depends upon the degree of infestation, price of corn, potential corn yield, cost of control, and level of control.

Treatments for corn borer control often are applied too late for best results. In any one field, there may not be more than 7-10 days when the location of borers on the plant is such that an insecticide will give satisfactory results. If treatment is delayed until borer damage becomes more evident, it is usually too late. By this time the borers may be nearly half grown and have entered the plant where an insecticide cannot reach them.

MONITORING MOTH FLIGHTS

Black light and pheromone traps are used to monitor corn borer moth numbers and their flight periods. The duration of flights and time of occurrence of peak flights (when more adults are flying than at any other time) vary from year to year. Yearly differences are primarily the result of changing weather conditions.

Many pest managers use black light and/or pheromone traps as tools for monitoring corn borer flight and predicting borer development. Although "real-time" data are best for determining the status of the current population, historical data can be used to determine the average peak flight date for a particular generation in a particular region. This should only be used where "real-time" monitoring is not available.

Average dates for peak flights have been established using 15 years of adult corn borer flight data (black light trap catches) from different areas of Indiana (Figure 2). These average dates can be very helpful in estimating the time of year that corn borers may cause problems; however, they should not be completely depended upon for timely sampling or making treatment decisions. For more up-to-date information on peak flights and borer development, contact your county extension agent or refer to the Pest Management & Crop Production Newsletter (available through subscription from P&CN, Extension Entomology, 1158 Entomology Hall, Purdue University, W. Lafayette, IN 47907-1158).

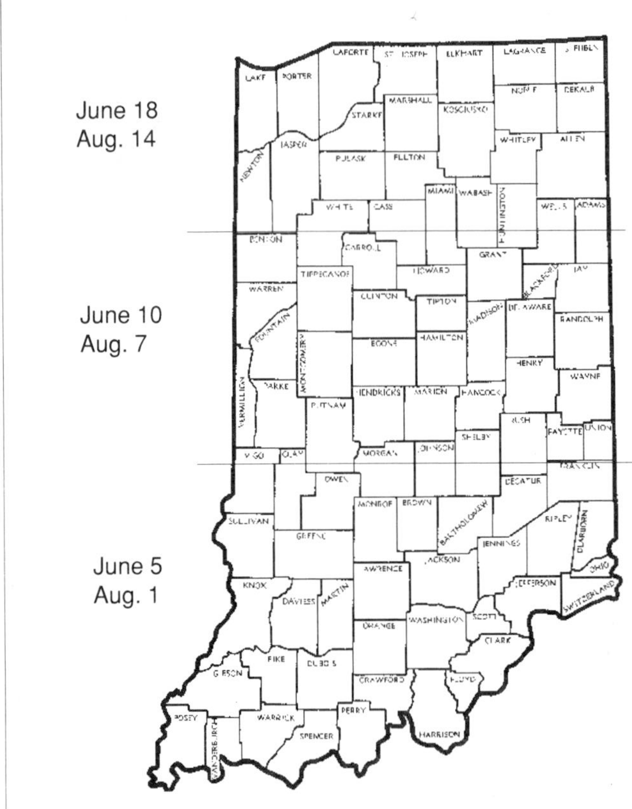

Figure 2. Mean date for peak adult corn borer flights in three areas of Indiana (earlier date in each area = first generation mean peak flight; later date = second generation mean peak flight). Third generation moths do not occur each year, mean peak flight dates have not been established.

CORN BORER DEVELOPMENT AND SAMPLING

First Generation.

First generation eggs, in masses of 15-30 eggs per mass, normally are laid on the undersides of leaves near the midrib. Young larvae migrate from the mass to the whorl area to feed. The larvae feed on the leaves in the whorl or in the midribs of leaves up until the 3rd larval stage, at which time they migrate to the stalk and burrow into it. They continue to feed in the stalk until pupation takes place.

A higher proportion of the larvae survive if the corn plants are in the mid-whorl stage (i.e., 22-36 inches in extended leaf height). Corn borer larvae do not establish well on corn less than 16 inches in extended leaf height due to the chemical DIMBOA (a plant aglucone).

Sampling. Begin sampling for first generation borers when corn is 16-22 inches in extended leaf height (from base of stalk to the tip of the stretched-up leaf). Examine the whorl leaves of 20 consecutive plants for shot-holes in at least five areas of a field. Calculate the percentage of plants with shot-hole feeding damage. Pull out the whorl from at least one damaged plant in each sample area, unroll the leaves, and examine them for live larvae. Determine the average number of live larvae per plant.

Second and Third Generations.

Like the first generation, second and third generation moths lay their eggs in the middle third of the plant on the undersides of the leaves near the midrib. Second and third generation larvae are more difficult to locate than the first but usually can be found feeding on pollen around the leaf axil, on plant tissue in the leaf midrib, on pollen and plant tissue behind the leaf sheath, or on the ear itself. This feeding generally occurs in the "ear zone" (two or three leaves above and below the primary ear). These areas should be carefully examined for borers and feeding activity.

Like the first generation, second and third generation larvae bore into the plant once the third instar stage is reached. Pupation takes place within the plant at the end of the fifth instar stage (this may occur in late summer and/or next spring, depending on how early the second and third generations occur).

Sampling. Field observations should begin approximately 7 days prior to the projected or average moth peak flight date. In at least five areas of a field, inspect leaves in the "ear zone" of 20 consecutive plants. Note if egg masses and/or live larvae are present. The larvae may be observed around the egg masses, in leaf axils, behind leaf sheaths, on tassels, or on the ear. Determine the percentage of plants infested and the average number of live larvae per plant.

TREATMENT DECISION GUIDELINES BASED ON FIELD CONDITIONS & ECONOMICS

The need for European corn borer control can be determined by using a system developed by researchers at Kansas State University and modified at Purdue University. This method produces variable treatment thresholds depending on level of infestation, control costs, stage of corn development, estimated yields, market value, and anticipated control.

Use the following steps to determine whether treatment is economically justified:

1. Preventable yield loss (bu/A) = anticipated yield (bu/A) x yield loss figure (Table 1) x level of infestation (decimal) x anticipated level of control* (decimal)
   * It is probably impractical to expect 100% control. A good estimate of control might be 75%.
2. Preventable dollar loss/A = Preventable yield loss (bu/A) x market value ($/bu).
3. Compare preventable dollar loss/A to cost of insecticide and application to determine if treatment is warranted.

TABLE 1. YIELD LOSSES CAUSED BY EUROPEAN CORN BORERS FOR VARIOUS CORN GROWTH STAGES.[1]

Plant stage	Percent yield loss - # borers/plant 1	2	3
Early whorl	5.5	8.2	10.0
Late whorl	4.4	6.6	8.1
Pre-tassel	6.6	9.9	12.1
Pollen shedding	4.4	6.6	8.1
Blister	3.0	4.5	5.5
Dough	2.0	3.0	3.7

[1] These percentages are based on physiological stresses and do not include losses due to stalk breakage and/or ear droppage.

Example: A field in the pre-tassel stage has 80% of the plants with shot-hole feeding and an average of 2 live larvae per whorl. Anticipated yield is 150 bu/A and the crop is valued at $2.00 per bushel. The cost of the insecticide and application is $10.00 and 75% control can be expected. Would it pay to apply the insecticide?

1. Preventable yield loss (bu/A) =
   150 bu/A x .099 (9.9% loss for 2 borers/plant) x .80 (80% infestation) x .75 (75% control) = 8.91 bu/A
2. Preventable dollar loss/A =
   8.91 bu/A x $2.00/bu = $17.82/A
3. Compare preventable dollar loss/A with cost of control/A
   $17.82/A - $10.00/A = $7.82 return from treatment.

CONTROL IN FIELD CORN (See Table 2)

Granules. The best corn borer control is usually obtained by applying an insecticide in granular form. This is because the granules lodge behind the leaf sheaths and in the plant whorl where most of the borers are or soon will be located. Granules can be applied with either ground or aerial equipment. Aerial applications are broadcast applications. Ground applications are band applications and are most effective when the insecticide is directed into the whorl or leaf axil.

Liquids-Air or Ground. By the time corn borer treatments are justified, most of the borers already have reached the plant whorl, leaf sheath, or ear. For this reason, the spray must be applied directly into the plant whorl or on the leaf sheath or ear. A spray application has little value if it is simply broadcast over the surface of exposed leaves. The use of raindrop nozzles, which results in larger droplet size and greater whorl and leaf axil penetration, should provide better control than using cone nozzles.

Liquids-Irrigation. Producers who utilize sprinkler irrigation have the potential for injecting labelled pesticides through that system. This method of application can save time and energy as well as increase the uniformity of application and reduce in-field exposure to the applicator. However, successful application depends upon proper design, installation, and utilization of the system. Those insecticides listed in Table 2 under Liquids-Irrigation Equipment may be used provided: 1) an anti-backflow check valve is present between the injection point and the water source, 2) the injection system has a check valve in the line to prevent irrigation water from entering the chemical supply tank, 3) the irrigation injection system has interlocking on-off switches, and 4) state and/or local regulations allow their use. For some insecticides, crop oil or non-emulsifiable oil may enhance control. Refer to the label for specifics on the use of oil.

TABLE 2. INSECTICIDES FOR EUROPEAN CORN BORER CONTROL IN FIELD CORN.

Insecticide	Formulation	Rate per acre
Granules		
Bacillus thuringiensis [4]	[6]	[6]
chlorpyrifos (Lorsban)	15 G	7 lb
fonofos (Dyfonate II)[2,8]	20 G	5 lb
phorate (Thimet, Phorate)[1,2,3]	20 G	5 lb
permethrin (Pounce)[2]	1.5 G	6.7 lb
Liquids - Air & Ground		
Bacillus thuringiensis [4]	[6]	[6]
carbofuran (Furadan)[1,2]	4 F	1 qt
chlorpyrifos (Lorsban)[1]	4 E	1 qt
methyl parathion (Penncap-M)[1,2]	2 FM	1 qt(band) 2 qt(broadcast)[7]
permethrin[1,2,5]		
(Ambush)	2 EC	6.4 oz
(Pounce)	3.2 EC	4 oz
Liquids - Irrigation Equipment		
carbaryl (Sevin)[1]	80 S	2.5 lb
chlorpyrifos (Lorsban)[1]	4 E	1 qt + 1 qt non-emulsifiable crop oil
methyl parathion (Penncap-M)[1,2]	2 FM	2 qt
permethrin[1,2,5]		
(Ambush)	2 EC	6.4 oz
(Pounce)	3.2 EC	4 oz

[1] Product highly toxic to bees if exposed to direct treatment.
[2] Restricted use pesticide.
[3] Use only on first generation European corn borer.
[4] var. *kurstaki* : Biobit, DiPel, Full-bac, Javelin
[5] Use prior to brown silk.
[6] See label.
[7] May be split as 2-1 qt. applications for second or third generations.
[8] Do not reenter treated field for 10 days.

CONTROL IN SWEET CORN (See Table 3)

Pre-silking Corn. 1) Begin looking for larval feeding in mid June or when the first moths are caught in blacklight traps. Blacklight traps are an efficient method for detecting the initial flight of corn borer moths. 2) Look at 20 consecutive plants in 5 different locations in each field. The damage is easy to see, so sampling can be done fairly quickly. Check at least one damaged plant in each location for the presence of live larvae. 3) If 15% or more of the plants sampled have feeding damage and live larvae are present, then an insecticide treatment is justified. Granular insecticides are generally more effective than liquids in the whorl stage, but are not effective after the tassels emerge. 4) Remember that ECB control in presilking sweet corn has two objectives, to keep the plants growing vigorously and to reduce the number of corn borers that may damage the developing ear. Whorl-stage corn plants can tolerate a substantial amount of damage without any yield loss. Insecticide treatments are usually not necessary until shortly before tasseling. As the plants approach tasseling and silking, control becomes more important because corn borers present at those stages may damage the ear.

When Silking Has Begun. 1) Look at 20 consecutive plants in 5 different locations in each field. Check plants thoroughly for egg masses or larvae feeding on the silks. Egg masses may be found on ears, tassels, stalks, or tillers, but are usually (98%) found on leaves. Egg masses usually are found on the underside of leaves. 2) The treatment threshold depends on the stage of development of the corn plants.

Stage	Sweet CornTreatment Threshold
Before 50% silks	5% or more with egg masses or larvae in silks
After 50% silks	10% or more with egg masses or larvae in silks
100% brown silks	20% or more with larvae in silks

CONTROL IN PEPPERS AND SNAP BEANS

(See Table 4)

In peppers, it is impractical to sample egg masses or larvae because of the extremely low infestation that can be tolerated in fruit (1-5%). Therefore, insecticide treatment should be initiated when black light trap catches average four or more female moths per night for three consecutive nights. The treatment program should consist of sprays of one of the insecticides recommended in Table 4 every 4-7 days until harvest is complete. Be sure to observe the harvest restrictions listed in Table 4 and on the product labels.

Sampling for corn borers in processing snap beans also is impractical because the insect is primarily a contaminant and, therefore, can be tolerated only in extremely low numbers. Treatment should be initiated 8-10 days before bloom when an average of five or more moths are captured in black light traps OR when egg

TABLE 3. INSECTICIDES FOR EUROPEAN CORN BORER CONTROL ON SWEET CORN.

Insecticides	Formulation	Rate per acre	Harvest restrictions
Granules			
permethrin (Pounce)[1,3]	1.5 G	6.7 - 13.3 lbs	1 day
chlorpyrifos (Lorsban)	15 G	6 lbs	35 days
fonofos (Dyfonate)[3]	10 G	10 lbs	30 days
	20 G	5 lbs	30 days
Bacillus thuringiensis var. *kurstaki* (Dipel)	10 G	10 lbs	0 days
Liquids - Air and Ground			
permethrin (Ambush)[1,3]	2 EC	6.4 - 12.8 fl ozs	1 day
	25 W	6.4 - 12.8 ozs	1 day
(Pounce)[1,3]	3.2 EC	4 - 8 ozs	1 day
	25 WP	6.4 - 12.8 ozs	1 day
methomyl (Lannate)[2]	1.8 L[3]	1 qt	0 days (ears), 3 days (forage)
	90 SP	0.5 lb	0 days (ears), 3 days (forage)
methyl parathion (Penncap-M)[1,3]	2 FM	2 qts	12 days
carbofuran (Furadan)[1,3,4]	4 F	1 pt Refer to label	For 2nd generation borers Machine Harvested Only 7 days
Bacillus thuringiensis [5,6] var. *kurtstaki* (several)	Several	See label	0 days

[1] Product highly toxic to bees if exposed to direct treatment.
[2] Product toxic to bees is exposed to direct treatment.
[3] Restricted use pesticide.
[4] For second generation only.
[5] Control may be highly variable and therefore unaccectable for many commercial producers.
[6] Biobit, DiPel, Full-bac, Javelin, MVP

masses on nearby corn exceed 10 per 100 plants. Treatment should be repeated at 7-day intervals if 5-10 moths are caught per night, at 5-day intervals if catches average 10-20, at 4-day intervals if 20-50 per night, or every 3 days if catches exceed 50 moths per night. If treatments have been faithfully applied, control measures usually can be terminated 7-10 days before harvest with little resulting damage to pods. By the time egg masses laid 7-10 days before harvest hatch and larvae reach boring stage, the beans will have been harvested.

TABLE 4. INSECTICIDES FOR CONTROL OF EUROPEAN CORN BORER ON PEPPERS AND SUCCULENT BEANS.

Insecticide and formulation		Snap beans	Harvest restrictions	Peppers	Harvest restrictions
acephate (Orthene)	75 S	1.3 lbs	14 days	1.3 lbs	7 days
methyl parathion (Penncap-M)[1,2]	2 FM	4 pts	15 days	None	Do not use.
permethrin (Ambush)[1,2]	2 EC	None	Do not use.	12.8 ozs (Bell)	3 days
	25 W	None	Do not use.	12.8 ozs (Bell)	3 days
(Pounce)[1,2]	3.2 EC	None	Do not use.	8 ozs (Bell)	3 days

[1] Product highly toxic to bees if exposed to direct treatment.
[2] Restricted use product.

European Corn Borer: *Ostrinia nubilalis* (Hübner)

READ AND FOLLOW ALL INSECTICIDE LABEL INSTRUCTIONS. THIS INCLUDES DIRECTIONS FOR USE, PRECAUTIONARY STATEMENTS (HAZARDS TO HUMANS, DOMESTIC ANIMALS, AND ENDANGERED SPECIES), ENVIRONMENTAL HAZARDS, RATES OF APPLICATION, NUMBER OF APPLICATIONS, REENTRY INTERVALS, HARVEST RESTRICTIONS, STORAGE AND DISPOSAL, AND ANY SPECIFIC WARNINGS AND/OR PRECAUTIONS FOR SAFE HANDLING OF THE PESTICIDE.

Rev. 12/91

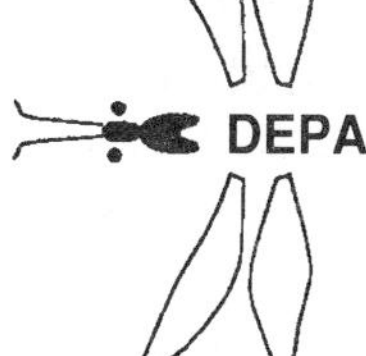

DEPARTMENT OF ENTOMOLOGY **household & public health insects**

CLOTHES MOTHS AND CARPET BEETLES

Gary E. Bennett and Timothy J. Gibb, Extension Entomologists

CLOTHES MOTH CONTROL

The clothes moth larva is a small white caterpillar that lives inside a silken case or web and feeds on wool, hair, fur and feathers. Damage done will depend upon the type of item being fed upon and the species of clothes moth involved. The adult is a tiny, buff-colored "miller" that avoids light. Adults do not feed, but their presence does indicate a moth infestation.

Likely spots to look for infestations around the home include boxes of old clothing, furs, feather pillows, piano felts, old over-stuffed furniture, carpets, and even lint that collects along baseboards or in corners. Mothproofing should be done as a precautionary measure when any of the above items are going into winter or long-term storage, or when these items will not be routinely cleaned.

Moth-Proofing Closets

Each spring and fall, remove all garments from closets, brush them beneath the folds, and hang them outdoors in the sun for several hours. Drycleaning, or washing and pressing the garments with a hot iron will also kill moth larvae and eggs. While the closet is empty, vacuum it clean and then spray the walls and floors until moist with a 0.5% Dursban or 0.5% Diazinon spray.

Clothing stored in little-used closets can be further protected by making the doors as tight-fitting as possible and keeping PDB or naphthalene balls, crystals or flakes in an open container on the top shelf. Follow label directions on the amount of balls, crystals or flakes for each 100 cubic feet of closet space. Never store soiled garments since perspiration and food stains favor moth development.

Moth-Proofing Storage Containers

Almost any kind of box or bag makes a satisfactory storage container if it is tight enough (or is taped) to keep out adult moths. Before storing clothing or blankets, first rid them of any insects by dry-cleaning, washing, pressing with an iron heated to 134°F, or brushing and sunning. Then place the garments in the storage container, and add PDB or naphthalene between sheets of white paper laid in with the articles. The label will instruct you on the amounts to use.

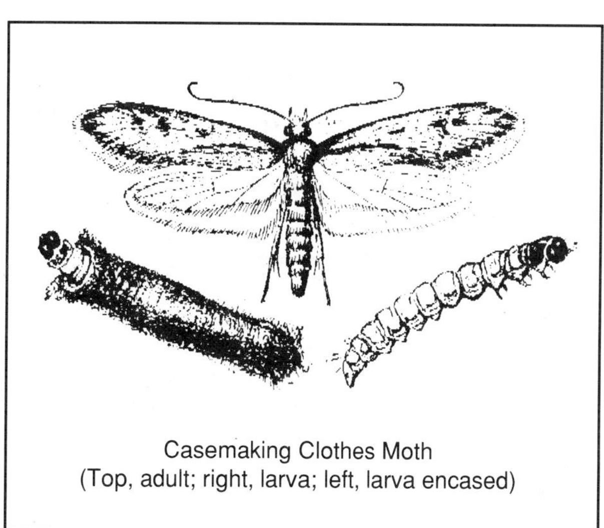

Casemaking Clothes Moth
(Top, adult; right, larva; left, larva encased)

Moth-Proofing Rugs, Carpets and Pads

First, eliminate any moth infestations by dry-cleaning, washing or brushing and sunning both sides of the rugs and rug pads. Before replacing them, spray both floor and rug pad lightly with 0.5% Diazinon or Dursban. This same treatment is also suggested before installing wall-to-wall carpeting, if the carpeting is made from natural fibers. Rug and carpet surfaces, especially around the edges and under heavy furniture, should also be sprayed. Read labels carefully before applying any product on a carpet. Specifically check for comments on potential staining.

CARPET BEETLE CONTROL

The carpet beetle larva is a fuzzy, slow-moving, light brown or blackish worm about 1/4-inch long. The damage it does is similar to that of the clothes moth larva but without webbing. The carpet beetle may be found crawling over the same items that are infested by clothes moths, but is more likely to be found in lint swept from beneath the edges of rugs or similar places. Skin which the larva sheds is often found mixed with lint and dust.

Preventive measures for carpet beetle are the same as for clothes moth, but special measures are needed to get rid of existing infestations. Carpet beetles usually live in lint and debris, including that which collects inside of walls, beneath floors and behind built-in storage spaces. Therefore, exposed areas should be swept frequently; and all cracks or openings where the insects might enter, such as beneath quarterrounds, should be sprayed with Diazinon or Dursban.

Carpet beetles, especially the black carpet beetle, also infest food and other stored products. When this occurs, control procedures are quite different. See Publication E-37, "Insect Pests of Home Stored Foods", for a discussion of this problem.

COMMERCIAL CLOTHES MOTH AND CARPET BEETLE CONTROL

Most pest control specialists provide dependable service for controlling clothes moths and carpet beetles. Since satisfactory prevention and control require a good understanding of these pests and how to properly use insecticides, most homeowners would be best advised to contact a professional.

Fur storage vaults are available in most larger cities.

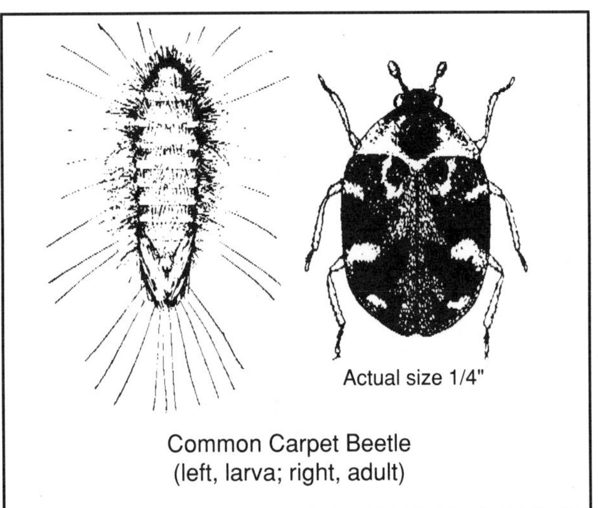

Common Carpet Beetle
(left, larva; right, adult)

Scientific Names:

Casemaking clothes moth—*Tinea pellionella* (Linnaeus)
Webbing clothes moth*—*Tineola bisselliella* (Hummel)
Black carpet beetle*—*Attagenus megatoma* (Fabricius)
Carpet beetles—*Anthrenus* spp.

---

*Colored picture contained in Purdue Extension Publication E-81.

READ AND FOLLOW ALL LABEL INSTRUCTIONS. THIS INCLUDES DIRECTIONS FOR USE, PRECAUTIONARY STATEMENTS (HAZARDS TO HUMANS, DOMESTIC ANIMALS, AND ENDANGERED SPECIES), ENVIRONMENTAL HAZARDS, RATES OF APPLICATION, NUMBER OF APPLICATIONS, REENTRY INTERVALS, HARVEST RESTRICTIONS, STORAGE AND DISPOSAL, AND ANY SPECIFIC WARNINGS AND/OR PRECAUTIONS FOR SAFE HANDLING OF THE PESTICIDE. Rev10/89

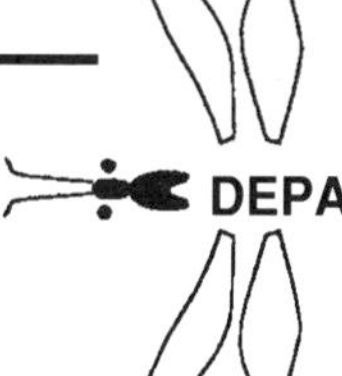

DEPARTMENT OF ENTOMOLOGY household & public health insects

ANTS

Gary W. Bennett and Timothy J. Gibb, Extension Entomologists

Ants can be a problem in and around the home. Most ants build nests in soil; those that invade buildings usually nest near foundation walls or under concrete slabs. One species—the carpenter ant— builds its nests in hollow trees, stumps, and sometimes in the timbers of buildings.

DISTINGUISHING ANTS FROM TERMITES

Sometime during the year, all ant colonies produce winged individuals, which homeowners often mistake for termites. Here is how to tell them apart:

An ant has a narrow "waist" like a wasp, while a termite has a straighter body and no waist. Ants have four wings of unequal length (front pair longer than the hind pair) that are clear like those of a house fly. Termites also have four wings, twice as long as the body, milk-colored and they are of equal length. Ants swarm during the spring, summer, or fall, but termites usually swarm only in the spring.

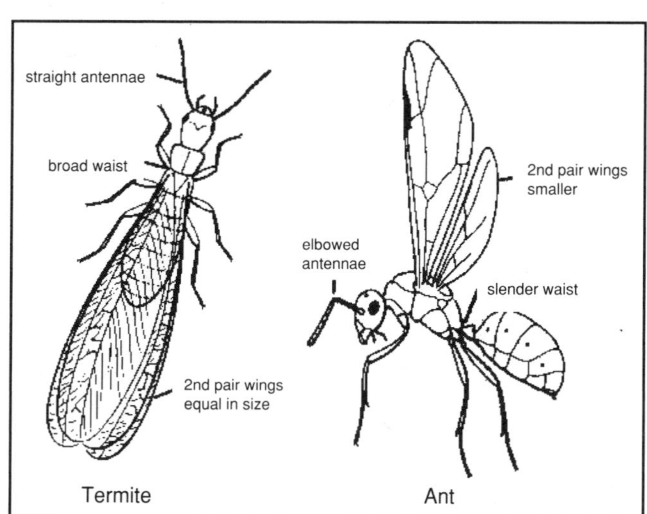

CONTROL IN BUILDINGS

The best way to prevent ants from invading a house is to locate and destroy their nest. Look in the soil around the building's foundation; control as you would for ants in the lawn (see directions at the end of this guide).

However, if ants still get into the house, apply insecticides where the ants gain entry or hide—at foundation walls, doorways, windowsills, baseboards, behind built-in cabinets and furniture, beneath refrigerators, and other heavy appliances. A 0.5% diazinon spray made by diluting concentrate diazinon in water according to label directions is an example of a good ant control insecticide.

A number of ready-to-use household sprays effective as spot treatments for ant control are available. Many of these contain one of the following: chlorpyrifos (Dursban) 0.5%, diazinon 0.5%, or propoxur (Baygon) 1%. These do not require mixing or extra application equipment.

Houses built on concrete slabs often have serious ant problems. The insects nest under the slabs and enter through cracks, heating ducts, and utility openings. Professional pest control may be needed in this situation, and for carpenter ants.

Carpenter Ants: These are large, black ants, either winged or wingless, measuring up to 1/2 inch long. They construct their nests in hollow trees, logs, telephone poles, posts, porch pillars, and other timber used in homes. Their trademark is a small pile of coarse sawdust beneath their nesting site. These nests usually are found in wood with a "higher than normal" moisture condition.

Carpenter ants differ from termites because they do not consume wood, but simply hollow it out to form nests. While usually not as serious as termites, they can weaken building structures.

PURDUE UNIVERSITY COOPERATIVE EXTENSION SERVICE • WEST LAFAYETTE, IN 47907

The secret to control is direct treatment of the nests. Look for the piles of sawdust to locate the entries. Then blow 5% Sevin dust into the "galleries" using a hand-held duster.

To prevent carpenter ant invasion, spray foundation walls and adjacent soil with a formulation of diazinon labeled for this use.

CAUTION

All insecticides are potentially hazardous. Therefore, do not apply on or near food or on surfaces where food comes into direct contact. Commercial household sprays contain oil that can harm plastic, rubber or asphalt tiles and counter tops. Wipe-up any excess spray, or use a water-base formulation. Be sure to read, understand, and follow all label directions.

CONTROL IN THE LAWN

Formulations of chlorpyrifos, diazinon and carbaryl (Sevin) are recommended for controlling ants in turf. Apply only one. A number of formulations of these insecticides are available for this use, including emulsifiable concentrates, sprayable powders and granules. Use only formulations labeled for ant control in lawns, and follow label directions. If a hose-attached sprayer is used, agitation must be maintained while spraying. The granular form is easily applied with a lawn fertilizer spreader. If a spray is applied, do not allow children or pets on the grass until the spray has dried.

Ant Mounds: To destroy mound-building ants, lightly soak the mounds with any of the sprays recommended above, or scatter the granules over them. Then water and roll the mounds to ground level.

Rev 4/89

DEPARTMENT OF ENTOMOLOGY

household & public health insects

COCKROACHES

Gary W. Bennett, Extension Entomologist

There are five kinds of cockroaches commonly found in Indiana. They vary somewhat in appearance and habits, but in general they are all rather large, flattened insects, brownish or dark in color and fast moving. Roaches seek concealment in the daytime and also when disturbed at night. They may be carried into homes in boxes, egg cartons, beverage cases and produce such as potatoes. In apartments and other large buildings, they readily migrate from one place to another along water pipes.

KINDS OF ROACHES

The German roach is a very common species and the one usually found in kitchens. The adults are comparatively small (about 1/2 inch long), tan in color and often occur in large numbers. The immatures (nymphs) have dark markings which make them appear dark brown to black.

The American roach is reddish-brown and is the largest of the common roaches (about 1-1/2 inches in length at maturity). It is found more often in food establishments, although houses and apartments near such establishments frequently become infested.

The Oriental roach is also large (about 1 inch in length) and shiny black or very dark brown. It is often called a "water bug" or "black beetle." This species is frequently found in dampness and may enter homes through sewer openings. It may likewise live outdoors during the summer months and move from home to home.

The brown-banded roach is a southern species but is often found in Indiana. It resembles the German roach in appearance and size but differs in habits. It may infest the entire home, rather than confining itself to the kitchen or where there is food. Infestations usually start from luggage, furniture or other materials shipped from one place to another.

The woods roach normally lives under the loose bark of dead trees, logs or stumps. It sometimes invades homes built in or near wooded areas, but it does not thrive indoors. Males are nearly 1 inch long and dark brown with a pale stripe on the outer margins of the wings. They are fairly good fliers and often enter homes this way. They can also be carried in on firewood. The females are short-winged and resemble the Oriental roach, but they are seldom found indoors.

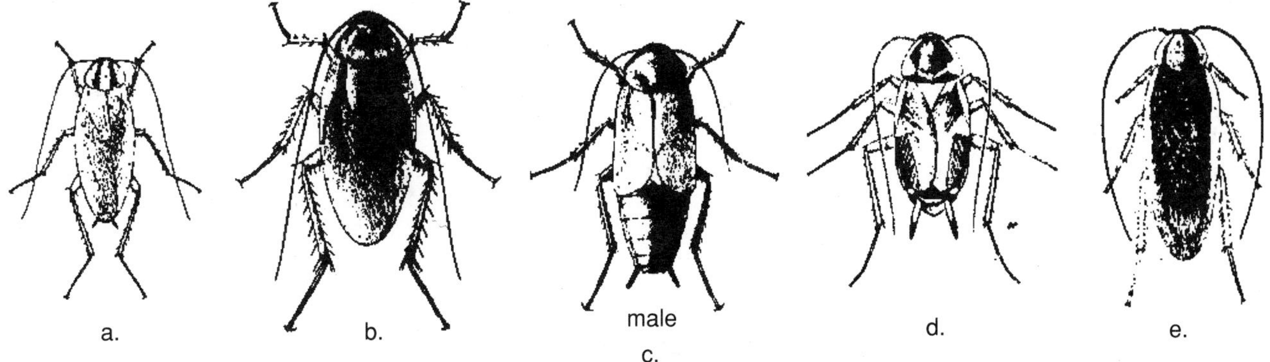

Cockroaches common to Indiana: a. German, b. American, c. Oriental, d. brown-banded, e. woods.

PURDUE UNIVERSITY COOPERATIVE EXTENSION SERVICE • WEST LAFAYETTE, IN 47907

CONTROL MEASURES AND MATERIALS

The chances of effective, lasting roach control are greatly increased if thorough sanitation preceeds proper chemical application. The destruction of breeding places (by clearing out trash and clutter, sealing cracks and openings, etc.) and the removal of food and water sources may reduce, or even eliminate, the necessity for chemical applications.

Table 1 shows the insecticides that may be used for cockroach control. Sprays are usually preferred to dusts because they are easier to apply and the deposits are invisible. However, dusts can sometimes be blown into places difficult to reach with a spray, such as wall voids.

Roach control materials are now available in low-pressure spray containers (cans) that apply a residual deposit of the insecticide. Pressurized sprays of this type are quite satisfactory. However, they should not be confused with the high-pressure "aerosol bombs" designed for applying space sprays. The latter are of limited use in roach control.

Insecticides to control roaches can be applied either as oil-base or water-base sprays. Oil-base sprays come in ready-to-use form, but they may dull or injure counter tops, linoleum or tile floors. It is best to use water-base sprays on such surfaces. They are made by diluting an emulsifiable concentrate or a wettable powder to the desired strength. Since concentrates may vary considerably in strength, it is extremely important to follow label directions in mixing the solution to be used.

A number of other insecticide formulations and devices can now be found in stores. These include baits, traps and ultrasonic/mechanical devices that are supposed to kill or repel cockroaches. Most ultrasonic/mechanical devices have not been tested thoroughly enough to know if they work. A number of these units have been removed from the marketplace by the Environmental Protection Agency after they were found to have no effect on insect pests. In many cases, traps and baits should be used in combination with sprays to obtain satisfactory cockroach control. Traps are most useful in pinpointing areas where cockroaches are located. Baits are most useful in areas where contamination with sprays or dusts might be a problem, such as near foods or dishes. One bait formulation, Combat, is very effective in German cockroach control without being supplemented by sprays or dusts.

If you have a serious cockroach problem, or if you are unable to obtain satisfactory control doing the work yourself, contact a reputable professional pest control company in your area.

TABLE 1. INSECTICIDES FOR ROACH CONTROL.

Insecticide	Spray	Dust	Remarks
chlorpyrifos (Dursban)	0.5%	—	Marketed for use by homeowners as a ready-to-use formulation that may also contain pyrethrins. Also available in bait form.
diazinon	0.5% or 1%	2%	The 1% spray concentration is to be used only by professional pest control operators. The homeowner is limited to a 0.5% spray, which may not be effective for German roach control.
malathion	3%	4%	Has less residual action than chlorpyrifos, diazinon and propoxur. Odor may be objectionable.
propoxur (Baygon)	1%	—	Available as a liquid concentrate or as a 2% ready-to-use bait.
pyrethrins	as labeled	—	Pyrethrins flush roaches from concealed places, but kill only those hit with the spray; there is no residual action. Use in combination with one of the other insecticides listed here.
hydramethylnon (Combat)			Available as a 1.65% bait for German and American cockroach control.

Scientific Names:

German cockroach — *Blattella germanica* (Linnaeus)
American cockroach —*Periplaneta americana* (Linnaeus)
Oriental cockroach — *Blatta orientalis* (Linnaeus)
Brown-banded cockroach — *Supella longipalpa* (Fabricius)
Woods cockroaches — *Parcoblatta* spp.

READ AND FOLLOW ALL LABEL INSTRUCTIONS. THIS INCLUDES DIRECTIONS FOR USE, PRECAUTIONARY STATEMENTS (HAZARDS TO HUMANS, DOMESTIC ANIMALS, AND ENDANGERED SPECIES), ENVIRONMENTAL HAZARDS, RATES OF APPLICATION, NUMBER OF APPLICATIONS, REENTRY INTERVALS, HARVEST RESTRICTIONS, STORAGE AND DISPOSAL, AND ANY SPECIFIC WARNINGS AND/OR PRECAUTIONS FOR SAFE HANDLING OF THE PESTICIDE.

Rev. 10/89

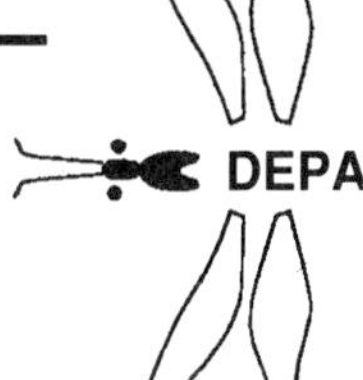

DEPARTMENT OF ENTOMOLOGY **household & public health insects**

MOSQUITOES IN AND AROUND THE HOME

Ralph E. Williams and Gary W. Bennett, Extension Entomologists; and Michael J. Sinsko, Public Health Entomologist, Indiana State Board of Health

Usually, the major reason for mosquito control is relief from the annoyance of mosquito bites and the irritating reaction that often follows. Many of the approximately 50 species of mosquitoes that occur in Indiana do significantly annoy by their biting activity. A potentially more important reason for control, however, is prevention of disease transmission. For instance, species of the genuses *Culex* and *Aedes* are capable of transmitting viruses that cause encephalitis in humans. In 1975, a strain of virus called "St. Louis encephalitis" resulted in illness and death in several Indiana counties. It is transmitted from birds to humans by *Culex* sp. mosquitoes. This publication explains briefly where and how mosquitoes develop, how to eliminate their breeding places, and how to control them around the home.

WHERE AND HOW MOSQUITOES DEVELOP

Mosquitoes always develop in water, but the type of breeding place varies with the species of mosquito. Common breeding places are flood waters, woodland pools, slow-moving streams, ditches, marshes, and around the edges of lakes. Mosquitoes may also develop in tree cavities, rain barrels, fish ponds, bird baths, old tires, tin cans, guttering, and catch basins — in other words, in anything that holds water. The extensive breeding of mosquitoes in such containers has often contributed to disease outbreaks. Mosquitoes lay eggs on the surface of water or in low places where water is likely to accumulate. In these low places, the eggs may hatch in less than 3 days after flooding occurs. The larvae, commonly called "wiggle-tails," mature in 7-10 days and change into a pupal or "tumbler" stage. Two or 3 days later, adult mosquitoes emerge. After taking a blood meal, each female lays 100-400 eggs or more. The entire life cycle may be completed in only 10 days.

ELIMINATING BREEDING PLACES

The most effective control of mosquitoes around the home is to prevent them from breeding. This can be done by eliminating or altering existing breeding sites as follows:

1. Destroy or dispose of tin cans, old tires, or any other artificial water containers.
2. Make weekly inspections of the water in flower pots and plant containers. If mosquito larvae are seen, change the water.
3. Change the water in bird baths and wading pools once or twice a week. Drain wading pools when not in use.
4. Stock garden and lily ponds with top-feeding minnows.
5. Keep rain gutters unclogged and flat roofs dry.
6. Drain and fill stagnant pools, puddles, ditches, or swampy places around the home.
7. Keep margins of small ponds clear of vegetation.
8. Place tight covers over cisterns, cesspools, septic tanks, fire barrels, rain barrels, and tubs where water is stored.
9. Fill all tree holes with sand or mortar, or drain them.
10. Remove tree stumps that may hold water.

PURDUE UNIVERSITY COOPERATIVE EXTENSION SERVICE • WEST LAFAYETTE, IN 47907

CONTROLLING MOSQUITOES OUTDOORS

In addition to the elimination of breeding sites, it may be necessary to control adult mosquitoes that migrate in from surrounding areas. The adults like to rest in vegetation. Therefore, do not allow weeds to grow uncontrolled near the home; and keep weeds in nearby lots well trimmed. For residual insecticide treatments, use carbaryl (Sevin) wettable powder or malathion emulsifiable concentrate. Select a product labeled for mosquito control. Apply either mixture with a hand sprayer, covering the lower limbs of shade trees, shrubbery, tall grass, flower beds, and shaded areas around buildings where mosquitoes congregate. Carbaryl sprays may injure Boston ivy, so they should not be used on this ornamental plant. Carbaryl is also highly toxic to bees and should not be sprayed where plants are in bloom. Selective application is very important. When using either carbaryl or malathion, follow all label directions carefully.

CONTROLLING MOSQUITOES INDOORS

Mosquitoes can be prevented in the home by keeping windows and porches tightly screened. Space sprays or aerosol "bombs" containing synergized pyrethrins are effective against mosquitoes found in the home. Use these materials as directed on the label.

USING MOSQUITO REPELLENTS

Repellents are very useful in protecting against mosquito bites. Available under various trade names, they include such active ingredients as diethyl toluamide, ethyl hexanediol, dimethyl phthalate, or dimethyl carbate. Repellents provide protection for up to 5 hours, depending on amount of perspiration, skin rubbing, temperature, and abundance of mosquitoes. Application should be made to clothing and to exposed skin areas but not around the eyes, nose, or lips. Follow carefully all directions on the label. A granular repellent containing napthalene compounds, Mosquito Beater, can be applied on lawns and other mosquito-infested areas. It effectively keeps mosquitoes repelled for several hours.

ELECTRONIC DEVICES

Devices that are advertised as physical attractants or repellents of mosquitoes are limited in use and should be thoroughly investigated before being purchased. Recent field tests have shown that electrocuting devices using ultraviolet light as an attractant are ineffective in reducing mosquito populations and mosquito biting activity.

READ AND FOLLOW ALL LABEL INSTRUCTIONS. THIS INCLUDES DIRECTIONS FOR USE, PRECAUTIONARY STATEMENTS (HAZARDS TO HUMANS, DOMESTIC ANIMALS, AND ENDANGERED SPECIES), ENVIRONMENTAL HAZARDS, RATES OF APPLICATION, NUMBER OF APPLICATIONS, REENTRY INTERVALS, HARVEST RESTRICTIONS, STORAGE AND DISPOSAL, AND ANY SPECIFIC WARNINGS AND/OR PRECAUTIONS FOR SAFE HANDLING OF THE PESTICIDE.

Rev. 6/89

The information given herein is supplied with the understanding that no discrimination is intended and no endorsement by the Purdue University Cooperative Extension Service is implied.

Cooperative Extension work in Agriculture and Home Economics, State of Indiana, Purdue University and U. S. Department of Agriculture cooperating. H. A. Wadsworth, Director, West Lafayette, IN. Issued in furtherance of the acts of May 8 and June 30, 1914. The Cooperative Extension Service of Purdue University is an affirmative action/equal opportunity institution.

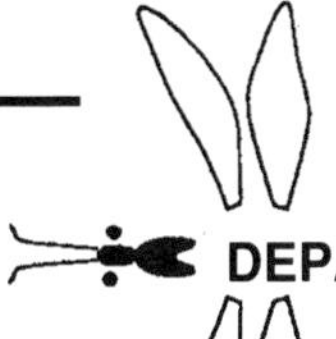

DEPARTMENT OF ENTOMOLOGY

stored product insects

INSECT PESTS OF HOME STORED FOODS

Gary W. Bennett and Timothy J. Gibb, Extension Entomologists

Many kinds of cereal products and other foods stored in kitchen cabinets or elsewhere in the home may become infested with insects or other organisms commonly referred to as "pantry pests." Practically all dried food products commonly found in the home are susceptible, including birdseed and dry pet foods. Pantry pests eat or contaminate the food, thus making it unfit for humans. They may also be annoying, in that they often leave the infested food and crawl or fly about the house. To eliminate infestations, it is necessary to identify the pest and then find and destroy or treat infested materials. Listed and illustrated below by groups are the most common pests of stored food products in Indiana.

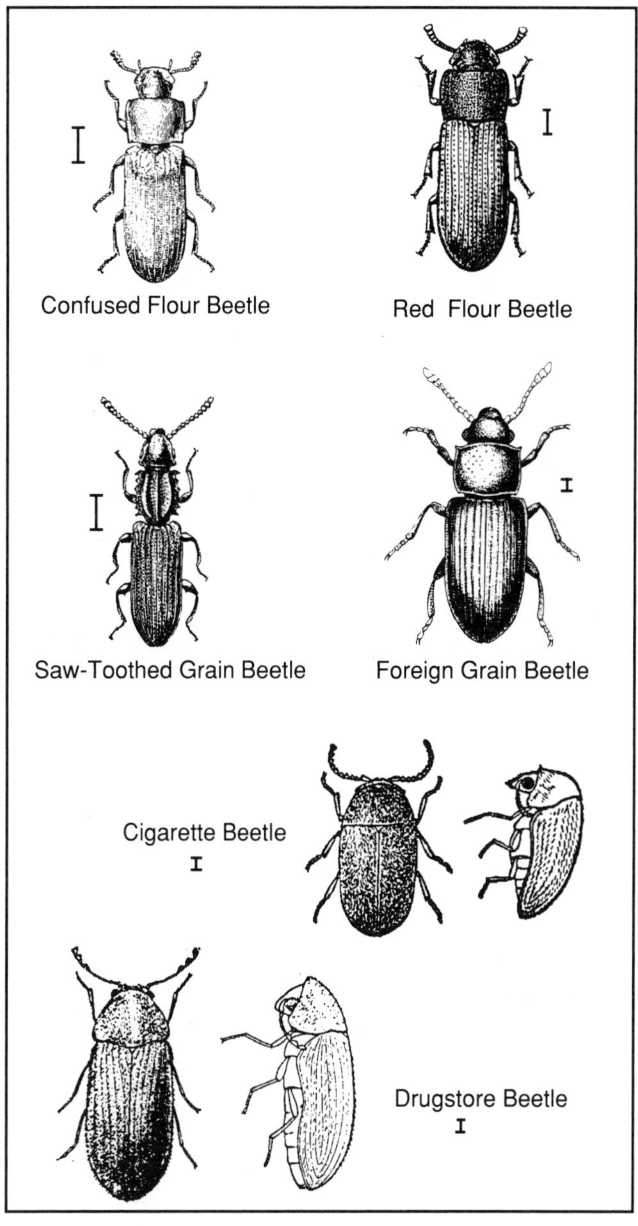

GRAIN AND FLOUR BEETLES

Sometimes collectively called "bran bugs," these reddish-brown beetles are usually less than 1/8 inch long. Their small, worm-like larvae (growing stages) are yellowish-white with brown heads. Larvae of the first four species illustrated are elongate and tubular; those of the latter two species are somewhat C-shaped in appearance and appear rather hairy. The larvae are usually found in infested material, whereas adult beetles often crawl about the kitchen or other areas as well as feed in the infested material.

PURDUE UNIVERSITY COOPERATIVE EXTENSION SERVICE • WEST LAFAYETTE, IN 47907

DERMESTID BEETLES

Members of this family are generally scavengers and feed on a great variety of products of both plant and animal origin including leather, furs, skins, dried meat products, woolen and silk materials, cheese and cereal grain products. Dermestids may be divided into three groups based upon the type of food preferred. Larder beetles prefer products of animal origin, such as dried meats and cheese. Only occasionally are they found in food materials of plant origin. Carpet beetles also prefer products of animal origin but may be found throughout the house feeding on carpets, upholstery, clothing and even on accumulations of lint. Their invasion of stored food products is more or less accidental. Cabinet beetles prefer cereal grain products and are the most common pantry pests of the group. Larval stages of these beetles do most of the damage. Adults are thought to feed mainly on flower pollen outdoors but may feed on stored products to some extent.

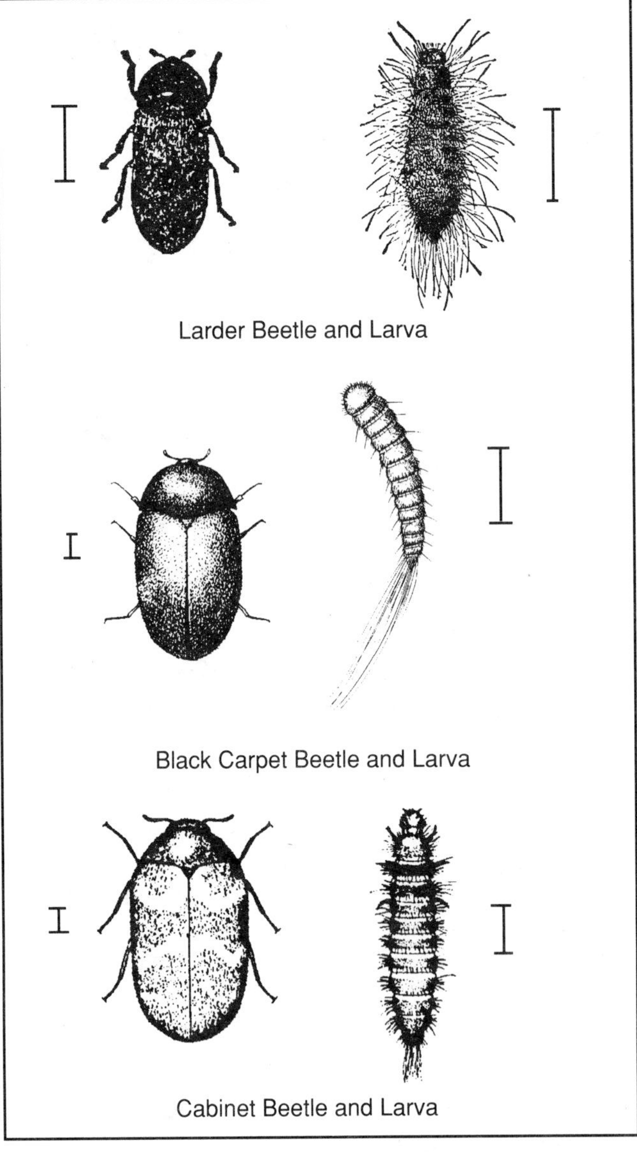

Larder Beetle and Larva

Black Carpet Beetle and Larva

Cabinet Beetle and Larva

SPIDER BEETLES

Several species of spider beetles (long legs and a general spider-like appearance) may be found infesting all types of stored food products. Both the C-shaped, grub-like larvae and the adults feed on the infested material.

Brown Spider Beetle

American Spider Beetle

GRAIN WEEVILS

These beetles, which have long snouts, feed primarily on stored whole grain but may feed to some extent on other plant matter. Their larvae are small, white, legless grubs that feed and develop inside individual kernels.

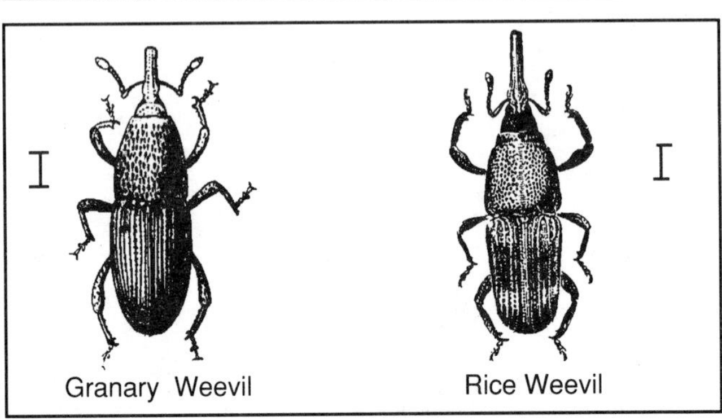

Granary Weevil

Rice Weevil

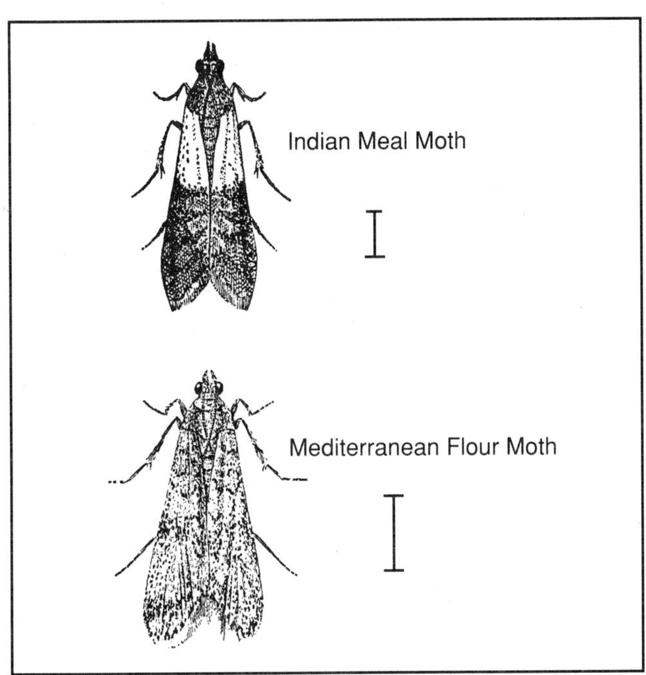

FLOUR MOTHS

These are small moths with a wingspread of about 1/2 inch. Of the two more common species, the Indian meal moth's forewings have a coppery color on the outer two-thirds and whitish gray at the basal end, while the Mediterranean flour moth's forewings are a pale gray with transverse wavy black lines. The larvae of both species are pinkish-white and web together the materials (grain products) in which they feed and develop. The adult moths fly about the house near the site of the infestation. The mature larvae may also leave their food and crawl about cupboards, walls and ceilings looking for places to pupate.

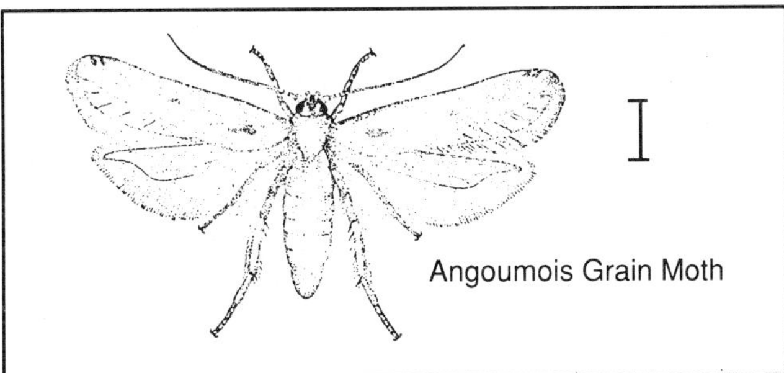

ANGOUMOIS GRAIN MOTH

These are tiny moths similar in size and color to clothes moths. They may be seen flying about the house in the daytime, whereas clothes moths shun light. The larvae develop within kernels of grain such as popcorn.

BEAN AND PEA WEEVILS

These are brownish-colored, short, stout-bodied beetles flecked with patches of black, gray and white. The larvae develop within dried beans and peas.

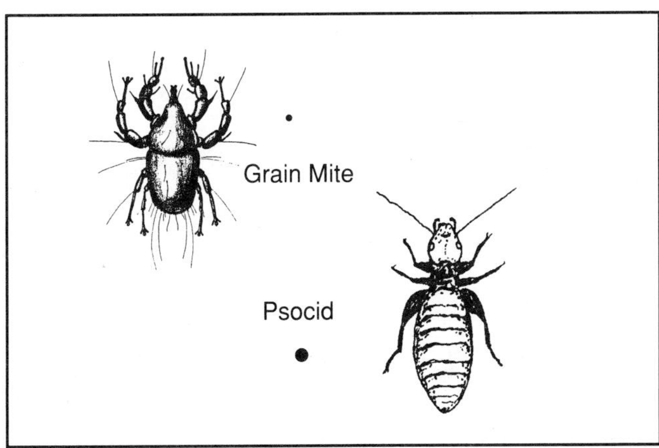

MISCELLANEOUS PESTS

A number of other pests, such as tiny scavenger mites and book-lice, may also infest stored food products. This is particularly true if the food is stored under moist conditions.

PREVENTION

The following procedures will help prevent infesta tions.

1. Purchase dried food in packages that can be used up in a short time. Keep foods in storage less than 2 to 4 months, if possible. Use older packages before newer ones, and opened packages before unopened ones.
2. When purchasing packaged food, be certain that the containers are not broken or unsealed. Check the packaging date to be assured of the freshness of the food. Packages with clear plastic or wax paper coverings should be checked for the presence of insects. (Foods are sometimes infested before being brought into the home.)
3. Store dried foods in insect-proof containers such as screw-top glass, heavy plastic, or metal containers. This will prevent entry or escape of insects. Ordinary metal kitchen canisters are generally not tight enough to exclude insects. Some plastic containers with very tight fitting lids may be acceptable. Cardboard, paper, or plastic wrapping will not prevent insect infestations.
4. Storing dried foods in a home freezer will prevent pests from developing.
5. Keep food storage areas clean and do not allow crumbs or food particles to accumulate, as exposed food will attract insects. Cleanliness is also important in areas where pet food and birdseed are stored.

STEPS IN CONTROLLING BEETLES AND FLOUR MOTHS

1. Determine sources of infestation by carefully examining all susceptible foods. Properly dispose of any that are heavily infested. Small amounts of highly susceptible foods can be kept in the refrigerator.
2. If infested material has further value or if infestation is questionable, heat the material in shallow pans in the oven at 130°F for at least 30 minutes or place in a deepfreeze at 0°F for 4 days.
3. Empty and vacuum cabinets and shelves to pick up loose infested material; then wash them with soap and hot water.
4. After dry from washing, spray shelves lightly with Diazinon, Baygon or Dursban (use only formulations labelled for use against stored product insects). Force spray into cracks and crevices where insects may hide. If a sprayer is not available, apply with a paint brush. Do not allow insecticides to come in contact with food or cooking utensils.
5. After the spray has dried, cover shelves with clean, fresh paper or foil before replacing food or cooking utensils, etc.
6. Avoid spillage and keep storage places clean.
7. Control moths or beetles flying around indoors by using a "flying insect" household aerosol insecticide. Total release aerosols containing synergized pyrethrins are also available for this use.

Insects infesting ornaments and decorations made from plant or animal products can be killed by placing the items in a freezer for 3 or 4 days. Insects in these items may also be killed by placing them in airtight containers along with aerosol fogs of the insecticides mentioned above. Leave the treated container closed for at least 8 hours. Retreatment may be necessary if all insects are not killed. Be careful when using plastic containers as some chemicals may react adversely with certain plastic materials. Pretesting the container with the insecticide to be used is always a sound practice.

Caution — if insects continue to appear, check other rooms in the home for possible sources. Tree seeds blown into ventilators or around windows may harbor these pests. Dermestids (carpet beetles) will develop in many products, including feathers, silk, wool, fur, stuffed animal skins, dead insects, lint, and many other materials.

If insect problems persist, seek help from commercial pest control operators.

Rev. 4/89

ornamental insects

TURF INSECT MANAGEMENT

Timothy J. Gibb, Extension Entomologist and Jeff Lefton, Turfgrass Extension Specialist

Problem-free turfgrass is usually the result of a combination of good management practices. Proper seed selection, good soil, sound watering, fertilizing, and cutting techniques all contribute to the production and maintenance of healthy turf. Healthy and vigorously growing grasses are more able to tolerate lawn pests than are weak and poorly maintained grasses, because of their increased capacity for producing new roots and leaves. Even under good management, however, insect pests can invade, cause unsightly turf damage and result in considerable repair costs.

The first step in successfully controlling turf pests is the early identification of potential insect problems. Routine and systematic inspections at several locations throughout the lawn may help detect early insect infestions. Above ground plant parts such as leaves and stems should be examined for feeding scars and discoloration. Inspect the crown areas for damage by pulling several handfuls of grass; if plants dislodge easily, the problem may be in the crown or root areas below the surface. To inspect plant parts below ground, cut three sides of a one-foot-square by four-inches thick section of sod; roll the sod back to expose the root zone and, possibly, the root-feeding insects.

DAMAGE SYMPTOMS AND IDENTIFICATION

Fertilizer burn, diseases, improper mowing, unsuitable grass variety, urine spots from pets, improper use of insecticides, fungicides or herbicides all cause symptoms which resemble insect feeding. For this reason, a thorough search should be made to determine whether insect pests are the cause of the problem. Many insect species may be found in the lawn. Fortunately, only a few cause damage. Other insects are either beneficial, or are of no real consequence. Some insects may be regarded as nuisance pests only on rare occasions when they become very abundant. Descriptions of the most common lawn-invading insect pests in Indiana, their biology, damage symptoms, and control recommendations are provided in this publication.

Lawn and turf insect pests can be grouped into one of three broad categories by where they are found: below-ground (root-feeders), thatch-dwellers (crown- and stem-feeders), and above-ground (blade- or leaf-feeders).

Below-ground pests.

Brown patches of dead or dying turf usually found in spring or fall may be caused by grubs. Symptoms also may include sod that pulls up easily (like a carpet) revealing the white grubs beneath. Sometimes raccoons, skunks, or flocks of blackbirds foraging in the lawn may indicate severe grub infestations.

Grubs are the immature stages of several species of beetles including Japanese beetles, June or May beetles, chafers and billbugs. Correct treatment of grub infestations depends upon proper identification of the species involved and understanding its particular life history.

White grubs are fat, white, C-shaped larvae with many wrinkles or folds on the front end of the body. The rear end is slightly larger in diameter and may appear bluish or black in color. White grubs have brown heads and six legs. Depending on species and age, they may range from 1/4 to 1-1/2 inches in length.

PURDUE UNIVERSITY COOPERATIVE EXTENSION SERVICE • WEST LAFAYETTE, IN 47907

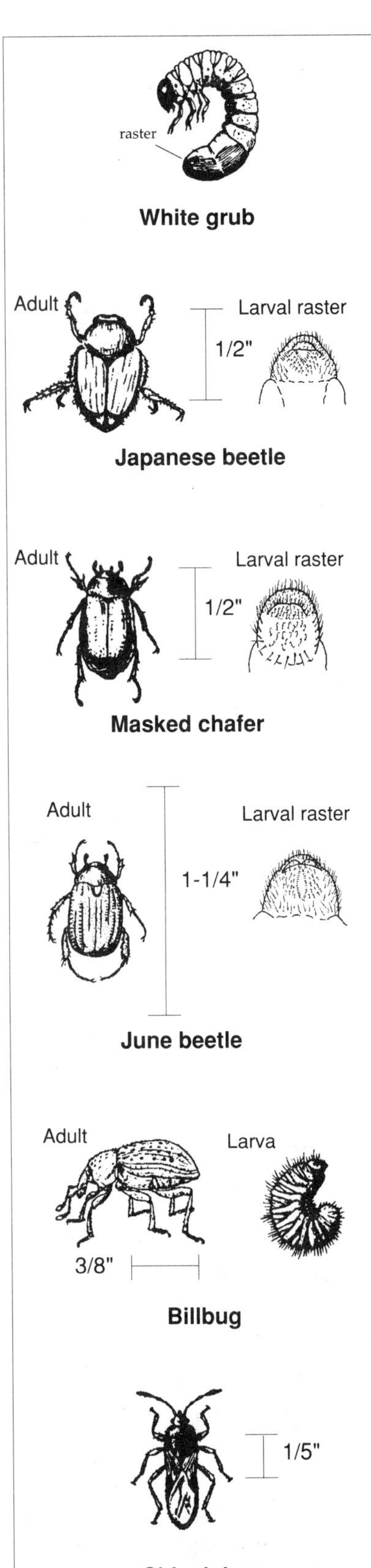

White grubs begin feeding on roots immediately after hatching. Larvae burrow below the freeze line to overwinter, and return to the root zone to resume feeding each spring. Depending on the species involved, grubs may feed for a single season or several seasons. To determine which white grub species is present, refer to the rastral (spine) pattern on the tip of the abdomen.

The **Japanese beetle** is now a very familiar insect in Indiana. Full grown larvae are approximately 1/2 inch in length and have a characteristic 'V' shaped rastral pattern. Adults are approximately 1/2 inch in length and have a shiny metallic-green head and body. The Japanese beetle has a one year life cycle. Eggs are laid during mid-July and hatch during the first few weeks of August. Therefore, chemical controls, should be applied in early August for newly emerged (more susceptible) larvae.

Masked chafer grubs are slightly larger than those of the Japanese beetle but lack any distinct rastral pattern. Adults are approximately 1/2 inches in length and have a darkened (or masked) area across the face. Unlike the Japanese beetles, chafers are short-lived and do not feed as adults. They are strongly attracted to house lights where they mate during late July and early August. Like the Japanese beetle, chafers require only a single year for larval development, thus, control chemicals should be applied in early August.

The larger **May or June beetle** grubs may grow to 2 inches in length. They require from 1 to 4 years for complete larval development. Since they must feed several years in succession, seasonal timing of insecticide application is not as critical as for other white grub species. Applications can be applied anytime throughout the growing season, but chemicals applied while the ground is warm are more effective. Adults are similar to the chafers in overall appearance, but much larger and often much darker. They will feed on leaves of deciduous trees but are seldom noticed except when they appear at lights in the evening.

Billbug larvae appear somewhat similiar to other white grub larvae, except that they are smaller (1/4 to 3/8 inch) and are legless. Damage also appears similar to that produced by other white grubs, because billbug larvae also feed on roots and stems of grasses. Damaged grass stems turn brown and may be pulled up easily, often exposing brown saw-dust like frass. Adults also may damage lawns by eating small holes in the blades and stems. Areas around the holes may turn yellow and the grass may take on a "speckled" appearance. Billbug adults are small, black or brown weevils ("snout" beetles).

Thatch-dwelling pests.

Chinch bug adults are small (1/5 inch), white and black insects that fold their wings flat over their bodies. Immatures appear similar in shape to the adults but are usually bright red in color, often posess a white band behind the neck, and lack wings. Both nymphs and adults damage lawns by sucking sap from grass blades. Grass may turn yellow and then brown as feeding continues. Chinch bugs may be found on the margin between the damaged and healthy lawn. They may occur in large numbers and because of their relatively small size, may remain unnoticed for some time.

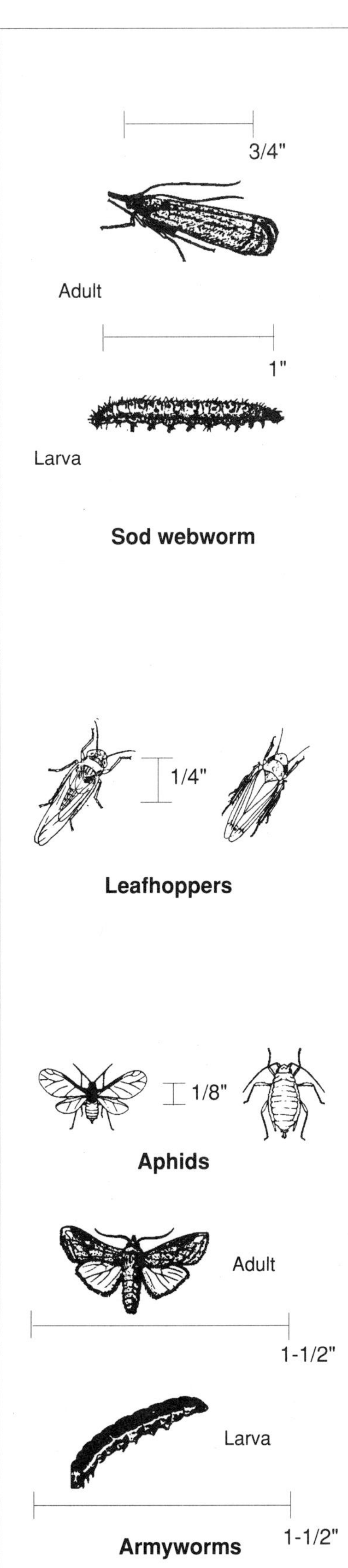

Two generations often occur in Indiana. Adults become active in the spring and move to rapidly growing grasses where they mate and lay their eggs. Females may oviposit up to 200 eggs each, which hatch within two weeks. Small nymphs begin feeding immediately and damage is more severe in hot dry weather. As bugs mature, they mate and produce a second generation. Second generation adults overwinter in grass clumps and leaf litter.

Sod webworm larvae are the caterpillar stage of several species of small 'lawn moths'. Mature caterpillars are about 1 inch long, slender, grayish-black and may be covered with small spots. Adults are whitish or buff-colored moths with long snouts and have a 1 inch wing span. They roll their wings close to the body when at rest and appear very slender. Adults hide during the day and become active (sometimes attracted to lights) at night. They may be noticed flitting just above the grass in very short and erratic flight patterns at dusk. Adults do not feed, but only mate, and oviposit eggs in the grass. New lawns seem to be preferred by this pest, and several generations may occur each season. Larvae overwinter in silken tunnels, and emerge in the spring to feed on grass blades, growing tips and greener portions of the crown but not on the roots. Damaged areas appear as scattered, irregular, brown patches. Grass also may take on a "ragged" appearance. Presence of larvae together with visible damage symptoms justifies chemical controls for sod webworm.

Above-ground pests.

Leafhoppers are small (1/8 to 1/4 inch) generally pale yellow-, white- or green-colored insects that jump or fly short distances when disturbed. Both adults and nymphs damage plants by sucking plant juices from leaves and stems. They may be very abundant and may feed on nearly all species of plants. There can be two or more generations per year depending on the species and the weather. Leafhopper feeding causes grasses to become yellow-spotted and to appear "bleached". Severe infestations may cause the lawn to appear wilted as if from drought.

Greenbugs are actually aphids or plant lice. They may be less than 1/8 inch in size, and either black with wings, or green in color. Greenbugs are quite common. Because they suck plant juices, their damage may appear similar to leafhopper feeding or they may impart a yellow to burnt-orange coloration to the turf. Greenbugs arrive in Indiana from the southern states each spring and may reproduce rapidly under favorable conditions. They are common in agronomic crops, but also can cause considerable damage in turf. This insect can produce many generations each season under ideal conditions and prefers healthy green lawns.

Armyworms and cutworms are the caterpillars of several species of night-flying moths. The dull-colored caterpillars may grow to two inches in length and feed on the above ground parts of plants. They are usually considered pests of crops, but may infest lawns and turf, especially in those areas which border crops or large, untended fields. Armyworms may migrate in large numbers from one area to another to feed. Usually, the caterpillars hide by day and feed by night, thus often go unnoticed. They feed on grass blades or cut off the plants at crown level. Turf may show brown patches and have an overall "ragged" appearance.

TREATMENT

If destructive insects are found in sufficient numbers to cause damage, chemical controls should be considered. Table 1 contains a list of insecticides recommended for control of the most common turf pests in Indiana. More than one chemical and formulation is usually available. Always read and follow label directions.

CONTROL EVALUATION

Remember that insecticides are designed to kill insects — not bring dead grass back to life. Do not expect immediate improvement in the appearance of your turf after insecticide application. Killing the turf pests only prevents further damage. Even under optimum conditions, lawns may require several weeks to recover.

TABLE 1. RECOMMENDED TURFGRASS INSECTICIDES.

Insecticide	Armyworms & Cutworms	Billbugs	Chinch bugs	Fall armyworms	Greenbugs (Aphid)	Leafhoppers	Sod webworms	White grubs
acephate (Orthene)	x			x	x	x	x	
Bacillus popillae (Japademic, Milkyspore, Grub attack, Doom)								x[1]
bendiocarb* (Turcam)		x	x[2]			x	x	x
biosafe (Biological pest control, Parasitic nematodes)	x	x		x			x	x
carbaryl (Sevin)	x	x	x			x	x	x
chlorpyrifos (Dursban)	x	x	x	x	x	x	x	x
cyfluthrin* (Tempo)	x	x[3]	x				x	
diazinon** (Spectracide)	x	x	x	x		x	x	x
ethoprop (Mocap)*		x	x				x	x
fluvalinate* (Mavrik)	x		x			x	x	
isazophos* (Triumph)	x		x				x	x
isofenphos (Oftanol)		x	x				x	x
trichlorfon (Dylox, Proxol)	x			x			x	x

1 Effective only on Japanese beetle species.
2 Label for larval control only (not adults).
3 Label for Adult control only (not larvae)
* For professional use only
** For homeowner use only

After insecticide application, always evaluate the performance of the chemical. Insecticides may require 2-3 days to kill above-ground insects and 2-3 weeks for those below-ground. Biological controls may require 1 month or more. If you suspect that a treatment failed, try to determine the cause. Most insecticide failures can be attributed to one of the following:

- *Enhanced bio-degradation.* Continued use of the same chemicals on turfgrass year-after-year can select for a population of soil inhabiting microbes which feed on the insecticides applied. If populations are allowed to build up, insecticides may be rendered ineffective very quickly. Periodically switching from one chemical to another will prevent this buildup from occurring.
- *Tank hydrolysis.* If chemicals are mixed with water which has either a high or a low pH value, insecticides will begin to break down inside the sprayer. The longer they are held in the tank, the more hydrolysis will occur. Mix only what is required for the job and do not 'save' spray mixture.
- *Improper calibration of applicatiors or poorly maintained equipment.* Equipment should be re-calibrated each season and for each product. Applications of improper rates can be very expensive and may cause undue problems.
- *Improper irrigation.* Label directions for most white grub insecticides recommend watering with at least 1/2 inch of water immediately after application. This procedure not only washes the chemical off the grass blades, but also causes the grubs to rise nearer the soil surface where the chemical is located. Purdue entomologists recommend watering both before **and** after chemical application when possible.
- *Improper timing.* Insecticides applied too late or too early in the season are often ineffective. Be sure insects are present before applying chemicals. In the case of white grubs, time chemical applications to coincide with activity near the soil surface.
- *True insecticide failure.* Product distributed did not perform as advertised. Contact manufacturer.

READ AND FOLLOW ALL LABEL INSTRUCTIONS. THIS INCLUDES DIRECTIONS FOR USE, PRECAUTIONARY STATEMENTS (HAZARDS TO HUMANS, DOMESTIC ANIMALS, AND ENDANGERED SPECIES), ENVIRONMENTAL HAZARDS, RATES OF APPLICATION, NUMBER OF APPLICATIONS, REENTRY INTERVALS, HARVEST RESTRICTIONS, STORAGE AND DISPOSAL, AND ANY SPECIFIC WARNINGS AND/OR PRECAUTIONS FOR SAFE HANDLING OF THE PESTICIDE.

Rev. 9/89

Index